MELISSA GRAHAM was born in Sunderland, in the north of England, and grew up only yards from a railway line. Along with half of County Durham, she claims to be a direct descendant of George Stephenson, the Father of Railways.

In 1988 she ventured south to read French and Spanish at Cambridge University. Subsequent travels have taken her rather further afield and have included large tracts of Europe, Southern Africa, South-East Asia and South America.

On the research trips she made across Canada for the first two editions of this guide she travelled from the Atlantic to the Pacific and north to Hudson Bay covering 15km by dog sled, 40km on foot, 45km by bus, 60km by car and over 20,000km by rail.

Melissa is also co-author of *The Rough Guide to Chile* and *The Rough Guide to Ecuador* and is now an editor for Trailblazer. She lives in London with her husband and fellow Trailblazer author, Richard Danbury, and their three young children.

KATIE O'BRIEN researched and updated this fourth edition of the Trans-Canada Rail Guide. Like the author, Melissa, Katie was born in Sunderland, UK and has had a passion for travel since family holidays introduced her to the Lake District and France at an early age. After travelling across the USA by Greyhound bus at 18, Katie returned to North America on an exchange programme to study at the University of Western Ontario in Canada. She fell in love with the country and enthusiastically welcomed the opportunity to travel across Canada on behalf of Trailblazer.

Trans-Canada Rail Guide
First edition: 1996; this fourth edition: 2007

Publisher
Trailblazer Publications
The Old Manse, Tower Rd, Hindhead, Surrey, GU26 6SU, UK
Fax (+44) 01428-607571, info@trailblazer-guides.com
www.trailblazer-guides.com

British Library Cataloguing in Publication Data
A catalogue record for this book is available from the British Library

ISBN 978-1-905864-01-0

© **Melissa Graham 1996, 2000, 2003, 2007**
Text, maps and photographs unless otherwise credited

The right of Melissa Graham to be identified as the author of this work has been
asserted by her in accordance with the Copyright, Designs and Patents Act 1988

Reproduced by permission of VIA Rail, the cover photograph; by permission of Rocky
Mountaineer Railtours, the photograph opposite p65; by permission of Tourism BC and
Manitoba Tourism, the photographs between p64 and p65

Editor: Henry Stedman
Series editor: Patricia Major
Layout: Henry Stedman, Bryn Thomas and Laura Stone
Proof-reading: Clare Weldon
Cartography: Melissa Graham and Nick Hill
Index: Jane Thomas

Cover photo: VIA Rail's service between Toronto and Vancouver, known as
The Canadian, is operated three times a week in both directions. Photo © VIA Rail

Every effort has been made by the author and publisher to ensure that the information
contained herein is as accurate and up to date as possible. However, they are unable to
accept responsibility for any inconvenience, loss or injury sustained by anyone as a result
of the advice and information given in this guide.

Printed on chlorine-free paper from farmed forests by
D2Print (☎ +65-6295 5598), Singapore

TRANS-CANADA RAIL GUIDE

MELISSA GRAHAM

FOURTH EDITION RESEARCHED AND UPDATED BY
KATIE O'BRIEN

TRAILBLAZER PUBLICATIONS

Acknowledgements

From Katie: First of all I'd like to thank Melissa for the great opportunity and Bryn for taking a chance on a new writer.

Many thanks to everyone at VIA Rail for their support and time: Françoise LaFleur, Malcolm Andrews, Josephine Wasch, Adrienne Douglas, Anne Clover, and especially Lee George, whose assistance was invaluable. Thanks also to Bernadette Lynch and Michelle Dunn of Rocky Mountaineer Vacations.

I am also indebted to the tourist board representatives across Canada (and those based in the UK) who helped me in so many ways, particularly Caroline Corfield-Rose in Quebec; Becky Addley in Ontario; Colette Fontaine in Manitoba; Nadine Le Jeune in Jasper; Barbara Heimlich in Banff; Sarah Falkingham, Rachele Grieve and Emily Armstrong in Vancouver; Nim Singh in London; and the incredible Eugene Roberts in Alberta. A huge thank you to Marla Daniels from Edmonton Tourism and Ken Sears from Magic Tours in Edmonton for taking such good care of me, and to Scott Eady at Jasper Raft Tours.

I am also indebted to Alice Swinhoe of Fairmont Hotels; to Sherraine Christopherson at the Fort Garry Hotel in Winnipeg; to Kevin Schmidt at the Fairmont Palliser in Calgary; and to Kim Ellsworth and Angela Anderson of Calm Air for flying me back to Winnipeg from Churchill.

In addition, a few personal thank yous ... to the HI Montreal gang for their friendship; to my fantastic hosts in Toronto, Amber, Brian and my flatmate, Viv; to Luke and Anthony Bristow, Mark Torrance and all at Peller Estates winery; to Doug for all of his time and knowledge regarding the Prairie Dog Central Railway; to Jenn McMillan for being a great companion in Jasper; and also to Jen B who took care of me on Vancouver Island. A huge thank you to all the fascinating people I met on board trains across Canada, both fellow travellers and staff, especially Bill and Elaine Marsh on the Rocky Mountaineer. Thanks also to Ten Bottonis for useful tips on Churchill.

Finally, to my family, especially my Mam and Dad, Alex and Teddy, for their love and support throughout the whole experience.

From Melissa: Thanks to Henry Stedman for his superb edit, Nick Hill for the splendid new maps, and, of course, Katie for her dedication and great work.

A request

The author and publisher have tried to ensure that this guide is as accurate and up to date as possible. Nevertheless things change. If you notice any changes or omissions that should be included in the next edition of this book, please write to Melissa Graham at Trailblazer (address on p2) or email her at melisssa.graham@trailblazer-guides.com. A free copy of the next edition will be sent to persons making a significant contribution.

CONTENTS

INDEX

INTRODUCTION

The overwhelming thing about Canada is its sheer size. How can one train ride in a single country take three whole days and three whole nights? And you've still got further to go. No other mode of transport conveys such an acute sense of Canada's vastness, of its beautiful, desolate, wide-open spaces. Endless stretches of track take you through a wilderness scarcely touched by man. You can travel for hours without seeing a road or a house, or indeed any sign of habitation – it's an incredible, almost haunting, experience. Back in 1872 an early traveller wrote a book about Canada's interior called *The Great Lone Land*. It captured the North American imagination and became an instant best seller. Today, much of Canada is still a 'great lone land' that continues to fire the imagination of the modern traveller; the huge iron artery stretching across the continent is truly the best way to cross it.

It is also the reason why this massive country exists at all. When the Dominion of Canada was created in 1867 it was no more than a set of loosely-connected colonies with no sense of unity or nationhood. It was, moreover, under a very real threat of being swallowed up by its powerful southern neighbour. The railroad was the single most important reason why this never happened: it gave the new country its life-blood and bound the provinces together into a transcontinental nation. When the last spike was driven in on 7 November 1885 it paved the way for rapid expansion, mass immigration and economic boom. Urban development ran parallel to the tracks and the stops along the line became the backbone of a new nation – which makes a rail trip today a fascinating journey into this young country's history.

What you'll probably remember about the trip more than anything, though, is the dazzling scenery you travel through. In 1885 the General Manager of the Canadian Pacific Railway Company realized that travellers would flock from all corners of the world to ride through such magnificent landscape. 'If we cannot export the scenery,' he declared, 'we shall have to import the tourists!' And tourists have quite joyfully been imported ever since. Imagine the snow-capped peaks towering right over the tracks; the sweeping panoramas of lakes, waterfalls and glaciers gliding past you. Better still, imagine looking out of the window onto a jade-green lake to find yourself staring at a moose. The whole thing takes your breath away.

On top of all this, a rail ride across Canada is a supremely relaxing experience, a rare joy in today's climate of rapid communications and jet-travel. In the words of Robert Louis Stevenson, 'the train disturbs so little the scenery through which it takes us, that our heart becomes full of the placidity and stillness of the country'. Nowhere is this more true than in Canada.

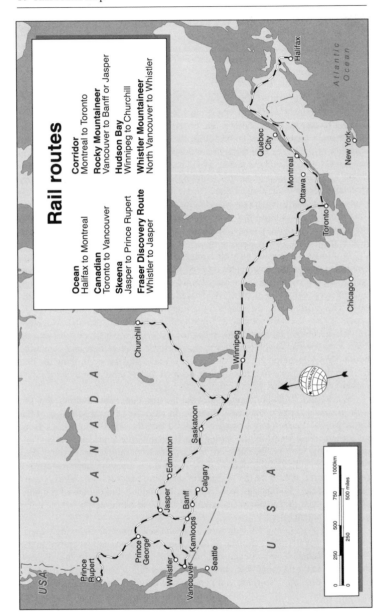

Rail routes

Ocean
Halifax to Montreal

Canadian
Toronto to Vancouver

Skeena
Jasper to Prince Rupert

Fraser Discovery Route
Whistler to Jasper

Corridor
Montreal to Toronto

Rocky Mountaineer
Vancouver to Banff or Jasper

Hudson Bay
Winnipeg to Churchill

Whistler Mountaineer
North Vancouver to Whistler

PART 1: PLANNING YOUR TRIP

Routes and costs

Travel a thousand miles up a great river; more than another thousand miles along great lakes; a thousand miles across rolling prairies; and another thousand through woods and over the great ranges of mountains, and you have travelled from Ocean to Ocean.

Rev Grant, *Ocean to Ocean*

ROUTE OPTIONS

Canada's **transcontinental through service** is operated by VIA Rail (the national passenger rail network) three times a week between **Toronto** and **Vancouver**. You can take **connecting trains** to extend or alter your route in several ways. For a start, if you want to make it a truly transcontinental journey from coast to coast, you can begin or end it in **Halifax** on the Atlantic. Alternatively you can make **Montreal** or **Quebec City** the eastern terminus of your trip. Another option is to start or end in **Prince Rupert** on the Pacific instead of Vancouver; this is very popular with travellers who want to combine their rail trip with the Inside Passage ferry ride between Prince Rupert and Vancouver Island.

Which direction?

Once you've chosen your route, the next thing to decide is in which direction to do it. You see the same scenery whichever way you go since scheduling by VIA has eastbound and westbound trains travelling through the same stretches of the journey at night. That said, there's no doubt that the approach to the Rocky Mountains is far more dramatic from the prairies than from the Pacific.

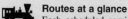 **Routes at a glance**

Each scheduled service is given a different name by VIA. The most famous is *The Canadian* from Toronto to Vancouver but there are several other services that we cover in this guide.

The Ocean: Halifax to Montreal (outline of service p66; route guide p187).
The Corridor: Montreal to Toronto (outline of service p66; route guide p194).
The Canadian: Toronto to Vancouver (outline of service p62; route guide p198).
The Skeena: Jasper to Prince Rupert (outline of service p66; route guide p214).
The Hudson Bay: Winnipeg to Churchill (outline of service p67; route guide p121).
The Rocky Mountaineer: privately run daylight-only train ride between Vancouver and Banff/Calgary or Jasper, and between Whistler and Jasper (outline of service p68; route guides p227 and p234).
The Whistler Mountaineer: Vancouver to Whistler (operated by the same company as *The Rocky Mountaineer*; outline of service p68; route guide p237).

Furthermore, if you're interested in charting Canada's history on your rail trip, travelling from east to west follows the direction of railway development and settlement across the country. It's worth noting, however, that westbound trains get booked up far earlier than eastbound trains.

BREAKING YOUR JOURNEY

Few people want to spend their entire holiday sitting on a train; fortunately, the railway takes you through some superb cities where you can break up your journey. Some of the best, notably **Vancouver**, **Toronto** and **Montreal**, are conveniently located at the beginning or end of a line, so spending time there is no problem as far as your ticket's concerned. There are, however, some restrictions on stopping off on a **through ticket**, with only one break allowed on *The Canadian*. If I had to recommend a single stopover en route it would be in **Jasper**, simply because the Rocky Mountains are so spectacular it would be a sin not to spend some time walking (or at least strolling) around them.

If you want to make more than one break on *The Canadian* you need either to buy **separate tickets**, which works out more expensive than a through ticket, or a **rail pass** (see p13), which allows **unlimited stops** within a given time period. In this case, **Winnipeg** is a good place to stop off: it's right in the middle of the journey and you're likely to be in serious need of a leg-stretch at this point.

On *The Corridor* only passengers with an undiscounted economy-class ticket can break their journey on a through ticket but all passengers can make unlimited stopovers on *The Hudson Bay* and *The Ocean*; if travelling on the latter, you should try to stop off at **Quebec City** (served by Charny station), perhaps the most beautiful city in Canada. The daylight-only *Skeena* has an obligatory overnight stop at **Prince George**, with no other stops allowed on a through ticket.

OVERALL COSTS

The overall cost of a rail trip across Canada will vary enormously, depending mainly on when you go, how many nights you spend off the train (and the kind of accommodation you choose to stay in), the length of your rail journey, the type of ticket you buy and how you get to Canada.

The cheapest possible **rail fare** from **Toronto to Vancouver** is $428 (off-peak; advance purchase economy class); the most expensive is $1958 (for a private bedroom in high season). From **Halifax to Vancouver**, the cheapest possible fare is with a Low Season Canrail Pass for $523. Otherwise, you can buy regular tickets from Halifax to Toronto and then on to Vancouver for a combined total of $625 (off-peak; advance purchase economy) and you can pay up to $2458 (for a private deluxe bedroom in high season).

❑ **Prices in the book – Canadian $**
Note that all prices in this book are given in Canadian dollars unless otherwise indicated. The current exchange rate is Canadian $1 to US$0.86 or UK£0.44.

❏ **Room rates – high season, double occupancy**
Unless otherwise stated, the hotel room rates given are for high-season double rooms, before tax. Prices in most hotels drop a lot in low season (around November to April).

When you add the cost of accommodation to these prices, it can sometimes work out cheaper to get a **package deal**, particularly if you plan to stay in upmarket accommodation. Packages start at around £1300 for a 10-day trip from Toronto to Vancouver including flights from the UK, going up to around £4000 for the more expensive luxury tours.

If you're not on a package and need to get your own **flights**, there are some good charter deals from London: from around £280 (low season) or £450 (summer) flying into Toronto and out of Vancouver; and from £450 (summer) into Halifax and out of Vancouver. Equivalent Apex scheduled flights are around the £600 mark. Note that all these prices exclude airport taxes. Online sites such as Zoom Airlines (🖳 www.flyzoom.com) or Fly Globespan (🖳 www.flyglobespan.com) provide competitive flights from a number cities across the UK.

Hotel costs

Prices are nearly always per room rather than per person, with most doubles only a few dollars more expensive than singles. This makes travelling in a pair extremely good value but lone travellers can end up feeling rather badly done by. Bear in mind that room rates are always quoted before taxes are added on (an extra 12-14% – see p49).

Upmarket hotels tend to offer exceptionally good value compared to their European counterparts, with rooms going from around $200 – just $100 (about £43) each if there are two of you. Note that it's usually cheaper to stay in these places at weekends, since weekday 'rack rates' are designed with business travellers in mind. Also, when you're quoted a room price, you should always ask if there are any 'specials' going, particularly during low or mid-season.

Typical **mid-range accommodation** will give you a double with a private bathroom for around $70–100, though prices can vary significantly depending on location and the general state of the place.

Budget travellers can count on paying about $22 for a youth hostel bed in the smaller cities, and about $28 in the bigger places (more for non-members). Single rooms in university residences and YMCA/YWCA hostels usually cost around $50-60. In university residences, discounts are normally given to students.

RAIL TICKETS, PASSES AND FARES

Types of ticket

You can buy either an **economy-class** ticket (known as Comfort class) or a **sleeper ticket** (known as Silver & Blue class on *The Canadian*). Sleeping accommodation comes as an upper or lower berth, a single bedroom or a double bedroom. See p64 for a description of each type.

PLANNING YOUR TRIP

 RAIL PASSES
There are several rail passes which are good value; some also include the US.

Canrail Pass
This gives 12 days of economy-class travel throughout the VIA national network within a 30-day period. Up to three extra days can be bought (for travel within the 30-day period) and in some cases passengers can upgrade to sleeper class. Unlimited stops are allowed on the pass.

	High season (1 June–15 Oct)		Low season (all other dates)	
	Basic pass	extra day	Basic pass	extra day
Adult	$837	$71	$523	$45
Concessions	$753	$64	$471	$41

North America Rail Pass
Gives unlimited economy-class travel on all VIA and Amtrak trains within a 30-day period. Upgrades to sleeper class, VIA 1 or equivalent Amtrak first-class tickets are usually available for a surcharge.

	High season (26 May–15 Oct)	Low season (all other dates)
Adult	$1149	$815
Concessions	$1034	$734

Discounts
Seniors (aged 60 and over) are entitled to a 10% discount on all regular fares; in addition, VIA sometimes run a fantastic promotion for Seniors, 'Bring A Friend For Free', which does exactly what it says on the tin (check with 🖳 www.via.ca to see if the offer is available when you want to travel). **Students** (with an ISIC card) and **youths** (aged 12 to 17) receive a 35% discount on economy-class tickets. Students also get a 10% discount from VIA 1 or sleeper tickets. For students intending to make regular trips between their hometown and university, the VIA 6 Pak is a fantastic deal, made up of six pre-paid vouchers between two designated towns or cities. **Children** aged two to eleven are given a 50% discount in economy class and a 25% discount on VIA 1 or sleeper tickets; under-twos travel free when not occupying a seat.

In addition, **advance purchase discounts** (tickets must be bought at least five days in advance) are available to all passengers on regular economy fares (year-round) and on off-peak sleeper tickets. In economy (Comfort) class, these advance purchase tickets are known as **Flexi Fares**: passengers can choose between two different tickets – the **Discounted fare** (refundable) and the **Supersaver fare** (non-refundable). Both allow you to change the dates of travel, though the Supersaver has more restrictions. Note that demand is often great so tickets should be bought as far in advance as possible.

Fares
The fares for routes covered in this guide are given opposite. Note that these **prices do not include taxes**, typically an extra 15%. The fares we give for **Advance Purchase** must be bought at least five days in advance – otherwise, higher rates

apply. Fares given under '**Berths**' refer to upper berths; a supplement is added for lower berths. '**Room**' refers to a private bedroom per person in sleeper class.

The Canadian: Silver & Blue (Sleeper)

	Peak (1 June–21 Oct)		Off-peak (rest of year)		Adv purchase (rest of year)	
	Berth§	Room	Berth§	Room	Berth§	Room
Toronto to:						
Winnipeg	$719	$1087	$539	$815	$453	$685
Edmonton	$877	$1321	$658	$991	$553	$832
Jasper	$972	$1466	$729	$1100	$612	$924
Vancouver	$1298	$1958	$974	$1469	$818	$1234
Edmonton to:						
Vancouver	$671	$1011	$503	$758	$423	$637
Jasper to:						
Vancouver	$581	$876	$436	$657	$366	$552

§ Supplement for lower berths start from $77.
Fares include all meals on the train.

The Canadian: Economy class

	Peak (1 June–21 Oct)	Off-peak (rest of year)	Supersaver (Peak/Off-peak)
Toronto to:			
Winnipeg	$369	$277	$277/$210
Edmonton	$548	$411	$411/$312
Jasper	$618	$464	$464/$352
Vancouver	$750	$563	$563/$428
Edmonton to:			
Vancouver	$306	$230	$230/$174
Jasper to:			
Edmonton	$164	$123	$123/$93
Vancouver	$227	$170	$170/$129

The Canadian: Romance by Rail (see p66)

	Peak (1 June–21 Oct)	Off-Peak (rest of year)
Toronto to Jasper	$5964	$2872
Jasper to Vancouver	$3554	$1706

Service available year-round; price is per couple, not per person.

The Ocean: Halifax to Montreal

Economy class:	Full-fare (year-round)	Supersaver (year-round)
	$211	$120

Sleeping Accommodation

	Berth§	Room‡	Deluxe Room
Easterly class*(13 June–14 Oct)	$319	$406	$423
Comfort Sleeper			
Peak (13 June–3 Sept)	$281	$368	$384
Off-Peak (rest of year):	$273	$357	$372
Adv purchase (rest of year):	$169	$221	$230

* Easterly class is a tourist class, including all meals, on-board commentary and other extras. For more details, see p66.
§ Supplement for lower berths start from $25.
‡ 'Room' rates are based on double occupancy, per adult.

PLANNING YOUR TRIP

The Skeena: Jasper to Prince Rupert
The Skeena now operates as a two-day, daylight-only service. The train stops overnight at Prince George, where you must arrange your own accommodation.

Jasper to Prince George:

Economy	Supersaver	Totem	Totem Deluxe
$90	$51	$335	$360

Jasper to Prince Rupert:

Economy	Supersaver	Totem	Totem Deluxe§
$186	$106	$599	$649

Totem and Totem Deluxe available only 13 May–30 September. For more details, see p67.
Regular economy-class and advance purchase Supersaver fares are the same year-round.

The Hudson Bay: Winnipeg to Churchill

Economy class:	**Full-fare** **(year-round)** $271		**Supersaver** **(year-round)** $154	
Sleeper class:	**Peak** (July & Oct)		**Off-peak** (all other dates)	
	Berth	**Room**	**Berth**	**Room**
	$564	$850	$271	$408

Regular economy-class and advance purchase Supersaver fares are the same year-round.

The Corridor: Montreal to Toronto

	Full fare (year-round)	Supersaver (year-round)
Economy class:	$122	$77
VIA 1:	$196	$149

The Rocky Mountaineer

	Peak June 3–Sept 30	Mid-Season May & Oct 1–Oct 14	Off-peak Apr 3–Apr 29
Kicking Horse Route			
(Vancouver-Banff)			
Red Leaf:	$769	$639	$559
Gold Leaf:	$1569	$1439	$1159
(Vancouver-Calgary)			
Red Leaf:	$869	$739	$659
Gold Leaf:	$1719	$1589	$1309
Yellowhead Route			
(Vancouver-Jasper)			
Red Leaf:	$769	$639	$559
Gold Leaf:	$1569	$1439	$1159
Fraser Discovery Route			
(Whistler-Jasper)			
Red Leaf:	$769	$639	$559
Gold Leaf:	$1569	$1439	$1159

Prices are per person, based upon double occupancy. Fares include overnight accommo-
dation in Kamloops or Quesnal and meals on the train.

❑ Note that all fares exclude taxes, which typically add an extra 15% to the price.

❑ **Useful websites**
Check out schedules, fares and special offers for VIA services on 🖥 www.viarail.ca.
Visit Rocky Mountaineer Vacations' website at 🖥 www.rockymountaineer.com
or 🖥www.whistlermountaineer.com for their latest prices and schedules.

The Whistler Mountaineer

	Coast Classic	Glacier Dome
Vancouver to Whistler		
One Way:	$105	$175
Round Trip:	$189	$299

*The Whistler Mountaineer route operates between 1 May and 14 October; fares do not
include tax.*

When to go

Corny as it may sound, Canada is beautiful in every season. Autumn is a tourist
attraction in itself as the country's forests turn into a glorious blaze of reds and
golds. In winter the snow-covered landscapes are dazzling but best experienced
from the comfort of a train; you have to be pretty hardy to cope with sightseeing
in sub-zero temperatures. Canadians, like hedgehogs, tend to hibernate in these
cold months so city centres can be depressingly
empty. Spring is lovely in Canada (as spring usually
is anywhere) with May temperatures averaging 13-
15°C/55-59°F in most cities. The warmest and sun-
niest months are July and August when temperatures
average around 25°C/80°F in places on the line.

Of course, there's more than the weather to take
into account in deciding when to go. An important
consideration is the cost of the trip: rail fares and
hotel rates are considerably cheaper out of the
tourist season (with off-season generally considered

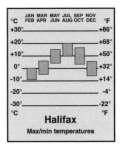

Halifax
Max/min temperatures

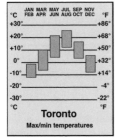

Toronto
Max/min temperatures

Winnipeg
Max/min temperatures

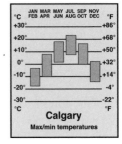

Calgary
Max/min temperatures

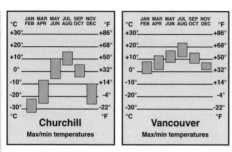

Churchill
Max/min temperatures

Vancouver
Max/min temperatures

PLANNING YOUR TRIP

to be between November and April). It's also much easier to get train reservations in the quieter months whereas peak period sleeper tickets should be booked five to six months in advance. Something else to bear in mind is the number of fellow tourists you can expect to be surrounded by on your visit: July and August are very, very busy so if you're going to Canada for its tranquillity and big empty spaces, give these months a miss.

Making a booking

WITH A TOUR OR ON YOUR OWN?

Canada is one of the easiest and most hassle-free countries in the world to travel in and arranging a trans-Canada rail trip is an extremely uncomplicated process. Simply choose the dates you want to travel, make the reservations with a VIA agent, then book your flights. Once you're in Canada there's no shortage of accommodation. In light of this, it hardly seems worth taking a package tour, particularly as you can decide exactly how much time you want to spend where if you organize it yourself, whereas this decision will usually be taken for you on a tour. Moreover, independent travel invariably works out cheaper if you plan to stay in mid-range or budget accommodation.

Tours come into their own if you want to stay in upmarket hotels. Many tour operators put you in luxurious establishments such as the former Canadian Pacific hotels now owned by Fairmont; they make block bookings which means a) they get big discounts, so you end up paying less than if you booked the accommodation yourself; and b) if you turn up at these hotels trying to book a room, there's often nothing left as tour companies have booked everything.

Escorted tours take most decision-making and the responsibility of getting from A to B out of your hands, which can be a good or a bad thing depending on what you're after. Bear in mind, though, that the pace of some tours can be considerably more gruelling than that of independent travel as you will be whisked off on countless sightseeing trips in between your days on the train.

VIA RAIL SALES AGENTS

VIA Rail has a number of general sales agents dotted around the world. These act as VIA's representatives: they answer rail enquiries, send out timetables and make reservations for you. You buy your tickets from them in local currency. This is extremely convenient and saves you making transatlantic payments in Canadian dollars. Many of them also act as agents for Rocky Mountaineer Vacations, who operate *The Rocky Mountaineer* and *The Whistler Mountaineer* trains (see p68).

MAKING A BOOKING IN BRITAIN

Reserving your rail tickets

VIA's UK sales agent is **1st Rail** (☎ 0845-644 3553, 💻 www.1strail.com) based at Trafford House, Chester Road, Manchester M32 0RS. They should be able to answer all queries relating to fares, routes and availability and can book all your tickets for you, both for VIA and *The Rocky Mountaineer*.

Getting to Canada

If you're organizing your rail reservations yourself you'll need to sort out your **flights** as well. The obvious choice is **Air Canada** (☎ 0871-220 1111, 💻 www.aircanada.com), as they have more flights to more places in Canada than any other airline and are the only one to offer non-stop scheduled flights to Halifax from London. Like most airlines, they offer 'open jaw' tickets which allow you to fly into one point and out of another; the fare is calculated by halving the cost of a return to each destination and adding them together. As a rough guide, typical fares to Halifax, Montreal and Toronto go from £349 in winter and £629 in summer; to Winnipeg, Edmonton, Calgary and Vancouver they go from £449 in winter up to around £700 in August.

Other scheduled airlines flying to Canada from the UK include **British Airways** (☎ 0870-850-9850, 💻 www.ba.com), 156 Regent St, London W1R 6LB, and **KLM Royal Dutch Airlines** (☎ 08705-074 074, 💻 www.klm.com), Plesman House, 2a Cains Lane, Bedfont, Middlesex.

You might also want to consider getting a cheap ticket from a **charter airline**. The charter season generally runs from May to October, with some destinations served only in July and August. Fares are difficult to pin down but as a rule you can get from London to Toronto from around £200 in low season and from £400 in high season; and to Vancouver from £300 in low season and from £500 in high season. Charter flights to Halifax (often just in July and August) go from around £420, while flights to Edmonton and Calgary start at around £300. Good-value charter deals can be found with **Canadian Affair** (☎ 020-7616 9184, 💻 www.canadian-affair.com), **Air Transat** (☎ 00800-2838 7673, 💻 www.airtransat.co.uk) and **Travelpack** (☎ 08705-747101, 💻 www.travelpack .co.uk). Some online companies also offer great deals, such as Zoom Airlines (☎ 0870-240 0055; 💻 www.flyzoom.com) and Fly Globespan (☎ 08705-561 522, 💻 www.flyglobespan.com) with flights leaving from Glasgow, Manchester and Newcastle as well as the London terminals.

Booking a package tour

If you're short of time and can't face the thought of planning all the details yourself, then package tours are a good solution. When choosing which company to go with, an important consideration – besides the itinerary and price – is whether you want an escorted tour or an unescorted one, as some companies offer only one or the other. Many tours combine a VIA rail trip with a ride on *The Rocky Mountaineer* (see p68); a common itinerary is Toronto to Jasper with VIA, Jasper to Banff by motor coach, then Banff to Vancouver on *The Rocky Mountaineer* (or the same in reverse). Also very popular are packages that concentrate on western Canada, sometimes combining VIA routes with Rocky Mountaineer routes – and in some cases incorporating a ferry cruise down the spectacular Inside Passage from Prince Rupert to Vancouver Island. Note that *The Rocky Mountaineer* is abbreviated to *RM* below, and all prices include flights unless otherwise stated.

● **Great Rail Journeys Ltd** (☎ 01904-521936, 🖳 www.greatrail.com), Saviour House, 9 St Saviourgate, York YO1 8NL. This excellent escorted rail-holiday specialist offers a 17-day 'Trans Canada' tour incorporating *The Canadian* from Toronto to Jasper and then the *RM* from Banff to Vancouver; prices go from £2690 in low season and from £3590 in the summer months, including flights and accommodation. Also on offer is an 18-day 'Coast-to-Coast' package from Vancouver to Halifax (£2790–3650).

● **Travelpack** (☎ 0870-121 2020, 🖳 www.travelpack.com/Canada), 73–77 Lowlands Rd, Harrow, Middlesex HA1 3AW. This Canadian specialist offers a range of VIA and RM unescorted rail packages. The 'Rail and Sail' (from £1366 low season and from £1599 high season) combines the *RM* from Vancouver to Banff with *The Skeena* from Jasper to Prince Rupert and then the Inside Passage cruise down to Vancouver Island. Their 13-day Trans-Canada package starts from £1282 in low season and from £1663 in high season.

● **1st Class Holidays** (☎ 0161-877 0433, 🖳 www.1stclassholidays.com), Trafford House, Chester Rd, Manchester M32 0RS. The sister company of 1st Rail, VIA Rail's UK sales agent, offers a good choice of rail-holiday packages, both escorted and unescorted. Their 13-day unescorted 'Trans-Canada by Rail' starts from £1409 in May and from £1835 in high season.

● **Bales Tours** (☎ 0845-057 1819, 🖳 www.balesworldwide.com), Bales House, Junction Rd, Dorking, Surrey RH4 3HL. Bales Tours have a 13-day deluxe 'Trans-Canada Rail Adventure' which is one of the most luxurious tours available with most off-train accommodation in the former Canadian Pacific hotels, including the famous Fairmont Chateau Lake Louise and Fairmont Jasper Park Lodge. Vancouver to Banff is on the *RM*, and Jasper to Toronto on *The Canadian*. Prices start at £3095.

Booking from Eire and Northern Ireland
● **CIE Tours** (☎ 0800-616760 from Northern Ireland, and ☎ 01-703 1888 from Eire; 🖳 www.cietours.ie). Cheap flights and package tours flying out of Dublin.

● **USIT** (🖳 www.usit.ie). Offices in Northern Ireland (☎ 028 90 327 111), Fountain Centre, College Street, Belfast, BT1 6ET and Eire (☎ 01-602 1904), 19–21 Aston Quay, O'Connell Bridge, Dublin 2. Discount flights focusing mainly on student and youth travel.

• **Air Canada** (☎ 01-679 3958, 🖳 www.aircanada.com), 7 Herbert St, Dublin. You can direct email enquiries to 🖳 aircanada@premair.ie.

MAKING A BOOKING IN CONTINENTAL EUROPE

From Austria
• **Canada Reisen** (☎ 2243-25994; 🖳 www.canadareisen.at), Buchberg-gasse 34, A-3400, Klosterneuberg. Sales agent for VIA and RMV.

• **Air Canada-AVIAREPS** (☎ 1-585 3630, 🖳 www.aviareps.com), Argentinierstrasse 2/4, A-1040 Wien.

• **Neckermann** (☎ 1-5020 2777, 🖳 www8.neckermann-reisen.at), Lassallestrasse 7A, A-1020 Wien. Package tours.

From Belgium
• **Air Canada-Deutsche Lufthansa** (☎ 2 627 4088, 🖳 www.aircanada.com), Troostaat, Rue de Trone 130, B-1050 Brussels.

• **Canada Tours** (☎ 456 8250), 572 Chaussée Romaine, 1853 Strombeek-Bever. Low-cost flights.

• **Thomas Cook Ltd** (☎ 9241 1611), Tramstraat 63, 9052 Ghent. Package tours.

From Denmark
• **Benns Rejser** (☎ 9742 5000, 🖳 www.benns.com), Hovedkontor Norregade 51, Holstevro 7500, Holstebro. Sales agent for VIA and RM.

• **Air Canada** (☎ 3311 4555, 🖳 www.aircanada.com), Suite 3425, Vester Farimagsgade 1, 3 SK-1606, Copenhagen.

From France
• **Express Conseil** (☎ 0144 778 700), 5 rue du Louvre, Paris 75001. Sales agent for VIA.

• **Air Canada** (☎ 08 25 88 08 81, 🖳 www.aircanada.com), 106 blvd Haussmann, Paris.

• **Havas Voyages** (☎ 01 48 51 86 19, 🖳 www.havasvoyages.fr), API 2B60, 74 rue de Lagny, 93107 Montreuil Cedex. Packages and low-cost flights.

From Germany
• **Canada Reise Dienst International** (☎ 040-3000 6160, 🖳 www.crd.de), Fleethof, Stadthausbruecke 1–3, 20355 Hamburg. Sales agent for VIA and RMV.

• **Marketing Services International** (☎ 069-629 282), Johanna-Melber-Weg 12, 60599 Frankfurt. Agent for RMV.

• **Air Canada** (☎ 018050-247226, 🖳 www.aircanada.com), Hahnstrasse 70, 60528 Frankfurt.

● **Thomas Cook AG** (☎ 061-716 500), Zimmersmuhlenweg 55, 61440 Oberursel. Package tours and flights.

● **Canusa Touristik** (☎ 040-2272-53-0) Hamburg, Nebendahlstrasse 16, Hamburg, D-22041. Flights and package tours.

● **DERTour**, (☎ 069 95 88 52 00) Emil-von-Behring-Strausse 6, Frankfurt, D-60439, Germany. Flights and tours.

From Italy
● **Kuoni Gastaldi Tours** (☎ 10 59 99-309, 💻 www.kuonigastaldi.it), Mura di S. Chiara 1, 16128 Genova. Sales agent for VIA; package tours.

● **Sundeck Rappresentanze** (☎ 06 353 47101), Via Festo Avieno 59, 00136, Rome. Sales agent for RMV.

● **Air Canada** (☎ 06 55 1112 or ☎ 800 919091, 💻 www.aircanada.com).

● **CIT Viaggi** (☎ 474 6555), Piazza della Republica, Rome. Package tours.

From the Netherlands
●　**Incento BV** (☎ 035 69 55111; 💻 www.incento.nl), Incento BV, PO Box 1067, 1400 BB Bussum, Netherlands. Sales agent for VIA and RMV.

● **Air Canada** (☎ 0 20 346 95 39, 💻 www.aircanada.com).

● **Thomas Cook** (☎ 023-513 5353), Scorpius 1, 2132 LR Hoofddorp. Flights and packages.

From Sweden
● **Tour Canada of Sweden** (☎ 54-552365, 💻 www.tourcanada.se), Box 268, 65107, Karlstad. Sales agent for VIA; package tours.

From Switzerland
● **Imholz/Western Tours** (☎ 1-455 4444, 💻 www.imholz.ch), Birmensdorfer-strasse 108, CH-8036 Zurich. Sales agent for VIA.

● **Air Canada** (☎ 22-0848 247 226, 💻 www.aircanada.com).

● **Thomas Cook** (☎ 55-415-8611, 💻 info.sag@thomascookag.com), Poststrasse 4, 8808 Pfaffikon/SZ.

MAKING A BOOKING IN NORTH AMERICA
From Canada
● **VIA Rail Canada Inc** (☎ 514-871-6000, 💻 www.viarail.ca), 3 Place Ville-Marie, Montreal, Quebec, H3B 2C9 (VIA's headquarters). You can phone for information from anywhere in Canada on the following toll-free number: ☎ 1-888-842-7245. If, however, you are calling from either Moncton or Montreal you can use their local numbers: Moncton ☎ 857-9830; Montreal ☎ 989-2626.

• **Rocky Mountaineer Vacations** (☎ 604-606-7245, 🖳 www.rockymoun taineer.com), Pacific Central Station, First Floor, 100-1150 Station St, Vancouver BC V6A 2X7. You can call them toll-free on ☎ 1-877-460-3200 from anywhere in Canada or the US, or fax the reservations department on fax 604-606-7250.

• **Air Canada** The toll-free number when calling from anywhere in North America is ☎ 1-888-247-2262; the website is 🖳 www.aircanada.com or www.aircanada.ca.

• **Travel Cuts** (call toll-free on ☎ 1-866-246-9762 or 416-979-2406, 🖳 www. travelcuts.com). Discount-flight specialist with branches throughout Canada.

• **Rail Travel Tours** (☎ 204-897-9551, 🖳 www.railtraveltours.com), Box 44, 123 Main St, Winnipeg MB, R3C 1A3. Established in 2001 and operating out of Winnipeg, this company offers a wide range of rail tours led by very knowl edgeable guides. A great choice for rail enthusiasts.

• **Marlin Travel** (☎ 416-979-9300, 🖳 www.marlintravel.ca), 161 Bay St, Toronto, with branches across Canada. Offers a range of rail package tours.

From the USA
VIA doesn't have a sales agency in America, since you can make reservations at most travel agents; you can also call and make reservations directly with VIA on ☎ 1-888-842-7245. The following are organizations you can get in touch with about getting to Canada, and some package-tour operators:

• **Air Canada** (☎ 1-888-247-2262, 🖳 www.aircanada.ca), 221 N La Salle St, Chicago, IL; 125 Park Ave, New York. Flights from the US to all over Canada.

• **STA Travel** (☎ 1-800-781-4040 from across the US or ☎ 212-822-2700 in New York, 🖳 www.statravel.com), many branches across USA. Low-cost flights.

• **Amtrak** (☎ 1-800-872-7245, 🖳 www.amtrak.com). Direct rail connections with VIA: New York to Montreal or Toronto (via Niagara Falls); Chicago or Detroit to Toronto; Seattle to Vancouver.

• **Maupintour** (☎ 1-800-255-4266, 🖳 www.maupintour.com), 1515 St Andrew's Dr, Lawrence, Kansas 66046. Package tours.

MAKING A BOOKING IN AUSTRALASIA
From Australia
• **Asia Pacific** (☎ 02-9319 6624), St David's Hall, 17 Arthur Street, Surrey Hills, NSW 2010. VIA and RMV sales agent.

• **Air Canada** (☎ 02-9286 8900, 🖳 www.aircanada.com), Level 1, Comaltech House, 117 York St, Sydney.

- **STA Travel** (☎ 134782 from anywhere in Australia, 🖳 www.statravel.com. au). Discount-flight specialist with branches throughout Australia.

- **Thomas Cook Ltd** (☎ 02-9229 6611), 130 Pitt St, Sydney. Package tours.

From New Zealand
- **Adventure World New Zealand**, (☎ 64 9 524 5118; 🖳 www.adventure world.co.nz) 101 Great South Road, Remuera, Auckland. RMV Sales Agent.

- **Air Canada** (☎ 09-379-3371, 🖳 www.aircanada.com), Level 1, 18 Shortland St, Auckland 1.

- **STA Travel** (toll free on ☎ 0800-474-400, 🖳 www.statravel.co.nz). Discount-flight specialist with branches around New Zealand.

- **Thomas Cook (NZ) Ltd** (☎ 09-849 2071), Shop 250A, St Luke's Sq, Auckland. Package tours and flights.

MAKING A BOOKING IN SOUTH AFRICA

- **Bill Paterson Ltd** (☎ 11-403 4444), 10th Floor Noswal Hall, 3 Stiemens St, Braamfontein 2017, Johannesburg. Sales agent for VIA and RMV.

- **Air Canada** (☎ 21-422 3232, 🖳 www.aircanada.com), Tarquin House, 8th floor, 79 Loop Street, Cape Town 8001.

- **Rennies Travel** (☎ 21-406 5757, 🖳 www.renniestravel.co.za), Table Bay Sun Hotel, Quay 6, Victoria and Albert Waterfront, Cape Town. Package tours.

MAKING A BOOKING IN ASIA

From Japan
- **Japan Travel Bureau Inc** (☎ 03-3820 8011), 1-6-4 Marunouchi, Chiyoda-ku, Tokyo 100 005. Sales agent for VIA.

- **Air Canada** (☎ 03-5405 8800, 🖳 www.aircanada.com), 1-16-1 Kaigan, Minato-ku, Tokyo.

- **Japan Tours System Co** (☎ 03-5436 6374), JTS Building, 3-7-10 Shimo-Meguro, Meguro-Ku, Tokyo. Package tours.

- **Universal Express Co Ltd** (☎ 03-5644 3604, 🖳 www.uniex.co.ip), Libra Building, 3-2 Nihombashi kobuna-chou, Chou-ku, Tokyo 103-0024.

From Hong Kong
- **Japan Travel Bureau** (☎ 2734 9288), Room UG305, UG 3rd floor, Chinachem Golden Plaza, 77 Mody Rd, Tsimshatsui East, Kowloon. Sales agent for VIA.

- **Air Canada** (☎ 2867 8111, 🖳 www.aircanada.com), Room 1612-Tower One, New World Tower, 18 Queens Rd, Central.

• **Thomas Cook Travel Service** (☎ 2544-4986), 18th Floor, Vicwood Plaza, 199 Des Voeux Rd, Central. Package tours.

From Taiwan

• **Air Canada** (☎ 2-2507 5500, 🖳 www.aircanada.com), 8F, No 61 Nan King East Rd, Section 3, Taipei 103.

• **China Travel Service** (☎ 2-395 5123), 7th Floor, No 16, Sec 2 Jen-Ai-Road, Taipei 100. Package tours.

• **CAL Travel & Tours** (☎ 2598-1111, 🖳 www.caltravel.com.tw), 7 Fl No 2 Ming-Tsu East Road, Taipei, Taiwan. Popular tour company.

Visas and medical insurance

VISAS

Visitors from the UK and Ireland don't need a visa to get into Canada, just a full passport. Nor are visas required by citizens of Australia, Austria, Belgium, Chile, Denmark, Finland, France, Germany, Greece, Hungary, Iceland, Israel, Italy, Japan, Luxembourg, Malaysia, Malta, Mexico, Monaco, the Netherlands, New Zealand, Norway, Saudi Arabia, Singapore, Slovenia, South Korea, Spain, Sweden, Switzerland, United States and Zimbabwe.

In addition, citizens of most Commonwealth countries or British dependent territories do not need a visa. Check with your nearest Canadian Embassy or High Commission.

If you do need a visa you should contact the Immigration section of a Canadian Embassy or High Commission and ask for a visa application form. This must then be submitted in English or French. You also have to pay a visa processing fee – $75 for single entry, or $150 for multiple entry. Visas are valid for six months.

MEDICAL INSURANCE

Since there is absolutely nothing to inoculate yourself against in Canada, the only health precaution you need to worry about is medical insurance. It's vital that you arrange this before your trip as medical treatment in Canada is extremely expensive.

Most all-round travel insurances contain comprehensive medical cover; popular companies in the UK include **Columbus** (☎ 020-7375 0011), **Endsleigh** (☎ 020-7436 4451) and **STA Travel** (☎ 020-7436 7779).

What to take

CLOTHES

If you're going in winter, warm clothing is absolutely essential and should include a heavy coat (or a good down jacket), a hat, gloves and generous supplies of thermal underwear. You should also take a pair of warm, water-resistant boots ('moon boots' are perfect, though the fashion-conscious may draw the line here). The key thing to remember when dressing comfortably for a Canadian winter is to wear lots of layers which you can easily remove when inside heated buildings and then throw back on when you head outdoors again.

For the rest of the year the weather is more or less comparable to that in the UK, though if you're taking the train up to Prince Rupert in spring or autumn or to Churchill at any time of the year, be sure to pack the hat, gloves and thermals.

One of the most important things to get right is footwear. Sightseeing is a tiring business and shouldn't be attempted in anything other than a pair of very comfortable shoes. Special walking shoes may be your best bet as these can double up for walking in the Rockies if you plan to get off at Jasper.

MEDICAL SUPPLIES

You won't have any trouble at all getting hold of any medical supplies in Canada, so only the most basic supplies need to be included in your luggage (paracetamol, antiseptic cream and plasters should be enough).

MONEY

Travellers' cheques are always a bit of a hassle so I would recommend getting most of your cash out of **automated teller machines** (ATMs) at banks, as and when you need it, using your debit card (see p43 for more on this). It would be unwise, however, to rely on the card as your sole means of obtaining money, just in case it's stolen. In this case, travellers' cheques are an invaluable back-up; even if they're stolen you can claim back their value very easily, though be very careful to keep the numbers in a safe place.

BACKGROUND READING

Trees and lakes are all very well but they can get a bit tedious in large doses. Reading of some sort is essential on the train and is all the more interesting if it's relevant to your journey. Here are a few suggestions:

Books about the railway
● *The National Dream* and *The Last Spike* by Pierre Berton. Eminently readable best-sellers on the trials, tribulations and dramas involved in building the

first transcontinental railway across Canada (turned into a mini-series in the 1970s). They're published together in an abridged version called *The Great Railway*, widely available throughout Canada.

● *Van Horne's Road* by Omer Lavallée. Detailed and exhaustively researched book chronicling the construction of the Canadian Pacific Railway – by the man who set up the Canadian Pacific Archives. Lots of wonderful old black-and-white photos.

● *Railways of Canada* by Jim Lotz and Keith McKenzie. Colourful and readable hardback book sold in major bookshops (like Coles) throughout the country.

● *All Aboard* by David J. Mitchell. Big glossy paperback focusing on rail travel through the Rocky Mountains. Well written (by BC historian) and with some excellent colour photography; available at Dulthie's in Vancouver (919 Robson St) or onboard *The Rocky Mountaineer*.

The following are out of print but should be available in libraries:

● *Scenic Rail Guide to Western Canada* and *Scenic Rail Guide to Central & Atlantic Canada* by Bill Coo. Collectively the bible of Canadian rail guides, written by a man who worked on the lines for over 30 years. Used to be given away free on *The Canadian* but now out of print. Copies are like gold dust but you could try Halifax and Montreal railway stations.

● *Ocean to Ocean* by Rev George M Grant. The author accompanied Sandford Fleming, head of the Canadian Pacific Survey, on his mammoth expedition across Canada in 1872. The book is a chronicle of the journey and a fascinating insight into Canada before the railway.

● *The Great Lone Land* by Capt W F Butler. The impressions of a young soldier as he journeys into the depths of Canada's North-West at the time of the Riel rebellion. The book was a best seller in its time.

● *The Queen's Highway* by Stuart Cumberland. Lively account of the railway journey from Port Moody to Halifax by one of the CPR's first passengers.

General books about Canada
For a more general spread of background material, you might like to try some of the following titles:

● *Oh Canada! Oh Quebec!* by Mordecai Richler. An incisive and witty send-up of some of the excesses of Quebec's independence movement.

● *The Betrayal of Canada* by Mel Hurtig. Typical Canadian anxiety about the state of the nation by one of the country's best-known writers.

● *The Will of a Nation: Awakening the Canadian Spirit* by George Radwanski and Julia Luttrell. More Canadian self-enquiry and meditation on the national identity.

● *A Short History of Canada* by Desmond Morton. Sensible and highly readable history book.

● *The Battle for Room Service* by Mark Lawson. Reflections of a British journalist as he travels through the 'world's safest places,' including Vancouver, Winnipeg, Toronto and Montreal. Cynical, scathing and hilarious.

● *The Edge* by Dick Francis. Dastardly doings on a private, luxury train as it crosses Canada, with some good landscape descriptions amongst the intrigue and suspense. Don't read it if you're travelling alone.

● *The Republic of Love* by Carol Shields. A superb comic romance by one of Canada's best contemporary novelists, set in the unlikely location of Winnipeg.

● *Cat's Eye* by Margaret Atwood. Excellent, sensitive novel about a painter who returns to Toronto to find it – and herself – indelibly changed.

● *Maria Chapdelaine* by Louis Hémon. Enduring best seller written in 1913 about a young girl's life in the backwoods of northern Quebec. It veers towards sentimentality but nonetheless paints a vivid picture of the uncompromising harshness of frontier life.

● *The Shipping News* by E Annie Proulx. Pulitzer prize-winning novel set in a remote village on the Newfoundland coast. Apart from being a wonderful read it gives you an insight into the incredible regional diversity within Canada.

● *The Unknown Country: Canada and her People* by Bruce Hutchison. Awarded the Governor General Award for non-fiction, this fascinating narrative gives a mid-20th-century perspective on transcontinental travel in Canada. Inspired by a conversation with a New Yorker who wanted to know more about the unknown neighbour to the north, it took Hutchison only six weeks to write.

● *Lost in the Backwoods* by Catherine Parr Trail. One of several books by Parr Trail offering a fascinating insight into the life of the early settlers building a new life in rural Ontario in the mid-19th century. The author moved to Canada from England in the 1830s with her sister, Susannah Moodie, who also chronicled her experiences with books such as *Roughing it in the Bush: Or, Life in Canada*.

Guidebooks

If you want to equip yourself with more **guidebooks**, there are dozens to choose from. *The Rough Guide to Canada* is packed with useful information on the whole country and contains some quirky and entertaining asides. There's also *Canada* from Lonely Planet. *Baedeker's Canada* is a good reference source, and has glossy colour pictures on just about every other page.

You could also take a look at the Fodor range. As well as *Fodor's Canada* there are numerous guides to various parts of the country including *The Upper Great Lakes region*, *Canada's Atlantic Provinces*, *the Rockies*, *Montreal & Quebec City* and *Toronto* – all of them full of good practical information.

If you're continuing your rail travel south over the border, *USA by Rail* by John Pitt (Bradt Travel Guides/Globe Pequot) is recommended.

PART 2: CANADA

Facts about the country

GEOGRAPHICAL BACKGROUND

Great stretches of wilderness, so that its frontier is a circumference rather than a boundary; a country with huge rivers and islands that most natives have never seen, a country that has made a nation out of the stops on two of the world's longest railway lines.
Northrop Frye, *Sudia Varia*, 1957

Canada is the second largest country in the world, covering a vast 9,970,610 sq km (almost four million square miles). It's flanked by the Atlantic on the east and the Pacific on the west, with some 6000km in between. Its southern boundary is the US border, which follows the 49th parallel from the Pacific to the Great Lakes, then loops all over the place between Lake Ontario and the Atlantic. To the north Canada stretches all the way up to Ellesmere Island in the Arctic Ocean, 4400km away from Toronto. In the north-west is the other US/Canada border, separating the Yukon and British Columbia from Alaska.

This colossal area is divided into ten provinces and three territories: Newfoundland, Nova Scotia, Prince Edward Island, New Brunswick, Quebec, Ontario, Manitoba, Saskatchewan, Alberta, British Columbia, North West Territories, Yukon Territory and the territory of Nunavut (see box p30).

Climate
In 1881 a British periodical called *Truth* described Canada as 'frost-bound for seven or eight months in the year....[and] as forbidding a country as any on the face of the Earth', a familiar but slightly unfair stereotype that persists to this day. Okay, so it does get a bit chilly in winter (everywhere except the west coast has average January temperatures well below freezing point and continuous snow cover) but the populated stretch along the south has very good springs and warm summers. A typical July on the prairies, for instance, is dry and hot (usually mid-20°sC/70°sF) while an average summer in Quebec and Ontario will be warm and humid. West coast summers tend to be temperate rather than hot but winters here are the mildest in the country thanks to the influence of the warm Pacific Ocean (Vancouver's average January temperature is 3°C/37°F, compared to Winnipeg's –20°C/–4°F).

Moving further north, the 'frost-bound' label is rather more justified, indeed much of the upper two-thirds of the country is continuously affected by *permafrost* (ground remaining at or below 0°C/32°F for at least two years). The only train taking you into this frozen region is *The Hudson Bay* to Churchill, where winter temperatures regularly drop to –30°C (–22°F).

CANADA

> **Nunavut – the new territory**
> On the somewhat inauspicious date of April Fool's Day 1999 a new territory was carved out of Canada's North West. Two million square kilometres in size, the place is one-fifth of Canada's total land mass and two-thirds its coastline. It's the traditional home of the Inuit, once called Eskimos by Europeans. The name of the new land is Nunavut, which means 'Our Land'.
>
> For at least four thousand years the Inuit lived on the barren tundra of what's now northern Canada, developing a harmonious relationship with their harsh lands. Their first contact with Europeans was in the mid-1700s when whalers started visiting the Arctic seas. They remained pretty much untroubled by Europeans until the 1940s but when the Canadian government began to establish itself in the area the Inuit were persuaded to abandon their traditional nomadic life and to base themselves in fixed settlements. Today there are 25,000 Inuit in Nunavut, living in 28 communities.
>
> The new territory faces a whole slew of problems. Not least is its sheer size: in Nunavut population density is just one person per 100 square km compared with 29 as the average for Canada as a whole. Other problems are economic: the average household in Nunavut earns only two-thirds of what a family in southern Canada earns yet the cost of living is about twice as much. Traditional ways of life such as hunting and trapping are under threat, particularly from ecologically minded Westerners who object to fur trading. The Canadian government has attempted to foster alternatives, particularly (and imaginatively) a craft industry, and Inuit soapstone carvings can now be seen all over the country (look for the trademark Igloo stickers and tags to check for authenticity).
>
> Despite its problems, the Canadian government is optimistic about Nunavut's future and sees the establishment of the territory as an indication of the more sensitive way in which aboriginal people are treated in the country.
>
> One example is the government of Nunavut itself. It has been designed with an eye on the people it is to govern – it's highly decentralized, spread across 11 different communities and the traditional knowledge of the Inuit elders is built into the government systems.
>
> In 2002 Queen Elizabeth II, on her jubilee tour of Canada, acknowledged the new territory by visiting Nunavut's capital, Iqaluit, on Baffin Island, which is more than she did for the people of Quebec who were not included in her itinerary.

Transport and communications

As might be expected in a country of this size and economic ranking, Canada's transport infrastructure is extensive and efficient. The majority of internal communications run east–west, such as the Trans-Canada Highway connecting St Johns (Newfoundland) to Vancouver – the longest national highway in the world at 7821km.

Rail remains an important means of transporting freight, principally bulk commodities like grain, lumber and coal, which are often carried in 'unit trains' of one hundred or more cars. It has been overtaken, however, by the motor car and the aeroplane as the chief transporters of people around the country. Shipping provides another important means of freight transportation, both from ocean ports like Vancouver and Halifax, and along the Great Lakes/St Lawrence Seaway system.

Landscape zones: flora and fauna

The main landscape zones you'll travel through on your trans-Canada rail journey are as follows:

● **St Lawrence Lowlands** Spreading across the northern shores of the Great Lakes and east along the St Lawrence River towards the Atlantic Ocean, this is the most densely populated area of Canada. The high degree of urbanization and industrialization in this region is interrupted by large areas given over to agriculture and forestry, mainly mixed conifers such as red spruce and pines, and various deciduous trees, red and sugar maple in particular. In autumn their blazing red foliage is spectacular and draws thousands of tourists each year.

● **Canadian Shield** This is Canada's dominant geographic feature, stretching in a massive band from Hudson Bay down to the Great Lakes and east into Labrador. It spreads over 4.5 million sq km, much of it covered by Precambrian rock (570–1100 million years old). The erosive effects of glaciation over the last million years have scoured the Shield's surface, leaving a striking landscape of bare rock and countless lakes, rivers and streams. Much of the Shield is covered by coniferous **boreal forest** (millions of spruce, larch and pine, plus some poplar and aspen).

● **Tundra** As they approach Churchill, travellers aboard *The Hudson Bay* will find themselves in the most barren and inhospitable part of the country covered by rail track. Tundra is a region of permafrost and bitter cold where vegetation is stunted and sparse. The few trees that can survive here (mainly birch) rarely grow higher than a metre and most of the earth is covered by lichens, shrubs and mosses, though the most beautiful wild flowers spring up for a few weeks in summer. Wildlife, on the other hand, is plentiful, though most of it is well camouflaged: arctic fox, arctic ptarmigan, white squirrels and caribou are all local inhabitants.

● **The prairies** The vast expanse of land between the Shield and the Rockies is part of the Interior Plains spanning the whole length of Canada from the US border up to the Arctic coast. The famous part of the plains is the southern fertile belt, known universally as 'the prairies'. This is where Canada's wheat is produced, an average of 25 billion tonnes of it each year. It's known for its extreme flatness, especially in Saskatchewan; the Alberta prairies are a little more undulating. The area was once home to enormous numbers of bison: an estimated 50–60 million roamed the plains in 1800 but had been hunted almost to extinction by 1885. These days you'll probably see little more than crops and grain elevators as you pass through.

● **Western Cordillera** The western mountains are part of the massive 14,000km-long chain that spans the length of the continent from Tierra del Fuego right up to Alaska. In Canada they're made up of several ranges, the most famous and most easterly being the **Rockies**. West of these is the Columbia system (the Purcell, Selkirk and Monashee ranges) followed by the Coast Mountains.

> **The Great Lakes**
> Lakes Superior, Michigan, Huron, Erie and Ontario are known collectively as the Great Lakes. Together they make up the largest body of freshwater in the world, with a total area of over 246,000 sq km. Apart from Lake Michigan, which lies entirely within the United States, they are located on the border between Canada and America. The largest is Lake Superior which is 563km long, 257km wide and reaches a depth of 406m. It is the largest fresh-water lake in the world.

The Rockies are your best bet out of the entire route for spotting wildlife (see colour section pp64-5). In spring and summer you'll also be treated to a profusion of wild flowers with beautiful names like Indian Paintbrush and Glacier Lily. As you move into central British Columbia the terrain becomes arid and is sparsely covered by low shrubs such as sagebrush and prickly pear. Much of the coastal range, in contrast, is covered by luxuriant green fir trees, particularly towards Prince Rupert, with its dripping rainforest, cliffs, mosses and fjords. These mountains are home to numerous bald eagles; sightings are almost guaranteed.

HISTORICAL OUTLINE

First Nations

The first inhabitants of what we now call Canada arrived from Asia between 12,000 and 20,000 years ago, having crossed the land bridge connecting Siberia to North America. A second wave of migration from Asia occurred around 3000BC. These people spread themselves around the continent, adapting and developing according to the different environments they settled in. By the time the European explorers 'discovered' Canada, it was populated by a range of distinct peoples with differing languages, belief systems, lifestyles and traditions. The tribes scattered between the Yukon and the Atlantic led a hunting-gathering existence and fell into two language groups: Athapaskan and Algonquin. To the south were the agricultural-based communities of the Iroquois. Far north were the Innu who had adapted to life in the harsh conditions of the Arctic tundra. Tragically, all native peoples were rapidly depleted with the arrival of European diseases to which they weren't immune.

French colonization

Early visitors to Canada's Atlantic coast included the Vikings around 1000AD, John Cabot in 1497 and scores of European fishermen soon after. It wasn't until the beginning of the 17th century that a permanent European settlement got going when Samuel de Champlain, following the course down the St Lawrence River taken by Jacques Cartier 70 years earlier, set up a small colony in 1608 at what is now Quebec City. It was a great success and another settlement was founded

---

(Opposite) Animals such as the eagle, the raven and the beaver are often used as symbols of spirits in the carving of totem poles. These examples are part of an impressive group standing in Vancouver's Stanley Park (see p178).

at present-day Montreal in 1642. The French presence gradually spread throughout the region and in 1663 New France was officially declared a royal colony.

The Hudson's Bay Company

New France was the source of a vast supply of furs which fed the insatiable demands of European fashion and it wasn't long before France's arch rival, Britain, decided to muscle in on the action and corner a share of the profits of this new land for itself. In 1670 the Hudson's Bay Company (HBC) was set up to exploit the wealth of fur-trading possibilities around Hudson Bay. Charles II claimed thousands of miles of land around the bay and granted this to the Company; they named it Rupert's Land after the King's cousin, Prince Rupert, who was instrumental in creating the company. Trading posts were erected throughout the area and intense rivalry developed between the HBC and French traders which continued for the next century, often spilling over into violence.

New France becomes British

Meanwhile, Britain's involvement in Canada was not limited to the fur trade: renewed efforts were being made to drive the French out of their Atlantic settlements in Acadia (the name given by the French to their territories bordering the Atlantic, that once spread over eastern Quebec, the Maritime provinces and New England), which the British had renamed Nova Scotia. In 1713 the Treaty of Utrecht gave Britain what it wanted and the French were forced to hand over their mainland Atlantic territories. Still not satisfied, Britain pushed for control of the remaining French strongholds, notably Quebec with its prime position on the St Lawrence River. In 1759 the conflict came to a dramatic head when the British attacked Quebec City, scaling the Heights of Abraham in the night and defeating the French in the famous battle on the Plains of Abraham. By now

CANADA

O Kanata!

It is ironic that the name of the second largest country in the world is derived from a word meaning 'village'. Cartier, in 1535, was directed to 'kanata' by a couple of Huron-Iroquois youths. They were referring to the village of Stadacona, where Quebec was later founded, but Cartier applied the word to the whole area subject to the rule of Donnacona, the chief of the village. The name somehow stuck and gradually came to be used for the region around the St Lawrence, and then for all of New France, but its boundaries were always vague and never officially delineated by the ruling French.

When the British took over New France they temporarily abandoned the name of Canada and called their new territory the Province of Quebec. The name was revived in 1791 when Quebec was divided into Upper Canada and Lower Canada, which were joined together again in 1841 as the single Province of Canada. Finally, when Nova Scotia, New Brunswick and Canada united in Confederation in 1867 they became 'One Dominion under the name of Canada'.

(Opposite) Dating from 1893 this magnificent CPR hotel, the Château Frontenac (see p90), has become the symbol of Quebec City and one of the most photographed buildings in the country.

France was ready to wash its hands of the troublesome North American colonies and in 1763 it officially ceded all of New France to Britain.

The division of Quebec

In contrast to the treatment meted out to the Acadians who were forcibly deported in the 1750s, the Quebec Act of 1774 safeguarded the rights of the French Canadians to speak their own language, practise Catholicism, hold civil appointments and keep their seigneurial land-owning system. However, they soon found themselves deluged with 10,000 Loyalist settlers (following the American War of Independence) who clearly did not expect to be governed according to the French system. In an attempt to get round this problem, the province of Quebec was divided into Upper Canada and Lower Canada in 1791. This way the French speakers, concentrated in Lower Canada, could remain separate from the English-speaking Protestants in Upper Canada with each side controlling their own local affairs.

The 1837 rebellions

In practice the French Canadians were increasingly discriminated against and the ensuing tide of resentment resulted in a violent but short-lived rebellion in 1837 led by Louis-Joseph Papineau. Upper Canadians had their own political grievances, too, expressed in a more scaled down and equally abortive rebellion led by William Lyon Mackenzie in the same year. The British government's response was to reunite the two provinces in 1840, forming the single province of Canada which would be granted greater powers of self-government. It was hoped that this would bring the French Canadians into line and curb their demands for self-rule. As time would show, it was to do nothing of the sort.

Confederation

Britain's North American colonies got bigger and bigger as immigration stepped up in the 1840s. Many politicians recognized that the separate provinces would be economically and politically stronger if they were to unite – and strength was an all important issue given the aggressive annexationist tendencies of the United States. At the same time, Britain was ready to give the colonies more autonomy: it was wearying of the huge cost of defending them for virtually no returns. So, after a big Confederation campaign and a few years of debate, the dominion of Canada came into existence on 1 July 1867 when the British North America Act became law. It consisted of the former colonies of New Brunswick, Nova Scotia and Canada (subsequently divided into Ontario and Quebec). These were shortly joined by Manitoba (1870), British Columbia (1871), and Prince Edward Island (1873).

Forging a nation

Canada's first Prime Minister was the Conservative leader, Sir John A Macdonald, a man blessed with both pragmatism and vision. Realizing that the links binding the provinces together were extremely tenuous, he set about strengthening the nation by expanding its territory and filling it with people. One of the major bedrocks of this policy was the creation of a transcontinental railroad which would physically join the provinces from east to west and transport a flow of goods, trade and immigrants across Canada. Accordingly, the first act of his government was to purchase from the Hudson's Bay Company the vast expanse of land between Ontario and British Columbia (still known as Rupert's Land) where settlers would be sent out to populate the southern, fertile stretch. This was not without its complications...

The first Riel rebellion

Rupert's Land had been almost but not completely unpopulated. At the meeting of the Red and Assiniboine Rivers (the site of present-day Winnipeg) was the small and isolated Red River Colony, made up principally of the Métis people (mixed French and Indian). When the government dispatched colonists and officials to 'settle' the area in 1870, the Métis, stirred up and organized by the passionate Louis Riel, staged a violent protest. Riel issued a series of demands to the Canadian government based on the creation of a French and English-speaking province with the provision of French-speaking schools. The government complied and the province of Manitoba was created but Riel was forced to flee to America following the execution of a Canadian by the Métis.

The second Riel rebellion

Fifteen years later, tensions between the Métis and the Canadian government broke out in a second rebellion. This time the Métis were supported by the Cree and Plains Natives whose lands had been encroached on by speculators and farmers. Louis Riel was whisked back from America (where he had been experiencing prolonged bouts of mental illness) to lead the rebellion, which he threw himself into with fervour. The uprising was crushed by Canadian troops, hastily transported to the scene by the almost completed railway, and Riel was captured and sentenced to death for high treason, even though he was clearly mentally unfit at the time. Riel was hanged in November, 1885 – immortalized for the French Canadians as a symbolic victim of brutal Protestant oppression.

Prosperity

It was prosperity, and not confrontation or drama, that characterized Canada's entry into the 20th century. Certainly the following decades were to bring their problems, such as the paralysing Depression of the '30s. On the whole, however, the nation followed a pattern of growth and success. New provinces were incorporated (Alberta and Saskatchewan in 1905); immigrants flooded in and the wheat empire of the prairies boomed. Meanwhile, successive Canadian governments, dominated first by the Conservatives and then by the Liberals after 1921, began to steer Canada along a more independent path, gradually severing all constitutional ties with Britain. In more recent decades, a series of prestigious projects such as the Trans-Canada Highway and the St Lawrence Seaway fostered a growing sense of nationhood, and in 1965 Canada finally adopted its own flag – the red maple leaf. This new-found national pride was further boosted by the hosting of major international events such as Expo '67 and the 1976 Olympic Games. However, national harmony was disrupted as French Canadian discontent took on a louder voice in the '60s and '70s.

THE QUEBEC ISSUE

Political awakening

French Canadians had been subjected to a multitude of social and economic injustices ever since the British had taken over New France in 1763. Incredibly, it wasn't until the 1960s that their needs and grievances were given a coherent political voice by Quebec's provincial government, under the Liberal premier, Jean Lesage. In response, a Royal Commission was set up in 1963 to investigate the situation. It concluded that Francophones earned less, had a lower standard of living and were less likely to advance economically and socially than their Anglophone counterparts. It also warned that the situation was heading towards a national crisis.

The crisis duly exploded in 1970 when the militant separatist group, the Front de Libération du Québec (FLQ), embarked on a wave of terrorism culminating in the kidnapping and murder of a Quebec politician, leaving the country in a state of shock.

Parti Québecois in power

Meanwhile the nationalist wing of the Liberal Party in Quebec had broken away to form the Parti Québecois (PQ) under René Lévesque. In 1976 the PQ won provincial elections and Lévesque became Quebec's premier. The party turned Quebec into an officially monolingual province with a series of controversial language laws that triggered an exodus of thousands of Anglophones from Montreal. However, it failed to achieve its goal of independence when 60% of Quebec voters rejected the mild form of separation ('sovereignty-association') proposed by the 1980 referendum.

The 1995 referendum

In 1990 the Bloc Québecois was formed to represent Quebec's cause at a federal level. It was phenomenally successful, gaining the highest number of votes after the Liberal Party in the 1993 federal elections, making the Bloc Québecois the official government opposition. In 1995, fifteen years after the original referendum, a new sovereignty referendum was called in Quebec, considerably more radical than the first. Under the charismatic leadership of Lucien Bouchard, the separatist movement gained massive momentum and Quebec seemed to be spinning inexorably towards independence. In the event, the separatists were defeated by just one per cent of the vote, leaving the issue far from resolved. However, in 1998 the Supreme Court of Canada ruled that if Quebec were ever to separate it would have to negotiate with federal government and the provinces.

ECONOMY

Voltaire somewhat underestimated Canada's potential when he dismissed it as 'several acres of snow' in 1759. In fact, it boasts one of the world's richest bases of natural resources including huge mineral deposits (potash, zinc, nickel, iron, copper and gold), generous supplies of coal, oil, gas and phenomenal quantities of trees. Almost half the country is covered in forests, providing pulp for the paper industry, as well as timber for the construction industry. In addition, the western prairies are among the world's biggest grain producers and Canada's great provisions of water (what isn't covered by trees seems to be covered by lakes and rivers) is the source of a massive supply of hydroelectric power.

All this has been carefully and efficiently exploited to make Canada one of the richest countries in the world. It has developed a highly successful industrial and manufacturing sector: major industries include vehicle manufacturing, logging, pulp and paper, and fish processing. Its most important trading partner is the US, which receives 75% of Canadian exports and provides 60% of Canada's imports, though Mexico looks set to play a larger role in Canada's economy now that NAFTA (North American Free Trade Agreement) is in operation. Most Canadians enjoy a very good standard of living but unemployment remains high at around 7%.

THE PEOPLE

Canada's population of just under 33 million people is concentrated in a thin east–west strip in the south of the country – indeed 90% of all Canadians live within 150km of the US border. This pattern of settlement follows the path taken by the transcontinental railways and, much later, by the Trans-Canada Highway. The climate is considerably milder here than in the more northerly parts of Canada and the land is more suitable for farming. The most densely populated provinces are Quebec and Ontario where about 62% of Canadians live. Even in the most populated areas of these provinces there are a mere 60 people to each square kilometre– compared to a miserable 230 per square kilometre in the UK.

Native settlement, Queen Charlotte Island; late 19th century.

The immigrants

Immigration has necessarily played a key role in boosting Canada's population and economy. Today, Canada's biggest ethnic group is of British origin (almost 50%) followed by that of French origin (about 27%). First the need to populate the prairies and then the shortage of a post-war workforce resulted in an influx of non French/British immigrants – mainly Germans, Italians, Finns, Ukrainians and Poles. Today, about 20% of Canadians are of non French/British European extract. Canada's immigration policies have often been characterized by racial discrimination; for example, Chinese and Japanese were virtually banned from settling in the country between 1885 and 1940. Since the 1970s, however, immigration policies have become increasingly liberal and Asians have constituted a high proportion of the annual 100,000 or so people settling in Canada over recent years.

The native peoples

At the time of early European contact, Canada had an indigenous population of up to two million people. The 2001 Canadian Census revealed that there are over 900,000 aboriginals in Canada and these consist of about 45,000 Inuit, until recently known as Eskimos, and around 600,000 descendants of the First Nations community. The remainder are 'non-status' Indians who have either abandoned their status rights or are of mixed blood, known as Métis.

The decline of these people is the saddest story of modern Canada. Initially, their numbers were ravaged with the arrival of Western diseases such as TB; then they were manoeuvred into a state of near-dependency on the fur traders and their European goods; finally they were forced off their land by British colonists and shunted into inadequate, isolated reservations where they witnessed a complete breakdown of the lifestyle that had served their people for thousands of years. For many native communities, the legacy of modern Canada has been high unemployment, alcoholism and depression.

On a more positive note, the Assembly of First Nations (AFN) has been formed to provide native peoples with political and legal representation. In 1992 the AFN scored a huge victory by negotiating a settlement for the Inuit land claim: in 1999 Nunavut (in the North West Territories) became a separate territory, governed by native Canadians. This is the first time in modern Canadian history that natives have been responsible for local government.

Canada's a great place to live – it's official
Ever since the UN started to publish its annual Human Development Index in 1990, Canada has been at or very near the top. From 1994 to 2000 it was ranked in first place for seven years running – an achievement matched by no other country. The index looks at standards of living, measured by GDP per capita, life expectancy and achievements in education, including adult literacy.

Canada has recently been nudged from the top spot by Norway but given that the index is composed of around 170 countries, it's unlikely anyone's too worried.

GOVERNMENT

Canada is a federal state with democratic parliamentary representation. It is also a constitutional monarchy (yes, Queen Elizabeth II is still the official head of state). The way it works is that each of the provinces has its own government with its own premier and its own legislative body. They're in charge of things like taxes, social welfare, education, transport and general administration. Then there's the federal government in charge of everything else. Executive power is in the hands of the Prime Minister and his or her cabinet. Legislative power rests with the Canadian Parliament in Ottawa, consisting of the House of Commons (elected) and the Senate (appointed by the Prime Minister).

Since Confederation in 1867, central power has swung between the Conservatives and the Liberals with few major differences between the two. The other main party is the New Democratic Party (mildly socialist). The current Prime Minister is Stephen Harper of the Conservative Party.

EDUCATION AND SOCIAL WELFARE

Canada spends a higher percentage of its GDP on education (over 7%) than any other country in the world. It has a universal, free and compulsory school system: all children are required to attend elementary and secondary schools from the age of six to about sixteen.

Education is the responsibility of the provinces, not the federal government, which results in distinct differences across the country. Newfoundland, for example, has an exclusively denominational school system, whereas BC's is totally non-denominational. Controversial issues have included the provision of minority language teaching (eg for Francophones outside Quebec, for Anglophones inside Quebec and for the children of immigrant groups) and the often ill-conceived programmes for the education of native children. There are 69 public universities in Canada and over 200 other post-secondary institutions.

Canadians are proud of their social welfare system, which provides free medical care, old age pensions, family allowance and unemployment insurance. The costs of these programmes are shared by the federal and provincial governments, and Canadians can generally take advantage of them whether they're in their own province or an outside province.

RELIGION

Religious mythology and ceremony were highly developed among the native peoples before the arrival of the Bible-brandishing Europeans. Beliefs and practices often differed from tribe to tribe but some were shared by many groups such as the myth of the Earth Diver in which the Transformer plunges into the ancient waters and gathers the mud from which he moulds the earth. Another common myth told of the mischievous Trickster who steals fire, light, water and food and sets them all lose to create a chaotic world.

Catholicism was, of course, imported by the French as soon as they arrived. Indeed, the Catholic Church provided the foundations for the society of New

France and continued to be a dominant power in Quebec until recent decades. British settlers, on the other hand, were Protestant and set about populating the country with more of their ilk. The resulting pattern continues today: over 90% of Quebeckers are Catholic, while Protestantism (of various sects) dominates all the other provinces. All in all, about 90% of Canadians claim to be Christian. These include significant numbers of Orthodox Christians, particularly in the prairie provinces. The remaining 10% are made up principally of Jews, Muslims, Sikhs, Hindus and Buddhists, large numbers of whom are centred in or around Toronto.

Practical information for the visitor

DOCUMENTS

Americans aren't officially required to show a passport when crossing the border (just solid ID), though it's very much preferred. For everyone else, a full passport is mandatory. You must also be able to provide evidence that you will be leaving the country within three months (eg a return or onward air ticket).

Travellers' cheques and a copy of your travel insurance policy should also be at the top of your document checklist and if you plan to rent a car remember, of course, to bring your driver's licence. Other useful ID includes student or senior citizen cards which will get you substantial reductions at most museums and tourist attractions.

ARRIVING IN CANADA

Before you touch down (or when you arrive at the border if you're coming overland), travellers who don't need a visa (see p25) will be given a waiver form to complete and hand in at passport control. If you do need a visa you'll have to line up in a separate queue at passport control and show your visa documentation. If you're travelling alone, and/or are staying for more than a few weeks and/or have a vaguely shifty look about you, be prepared to answer a long list of searching questions from a Port of Entry examining officer about your travel plans/job back home/childhood holidays in Brighton. If you're travelling as a couple or family, especially if you've got a couple of kids in tow, you should be spared the detective work.

❑ **Senior tip**
'It's worth mentioning the Senior Citizens' Discount. We always asked if it applied and in most places we were lucky and got a 10% discount.'
James and Joan Fundell (Cyprus)

Customs

Import allowances are: 200 cigarettes and 50 cigars; 200gm tobacco; 1.4 litres of spirits or 8.5 litres of beer (for persons aged 18 or over in Alberta, Manitoba and Quebec, aged 19 elsewhere in Canada) and gifts worth up to $60 each. Any food, plants and animals among your luggage must be declared to Customs.

HOTELS

Canada is well supplied with hotels and most of them are of a high standard. Many of the **upmarket hotels** are enormous and luxurious establishments, boasting grand lobbies, sumptuous dining rooms and state-of-the-art gym and pool facilities. Among the best – and certainly the most appropriate for the trans-Canada railway traveller – are the old Canadian Pacific railway hotels (now owned by Fairmont), many of them built to accommodate wealthy tourists travelling across the country at the turn of the 20th century.

Mid-range hotels are usually clean, well-equipped and comfortable. They fall into two broad categories: the large and faceless (usually with good facilities which nearly always include private bathroom, TV and phone) and the smaller inn or guest-house type of place ranging from the very elegant to the distinctly shoddy. It is these smaller places that have the most character, particularly in the numerous converted Victorian or Georgian homes in eastern Canada, but some of them can be a little spartan. Mid-budget travellers might also consider the private en-suite rooms increasingly on offer in many hostels – see below.

The most popular base for **budget travellers** seems to be the Hostelling International youth hostels. On the whole their standards are excellent (small dorms, cafeterias, laundry rooms, plenty of hot showers and usually internet access) though this is reflected in their prices. Many HI hostels now offer private rooms with en-suite bathrooms in addition to their traditional dormitory accommodation – they're usually immaculate and make an attractive alternative to mid-range hotels.

Other popular budget accommodation is provided by YWCA and YMCA hostels (often with free use of pool and gym facilities) and university residences during the summer. All these are typically quite spartan single rooms with a shared bath in the corridor but a few of the YWCAs offer first-rate en-suite rooms as well. Hostels in general are much cleaner and more pleasant than the really cheap 'hotels' you'll find adjoined to some of the less salubrious downtown bars, many of which are rowdy doss-houses left over from the days when alcohol could be served only in places that had rooms to let.

LOCAL TRANSPORT

Local transport in Canadian cities is exactly as you'd expect it to be: wide-ranging and frequent, clean, safe and efficient. In many remote areas, however, it is non-existent, so if jumping off the train at a trappers' flag stop in northern Ontario takes your fancy, don't expect to be greeted by a shuttle bus.

Taxis

These are numerous in all cities and even small towns have their fair share of them. Fares are comparable to those in Europe. Note that it's customary to give cab drivers a tip of about 10-15%.

Subway

There are subway systems in Montreal and Toronto. Both are clean, safe and always busy but since there are relatively few lines it's often as quick to walk or take the bus if you just want to get around the downtown core.

Buses

Bus travel is far better than taking the subway as you can see where you're going and get a better idea of the city's geography. Buses are the mainstay of local transport in Canada with extensive routes in every city. You'll be able to get a route map at the local tourist office or you can ring the local transport information line – for the number, see the Transport section of the relevant city guide in this book.

One irritating thing about buses is that to travel on them you need the exact change which you deposit in a plastic box in front of the driver. There's usually a flat fare of about $2 or so.

Internal flights

Canada's cities are spaced out over thousands of miles, which makes flying the quickest and most convenient way of getting between them. Accordingly, the country's internal flight network is highly developed and heavily patronized. The main carrier is Air Canada, serving hundreds of places in the country, including some of the most remote outposts such as Inuvik on the Arctic Coast.

Internal flights are cheaper if booked outside Canada (you don't have to pay tax); if you plan to take more than one flight enquire about air passes.

Ferries

Canada has plenty of busy local ferry services such as those from Halifax to Dartmouth, Lévis to Quebec City, Vancouver to Victoria, and from Newfoundland, Prince Edward Island and Cape Breton Island to the mainland. New Brunswick operates toll-free ferries across the Saint John and Kennebecasis rivers as part of the highway system. The most popular ferry service among tourists is probably the spectacular 15-hour ride up the Inside Passage from Vancouver Island to Prince Rupert.

Car rental

Renting a car in Canada is expensive (at least $400 a week). As well as your driver's licence it helps to have a major credit card, especially if you're under 25. People under the age of 21 aren't normally eligible to rent cars. If you're intending to hire a car in one city and drive to another part of Canada, it's usually possible to leave the car at the end of the journey – however, beware of 'drop-off fees' which can be fairly steep, and be sure to shop around to see who has the best offer.

Note also that International Driving Permits aren't valid without a supporting national driver's licence.

ELECTRICITY

This is 110 volts AC. Sockets take two-pronged flat-pin plugs or adaptors. Be sure to buy the adaptor before you get to Canada because they're very difficult to obtain once you're there as, understandably, most stores sell the other type of adaptor, for Canadians travelling to Britain.

TIME

Canada has six standard time zones which are between $3^{1}/_{2}$ and 8 hours behind GMT as follows:

- Newfoundland Time $-3^{1}/_{2}$ hrs
- Atlantic Time -4 hrs
- Eastern Time -5 hrs
- Central Time -6 hrs
- Mountain Time -7 hrs
- Pacific Time -8 hrs

On the first Sunday in April the clocks are put forward an hour into Daylight Saving Time, which lasts until the last Sunday in October. This does not happen in most of Saskatchewan. Train timetables always show local time and indicate when the transition into a new time zone is made.

MONEY

Currency

Canada has a decimal currency system: 1 dollar is divided into 100 cents. Coins come in 1, 5, 10, 25 and 50 cent denominations, as well as the $1 coin (referred to by Canadians as a 'loonie' after the bird on one side) and the $2 coin (rather amusingly known as a "toonie"). Notes come in $5, $10, $20, $50, $100, $500 and $1000 bills and unlike American currency, which is all the same colour, Canadian notes come in a number of different colours: $5 is blue, $10 is purple and $20 is green, which means there's less of a chance of handing over a $20 instead of a $5 once you've got used to the various colours.

❏ Rates of exchange	
USA$1	Can$1.16
Europe €1	Can$1.54
UK£1	Can$2.27
Australia $1	Can$0.94
NZ $1	Can$0.83
Singapore $1	Can$0.77
For up-to-the-minute rates of exchange visit:	
🖥 www.xe.com	

The Canadian dollar has been very weak against the US dollar for the last few years which is one of the reasons why American tourists are flocking to Canada.

Withdrawing cash

By far the easiest way to get your Canadian currency is to withdraw cash from an automated teller machine (ATM) at a bank, of which there are dozens in all Canadian cities, using your ordinary debit card. The amount you withdraw is then automatically debited from your account back home.

Most debit cards can be used worldwide at ATMs displaying either a Cirrus or a Maestro symbol. The advantages are obvious: most ATMs operate 24 hours

CANADA

a day, seven days a week, so you don't have to worry about bank closing times. Note, however, that many banks add a 1.5% handling fee to the amount you withdraw; check with your branch before you go. Also, you should check that your card actually carries a Cirrus or Maestro symbol before heading to Canada. If it doesn't, your card can still be used but acts as a credit card rather than a debit card which may make withdrawals more difficult or even limit the number of times you can take money out within a week (this applies to Barclays customers, so check with your branch before heading abroad).

From an ATM you can also get a cash advance on a credit card (Visa or MasterCard); all major Canadian banks accept one of these, eg the Royal Bank of Canada takes Visa and the National Bank of Canada takes MasterCard.

Travellers' cheques
The traditional way to get your dollars is, of course, to take travellers' cheques. Some banks don't change these (and if they do you usually have to pay a commission) but many restaurants, hotels and shops will accept small-denomination American Express or Visa cheques as cash.

Credit cards
All major cards – eg Visa, MasterCard, American Express, Diners – are accepted throughout Canada and are a very useful backup. They can also be used for payment in taxis across the country, though of course you should always check with individual drivers that credit cards are accepted before travelling, as certain places, such as Jasper, do not offer this service.

No extra charges are made when you use the card to pay for goods and services but if you use it to get a cash advance you are normally charged a 1.5% handling fee.

Banking hours
Standard banking hours are 10am–3pm, Monday to Friday but more banks are staying open much later during the week and on Saturday mornings as well.

Tipping
Tipping, usually around 15% of the bill, is practically obligatory in restaurants; some establishments even fill in the tip box for you on your credit card slip. It is also standard practice to tip bartenders, taxi drivers, porters and doormen.

POST AND TELECOMMUNICATIONS
Post services
Post offices are open 8am–5pm or 9am–6pm Monday to Friday; some big offices also open on Saturday mornings.

Many drug stores have post office counters inside (look for the Canada Post sign on the window) and you can buy stamps from countless newsagents, general stores, hotels or stamp machines.

It currently costs 65 cents to send a postcard to the US; $1.25 for a postcard overseas; prepaid aerograms are also $1.25. The service is very reliable and speedy: it takes about five days for a letter to get from Toronto to London (London, England, that is, not London, Ontario). Aside from the usual services, most post offices also now provide a free **internet** terminal.

Making phone calls

It is *extremely* cheap to make international phone calls from Canada if you use one of the more competitive **international calling cards** offered by companies such as Globo Call and Econo Call. These work on any phone; you simply dial the number on the back of the card, key in the card's pin (usually found by scratching away the foil strip) then dial the number you want to reach. Rates for calling Europe are often as low as 7 cents a minute with a $20 card. The trouble is, these cards are not always easy to obtain – the best places to find the cheapest ones are newsagents or corner shops (known as 'dime stores' or 'loonie stores') in the bigger cities. Youth hostels usually stock them as well but not always those with the lowest rates. When you do find a good deal, it's best to stock up on a few cards if you intend to call home often.

Another option is the **standard phone cards** that you insert directly into public phones. The problem with these is that the companies owning public phones differ across the country, which limits the usefulness of your card. You'll find MTT phones in Halifax, Bell phones in Toronto, Montreal and Quebec, MTS in Winnipeg, Telus in Edmonton and Calgary, and BC Tel in Vancouver.

A final option is to use the phones which allow you to swipe your **credit card** through – a very convenient way of calling but you need to watch the time or you can clock up a huge bill. Public phones in most of the big cities offer this facility; if you can't find one on the street try the phones in the lobbies of the big hotels. Attempting to make an international call with **coins** is so frustrating it's not worth thinking about.

NEWSPAPERS

The most widely read broadsheet is the *Globe and Mail*; it has good nationwide and some foreign news coverage and is the only paper circulated right across the country.

Many cities have their own quality newspaper (eg the *Toronto Star*, the *Vancouver Sun*) as well as a selection of tabloids. Canada's answer to *Time* magazine is *Maclean's* which is available throughout the country.

HOLIDAYS

As well as national holidays, which apply throughout Canada, there are a number of provincial holidays. In both cases banks, offices, schools and some shops are closed, though restaurants and tourist attractions usually remain open.

National holidays
- New Year's Day
- Good Friday
- Easter Monday
- Victoria Day: Monday before 25 May
- Canada Day: 1 July
- Labour Day: first Monday in September
- Thanksgiving: second Monday in October
- Remembrance Day: 11 November
- Christmas Day
- Boxing Day

Provincial holidays
- **Alberta** – Heritage Day: first Monday in August
- **British Columbia** – British Columbia Day: first Monday in August
- **New Brunswick** – New Brunswick Day: first Monday in August
- **Newfoundland and Labrador** – St Patrick's Day: 17 March or Monday before; St George's Day: 23 April or Monday before; Discovery Day: Monday nearest to 25 June; Memorial Day: Monday nearest to 1 July; Orangeman's Day: Monday nearest to 10 July
- **Manitoba, NWT, Ontario, Saskatchewan** – Civic Holiday: first Monday in August
- **Quebec** – St-Jean Baptiste Day: Monday before 24 June
- **Yukon** – Discovery Day: third Monday in August

FESTIVALS

The Canadians take their festivals very seriously and there are great numbers of these events throughout the year, right across the country. The great diversity and frequent bizarreness of their themes reflect the contrasts contained within Canada. Interesting examples include the Trappers' Festival in The Pas, Manitoba (February), the Indian Festival in Chilliwack, BC (June), the Potato Festival in Grand Falls, New Brunswick (July), the Trout Festival at Flin Flon, Manitoba (July), the National Ukrainian Festival in Dauphin, Manitoba (August) and the Whoop Up and Rodeo Festival in Lethbridge, Alberta (August).

The major festivals of interest to the trans-Canada rail traveller are the Montreal International Jazz Festival (June/July), the Carnival de Québec in Quebec City (February), the Festival d'été in Quebec City (July) and Caribana, the Caribbean carnival in Toronto (August). These and other festivals are listed in the relevant city guides in this book.

FOOD

At the lower end of the scale, Canada holds few gastronomic surprises. The most prolific food outlets you'll come across are the standard Western fast-food chains (McDonald's, Burger King, Kentucky Fried Chicken, Pizza Hut and the countless spin-offs) crammed into 'food halls' in shopping malls and lining main streets. Added to these are the typical North American diners and countless bagel stores.

If you can afford to give the cheapies a miss, however, you can eat very well in Canada, with most cities offering a range of good quality upmarket restaurants. Many of these are of the same ilk: stylish, minimalist places serving Californian-derived or West Coast cuisine – sort of healthy Mediterranean, with lots of 'pan-seared' (never just 'fried'!) fish and meat fillets, imaginatively cooked with fresh local produce. In addition, there are also some notable regional specialities. The Maritime provinces (New Brunswick, Nova Scotia and Prince Edward Island) are famous for their excellent fish, particularly their lobster, salmon, oysters and scallops. Then there's the province of Quebec, where the generally superb food owes far more to Gallic than to North American influences. At the same time, the choice in most big cities is considerably enlivened by a wide range of ethnic restaurants, typically Italian, Greek, Vietnamese, Chinese and Japanese.

DRINK

Non-alcoholic

The nation's favourite non-alcoholic drink is **coffee**, which is invariably the freshly ground variety, served with milk or cream. Canadians drink a lot of it and empty cups are nearly always refilled at no extra charge. Perhaps Canada's most popular coffee chain, and certainly one of its proudest establishments, is the delightful Tim Horton's which was created by, and named after, a successful ice hockey player who died tragically in a car accident in 1974, at the age of 44 – ten years after opening his first coffee and donut shop in Hamilton, Ontario. Today, you'll find Tim Hortons, or 'Timmy's' as the chain is affectionately known across Canada, dotted along highways and on street corners of towns throughout the country. Despite being part of an extensive chain network, the atmosphere is friendly, the coffee is really rather good and for a mere $2 you can fill up on coffee and a fresh muffin.

Tea, on the other hand, is not a Canadian speciality. British travellers may well be shocked by the manner in which this is prepared: instead of pouring the boiling water *over* the tea or tea bag (essential for a good brew), they simply fetch you a pot of vaguely hot water with a tea bag lying limply by the side. Their **milkshakes**, on the other hand, are a credit to the country.

Alcoholic

The most popular alcoholic drink is **beer**. Most of it is brewed by Labatt's or Molson and tends to be on the light and fizzy side.

Another favourite is **whisky** – as well as importing foreign labels, Canada distils its own stuff. A good and seriously strong Canadian malt whisky is Yukon

Jack, while popular rye whiskies are Canadian Club and Seagram's. Believe it or not Canada also has its own wine, produced from grapes grown in southern Ontario and BC and developing steadily in quality.

WHAT TO DO IN THE EVENING

While many of Canada's smaller towns offer little more than a seedy, rough-edged bar by way of evening entertainment, there's usually no shortage of options in the big cities.

Drinking takes place in numerous establishments including English-style pubs, super-trendy bars, mellow 'lounges' (sit-around-chat-and-relax kind of places) and hundreds of bog-standard dimly lit taverns. A lot of these places serve food, too, and some have regular **live music** slots (lots of folk, rock and indie – with the quality ranging from good to dire – and jazz, usually the safest bet).

If **dancing** is what you're after, the best place for this is Montreal which boasts hundreds of nightclubs catering to all ages and tastes. This activity is less widely pursued in the other cities, apart from in the prairies where the extraordinary country-and-western 'line dancing' is still enjoying its revival.

If this sounds a bit too energetic, there's always the **movies** – Canadian cities have plenty of cinemas showing all the mainstream American output, which is screened there ages before it reaches the UK. You'll usually find a couple of local art-house cinemas as well, or cinemas showing mainly Canadian releases.

Theatre is particularly well represented in Toronto which claims to be the third biggest theatre city in the English-speaking world after London and New York. Certainly there's lots to choose from, ranging from Andrew Lloyd-Webber to Shakespeare to new Canadian talent.

Ballet (from classical to contemporary) is widely performed not only in Montreal, Toronto and Vancouver but also in Winnipeg, whose Royal Winnipeg Ballet is internationally respected. **Classical music** and **opera** enthusiasts should find enough to keep them happy among companies such as the Montreal Symphony Orchestra, the Canadian Opera Company (Toronto) and Vancouver Opera. Moreover, all this high-brow cultural entertainment is very good value (much cheaper than in London) with tickets ranging from about $15 to $50.

Finally, if none of this takes your fancy you can always join the best part of Canada's youth and simply sit around with a bunch of mates in a shopping mall.

SHOPPING

Shopping in Canada is, on the whole, no different from shopping in the US. Most of it takes place in malls, of which there are thousands spread across the country. The advantage of these is that they protect shoppers from Canada's fierce winter weather. On the downside, they're often oppressively crowded and the absence of natural light makes them a bit depressing.

The big department stores are Eaton's and The Bay (part of the original Hudson's Bay Company), which you'll find in every city. Most shops are open 9am–6pm, or later in the bigger cities.

Souvenirs

Prints of Inuit paintings (originals are very expensive) and Inuit soapstone carvings are popular with tourists and Canadians alike. Indian crafts are also undergoing a revival; you'll find some beautiful and reasonably priced goodies for sale, such as beaded moccasins and handwoven sweaters. Look out for the cooperative stores owned and run by natives themselves so you can be sure that the profits are all going back to the people who produced the goods. Moving west, local specialities include stetson hats and cowboy boots (obligatory if you're thinking of taking up line dancing). Finally, wherever you go in Canada you'll come across zillions of bottles of maple syrup.

TAXES

When you first arrive in Canada you'll be amazed at how cheap everything seems until you go and buy something and watch the price shoot up by about 14% at the checkout. This is because most things you pay for including food, drink and accommodation are subject to a 7% **Goods and Services Tax** (GST). In addition, British Columbia, Saskatchewan, Manitoba, Ontario, Quebec and Prince Edward Island levy a 5–7% **Provincial Sales Tax** (PST) on goods, restaurant bills and sometimes hotel bills.

To complicate things further, Nova Scotia, Newfoundland and Labrador and New Brunswick have a **Harmonized Sales Tax** (HST) of 15% combining GST and PST, levied on goods, services and accommodation.

You can claim a rebate for GST/HST paid for goods subsequently taken out of Canada and for some accommodation **but you must keep all your receipts**. You can also reclaim PST on goods bought in Quebec and Manitoba.

Booklets containing a claim form and details on conditions and restrictions are available in tourist offices and many stores and hotels.

CRIME

Canada justifiably has a reputation for being one of the safest countries in the world in which to travel. That said, crime against tourists isn't unheard of. Use your common sense: don't stray into the rougher neighbourhoods waving a map about; don't wander around alone late at night, women in particular; keep your important tickets and documents in a money-belt, preferably with a belt-style strap rather than a quick release catch. Also, be careful about where you leave your luggage: if you're staying in a hostel leave valuables in a locker and remember that even the most expensive, security-conscious hotels aren't invulnerable to petty thieves.

❦ PART 3: TRANS-CANADA RAILWAY ❦

Building the first trans-Canada railway

What tempted the people of Canada to undertake so gigantic a work as the Canadian Pacific Railway? The difficulties in the way were great, unprecedented, unknown... We were under the inspiration of a national idea, and went forward. We were determined to be something more than a fortuitous collection of provinces.   ***The Century*** (1885)

The story of Canada's first transcontinental railway has a plot as thick as a Jeffrey Archer novel. The only thing missing is sexual intrigue; everything else is there: corporate greed, political skulduggery, brave men, bankruptcy, war, danger, death, glory... It's a story that has gripped Canadians for more than a century spawning countless books, an epic poem and, of course, the inevitable TV mini-series.

Canada's ongoing preoccupation with the railway is due not only to the drama surrounding its construction but also to the crucial role it played in shaping Canadian history. For the CPR did more than build a railway: it built a nation. 'It can be argued,' reads a display in Winnipeg's Union Station, 'that November 7th 1885 – the day on which the last spike was driven on the CPR line at Craigellachie – is a more appropriate day from which to date the existence of Canada than July 1st, 1867.' Rather a tall claim for a railroad. But to understand this railroad's significance it is necessary to abandon one's concept of modern Canada and take a look at the young dominion of the 1860s and 70s.

CANADA BEFORE THE RAILWAY

The infant country
Canada officially became a country when Queen Victoria signed the British North America Act on 1 July 1867 but in no way did it resemble the country we know today. The new 'dominion' was basically a disparate collection of eastern colonial provinces with no real sense of unity or nationhood. It covered a relatively small chunk of a vast territory, for the most part uninhabited. British Columbia, which remained under the jurisdiction of Great Britain, lay 3000 miles west of Ottawa, beyond the Rocky Mountains. Stretching east from the Rockies were the immense prairies, still controlled by the Hudson's Bay Company – barren and empty save the little Red River settlement where Winnipeg now stands.

Fear of the Yankees
To make matters worse, Canada lay in the shadow of a large, intimidating neighbour. The United States boasted an ever growing population of 40 million, an alarming number of people next to Canada's scanty three and a half million. Moreover, America had been pursuing an aggressive policy of expansion and annexation for a number of years.

'That the U.S. are bound finally to absorb all the world and the rest of mankind,' declared a San Francisco newspaper in 1869, 'every well-regulated American is prepared to admit. When the fever is on our people do not seem to know when and where to stop, but keep on swallowing, so long as there is anything in reach.' Canada understandably felt threatened.

Some twenty years earlier America had effortlessly absorbed Texas and California. Then, in 1867, it purchased Alaska from the Russians for $7.2 million. Any fool could see that the Americans now had their eye on British Columbia and the North West – natural extensions of California and Minnesota. Indeed, for these isolated communities, America was their closest link with the outside world; annexation would in many ways be logical and sensible. The future of Canada was by no means assured.

Macdonald reaches across the continent

Sir John A Macdonald, Canada's first Prime Minister, firmly believed that if Canada were to survive as a nation it would have to expand westwards and take control of British Columbia, the Pacific coast and the giant stretch of land in between. But this was easier said than done. How were these areas to be obtained and consolidated? How were settlers to be induced to move west with virtually no east–west transportation or communication? The answer came in the form of a demand put to the government by British Columbia as a condition of entering Confederation: a railway across Canada to the Pacific.

The railway is promised

The British Columbians got their way; the province joined Canada in 1871 and in return the government formally pledged to build the railway. The terms agreed were somewhat optimistic: it was guaranteed that construction of the line, which would take an all-Canadian route instead of cutting south of the Great Lakes through America, would begin within two years of union and that the railway would be completed within ten!

Macdonald rightly saw in this enterprise the key to the creation of a transcontinental nation. As well as securing Canada its sixth province, the railway would encourage immigration, carry thousands of settlers out west and open up trade with the Orient. But it wasn't going to be easy. The distances to cover were enormous, the expense would be colossal and the physical challenges of laying track across the mountains and the Precambrian Shield would be back-breaking. It took a man of Macdonald's expansive vision not to baulk at these difficulties. Others did indeed: the leader of the opposition, Alexander Mackenzie, was almost apoplectic in his outrage at what he repeatedly denounced as 'an act of insane recklessness!'

The survey begins

The first gigantic step was to survey the land and determine the route. The government formed the Canadian Pacific Survey to do this work and placed it under the direction of Sandford Fleming. Thousands of miles of wild and inhospitable land had to be covered on foot, and the towering mountains had to be climbed again and again by men searching for passes the railway could go through.

Over the next six years Fleming's team was to complete 46,000 miles of survey and 38 men were to die in the process.

THE PACIFIC SCANDAL

Macdonald seeks a private company

Meanwhile Macdonald was searching for a suitable private company to build and operate the new railway. This way the government would avoid having to pay for it by increasing taxation.

Two companies emerged in competition for the charter, one of them headed by the multi-millionaire, Sir Hugh Allan, backed by a group of Americans. Macdonald stipulated that the two companies should merge and insisted on Allan disassociating himself from his American backers; it was imperative that this should be a Canadian enterprise. Everyone complied and the charter was granted in March 1873, with Allan appointed as president of the new company.

Sir Hugh's double dealing

All the while, however, Allan had been engaged in a series of complicated secret agreements. In the first instance he and his American partners, owners of the Northern Pacific Railway lines in America, had plotted to delay completion of the all-Canadian route while they pushed on with a connection from the main line down to their own lines in the US. Later, Allan entered into clandestine talks with the government regarding his role in the new company. Then, when it became clear that he must disentangle himself from the Americans if he were to succeed in his plans, he proceeded to wriggle out of his previous US pact. The Americans were furious with him and decided to blow Allan's cover and reveal a few incriminating details to the Opposition...

Scandal erupts: the government collapses

The Liberals seized upon this gift horse with zeal. More investigations unearthed even better ammunition. Not only could the government be charged with handing over the railway to a bunch of American schemers disguised as a Canadian company: it also emerged that Allan had advanced large amounts of cash to fund Macdonald's 1872 election campaign – presumably in return for the promise of the presidency of the company.

Particularly indicting was a stolen telegram from Macdonald to Allan's lawyer: 'I must have another ten thousand; will be the last time of calling; do not fail me; answer today.' The Pacific Scandal, as it was known, filled all the newspapers and was on everyone's lips. Finally, charged with corruption in parliament, Macdonald resigned on 6 November 1873 and the government was dissolved.

THE RAILWAY UNDER THE LIBERALS

The dream gets watered down

The newly elected Liberal government found itself lumbered with a project it had never supported in the first place. Moreover, Canada was suddenly entering a continental depression. Private investment shrivelled up so the government was forced to undertake the railway as public works, handing out contracts for the construction of sections of track. The ambitious scheme was literally watered down as Mackenzie talked not of a single continuous track but of a land and water route. He planned to shorten the railway and use steam ships to cross the Great Lakes.

Slowly on

To avoid corruption, Mackenzie ruled that contracts should always be awarded to the lowest bidder. These men, however, were not always the most qualified or competent builders.

The first section of track to be built was, in fact, a branch line going south from Winnipeg to the US border. Its construction was characterized by costly incompetence and blunder. Work progressed slowly – the Pacific Survey seemed to be dragging on forever – and it wasn't until June 1875 that construction began on the main line, the section linking Lake Superior and Winnipeg. It was becoming clear that the railway was languishing in the hands of the government.

OVER TO THE CPR

Macdonald back in power

It had been generally assumed that Macdonald's career had ended with the ruin and dishonour of the Pacific Scandal. But Canada was fed up with the Liberals and in the 1878 elections 'the Old Chief' was returned to power with a landslide victory. Once more he took up his old vision of transforming Canada into a strong transcontinental nation. This policy depended on completing the railway as quickly as possible.

More government contracts were awarded for the 125-mile section between Yale and Kamloops, west of the Rockies; but Macdonald was on the lookout for a group of private capitalists to take over the venture. This time their credentials would have to be flawless.

The CPR is formed

Such a group presented itself in the form of the CPR Syndicate. Its key members were leading directors of the Bank of Montreal. They came with an impeccable reputation, considerable financial backing and experience in running a railroad (they had recently transformed a bankrupt line into a resounding financial success). They were clearly perfect for the job and, following lengthy negotiations with the government, the Canadian Pacific Railway Company was incorporated in February 1881, a decade after British Columbia had been promised the transcontinental line.

Macdonald pledged a $25 million cash subsidy and 25 million acres of land to the new CPR, and agreed to turn over all the government contracted lines to the company once they were completed.

The task ahead

The CPR was faced with a mammoth task: a total of 1900 miles of track remained to be laid. In the east, there was the formidable challenge of carving a way through the Canadian Shield north of the Great Lakes. In the prairies they had to lay 900 miles of track west of Winnipeg to the Rockies. In the west they had to take that track over or through the Rockies and the Selkirks to meet the government contracted line at Kamloops.

The company hoped to forge ahead with this work as quickly as possible: the more rapidly the railway was completed, the sooner it could turn in a profit. The building season usually lasted only from April to November. The first season's work, however, was very disappointing – only 130 miles of track were laid. It became clear that some dynamic force was required to galvanize the operation and push it full steam ahead.

Enter Van Horne

This dynamic force was provided by William Cornelius Van Horne, a rising star in American railroad management. The appointment of Van Horne as General Manager of the CPR was possibly the most important decision the company ever made – he was soon to be ranked as one of the world's greatest railway men. He took the railway by the scruff of the neck, established control of the entire line himself and began work in February 1882 by declaring he'd have 500 miles of track laid by the end of the season.

Whirlwind construction across the prairies

The press and politicians openly scoffed at Van Horne's extravagant boast. But soon their jaws were hanging open at the breakneck speed of the track-laying west of Winnipeg. Men worked around the clock to push the track forward and construction gobbled up a mountain of supplies. In the end, Van Horne's goal was not reached; he was thwarted by spring flooding. But by the end of the building season no less than 418 miles of track had been laid.

The next season, 1883, was to see the fastest construction rate of the entire project, with the record set in the month of July when 92.3 miles were laid under scorching temperatures.

By November the prairie section was completed. However, the track had been racing towards the mountains all summer with one crucial question remaining to be answered: which route was it going to take across them?

Problems with the route

Based on the results of the exhaustive Pacific Survey, Sandford Fleming had concluded that the best route west of Winnipeg would be north to Fort Edmonton, then over the Rockies through the Yellowhead Pass. When the CPR took over they rejected this decision in favour of a southerly route – partly to shorten the line, and partly because they realized it would be easier to control and profit from an area as yet unpopulated. The problem was that a suitable pass through the Rockies had yet to be established, and a pass through the Selkirks had not even been discovered.

The company dispatched Major A B ('Hells Bells') Rogers. It took him one and a half years of scouring the mountains to discover a pass through the Selkirks (still known as Rogers Pass) that the railway could take after crossing the Rockies via the Kicking Horse pass. Rogers himself had some doubts about the feasibility of this route and alternative passes were still being explored as the track was approaching the mountains from Winnipeg in 1883. It wasn't until autumn that year that the CPR confirmed, to Rogers' great relief, that his route would be adopted after all.

Meanwhile, the planned route across the Shield was also proving controversial. Although the government had always stipulated that the railway should take an all-Canadian route north of Lake Superior, some of the directors had believed that this would never be enforced given how much cheaper and easier it would be to connect the line with existing American tracks south of the lakes. When George Stephen, the CPR president, made it clear that he was determined to follow the all-Canadian route two of the directors resigned; they obviously felt that this plan was doomed to failure.

The track through the prairies had been straight and relatively easy to lay. Now the railway had to be forced across the two dreaded barriers: the Shield and the mountains. The challenges were to prove enormous.

DANGERS AND DIFFICULTIES

Muskeg, sinkholes and rock
Van Horne is said to have described the section north of Lake Superior as 'two hundred miles of engineering impossibilities'. Workmen had to blast their way through the granite of the Shield, often finding solid rock well below the level where earth had been expected. Track-layers also had to contend with the infamous muskeg and sinkholes, seemingly solid earth which would suddenly swallow up track under the weight of a train. One such sinkhole required fill to be dumped in it for three months before it could safely support trains.

Whisky peddlers
Life along the line in Ontario was frequently disrupted by the workmen's enthusiasm for liquor. A railway worker's life was particularly harsh and comfortless and for many whisky was the only diversion. They were easy targets for the illegal whisky merchants, and results were often colourful.

The problem became chronic in the summer of 1884 as this construction supervisor's report testifies: 'These whisky peddlers would get off in the woods near the supply roads – get the teamsters drunk, racing teams, breaking wagons; destroying property and supplies would follow. They would waylay men, get them drunk, rob them of everything of value and threaten the life of anyone who opposes the traffic...' These events took place in areas so remote that few policemen were available to halt the lawlessness.

The weather
All along the line the workers had to cope with the paralysing effects of the weather. In 1884 there was no winter break on the Ontario line. Track had to be laid in snow that was sometimes up to five feet deep and in temperatures occasionally as low as minus fifty. Freezing weather conditions were also a problem in the mountains. Track was laid between Blaeberry Creek and Donald in temperatures of minus thirty; then, when the warmer weather came, the rails expanded and it was found that the track was out of gauge.

TRANS-CANADA RAILWAY

Construction in the Selkirks took place under the continual threat of avalanches. James Ross, head of construction in the mountain division, wrote to Van Horne of the dangers: 'I find that the snow-slides on the Selkirks are much more serious than I anticipated, and I think are quite beyond your ideas of their magnitude and of the danger to the line.... at one point, ten slips came down within six days, piling the snow 50 feet deep and 1800 feet in length along the located line..... The great trouble we are labouring under at present is that the men are frightened. Seven have already been buried in different slides, though fortunately only two were killed...'

The CPR built numerous snowsheds to protect the railway's passage through the Selkirks; nonetheless, avalanches were to cause the deaths of two hundred people between 1885 and 1909, prompting the construction of the remarkable Connaught Tunnel.

Mountains, tunnels and bridges

Of course the biggest challenge facing the railway builders was the physical barrier of the mountains. Trains had to cross three major summits – Kicking Horse Pass, Rogers Pass and Eagle Pass – each presenting an engineering nightmare. Tunnels had to be blasted through rock, bridges built over precipitous gorges, track laid close to vertical drops. It took thousands of workers to get the line through the gruelling mountain division; the Kicking Horse pass alone required 12,000 men. Typical of the kind of construction that had to be built was the Mountain Creek bridge on the eastern slopes of the Selkirks. This amazing feat of engineering was 164 feet high, 1086 feet long and contained two million board feet of timber.

On Andrew Onderdonk's section from Yale to Kamloops the difficulties of drilling tunnels through the Fraser Canyon were so great his men were able to advance the track no more than six feet a day. In some parts, the men had to be winched down to the track on ropes. Scores of men died on this treacherous route, some as a result of rockslides, many as a result of careless handling of explosives. The nearby hospital at Yale had to be enlarged to cope with all the injuries.

ON THE VERGE OF BANKRUPTCY

The money runs out

Despite these enormous difficulties, the track moved ever on. Then, in 1884, the CPR found itself in the midst of a severe financial crisis that threatened to throw the company into ruin even as completion of the line was in sight. The railway was swallowing up vast amounts of money. George Stephen, the CPR president, had been frantically trying to raise capital at home and in London but the funds he secured were not sufficient to keep the operation going. The CPR's debt in January 1884 ran to $15 million and time was running out. In desperation he begged the government for a loan of $22.5 million.

Temporary relief

Macdonald knew he'd have a tough time getting this through parliament but he also knew that if the CPR went under so would the government. He forced his party to support the relief bill by threatening to resign if it was rejected. As parliament dragged out the issue in endless debate, the CPR was sinking fast. Stephen wrote to Macdonald: 'I do not, at the moment, see how we are going to get the money to keep the work going... If I find we cannot go on I suppose the only thing to do will be to put in a Receiver. If that must be done the quicker it is done the better.'

At the end of February the bill was passed and the money was loaned to the company. By the end of the year it was gone. The CPR had reached its darkest hour. Stephen and his cousin Smith, a fellow CPR director, had sunk their entire personal fortune into the company. There was no more money to be had. Wages were months in arrears all along the line and men were striking or rioting. There was virtually no chance of persuading parliament to loan yet more money. The CPR was done for.

The North-west rebellion
Events suddenly took a dramatic turn in the spring of 1885 when the bloody North-west Rebellion broke out in Manitoba. Van Horne ingeniously seized on this opportunity to demonstrate the importance of the railway to the government: he immediately offered to move troops out by train to crush the rebellion. The line was not yet finished; there were four gaps, totalling 86 miles, but by shifting the men across the gaps by sled or on foot Van Horne was able to get them to Winnipeg in a week. Just 15 years earlier, during the first North-west Rebellion, that same journey had taken three months. By the time the troops returned, the gaps had been closed and the section was completed.

The final loan
As summer approached the CPR's credit could stretch no further. Disaster seemed imminent, as this telegram from Van Horne to George Stephen indicates: 'Have no means of paying wages, pay car can't be sent out, and unless we get immediate relief we must stop. Please inform Premier and Finance Minister. Do not be surprised, or blame me, if an immediate and most serious catastrophe happens.'

Once more a desperate Stephen begged Macdonald to bail out the company. He knew that they could quickly recoup the money once the line was completed and a through service was in operation; without a loan, however, the CPR faced bankruptcy even at this eleventh hour. Given the railway's crucial role in dealing with the recent rebellion, parliament could hardly fail to back the CPR. In July it passed another relief bill. This was the last time the CPR had to ask the government for a loan.

COMPLETION OF THE RAILWAY

The last spike
It took just a few more months to complete the line; all that was left to do was to close the gap between Onderdonk's tracks in the Gold Range and James Ross's in the Selkirks. The tracks met on 7 November 1885 in Eagle Pass at a spot named Craigellachie. The driving of the last spike was surely an emotional

moment for all involved but it was a simple affair without pomp or ceremony. Van Horne declined to celebrate the occasion with the traditional golden last spike: 'The last spike will be just as good an iron one as there is between Montreal and Vancouver,' he said, 'and anyone who wants to see it driven will have to pay full fare.'

The spike was driven by Donald A Smith, the eldest member of the CPR Syndicate. His first blow bent the iron, the spike was quickly replaced with a new one, and Smith's second attempt was a success. The crowds cheered and demanded a speech of Van Horne. His response was typically succinct: 'All I can say is that the work has been done well in every way.'

EARLY RAILWAY SERVICE

Passenger service begins

The line had to be properly finished off and upgraded before a passenger service could be inaugurated. The CPR had extended the track to Montreal by taking over existing lines in eastern Canada and on 28 June 1886 the first regular passenger train, the 'Pacific Express', left Montreal at 20:00 hours. On 1 July it reached Winnipeg and on 4 July it reached Port Moody at 12:00 hours – exactly on time. This was the first scheduled trans-Canada rail trip and at the time the longest scheduled passenger train trip in the world. With the extension of the line from Port Moody to Vancouver in May 1887, the main line was 4675km long.

The rear platform on an early CPR train.

The first travellers

Until 1899, transcontinental trains ran on a daily basis; the westbound train was known as the Pacific Express and the eastbound train as the Atlantic Express.

The carriages were extremely luxurious with all sleeping cars boasting bathtubs, an unheard of novelty in North America at the time. The dining cars served fine international cuisine and vintage wines and were generally patronized by passengers travelling First Class. Coach passengers usually dined in the much cheaper Canadian Pacific restaurants located at division points along the line, while the train was being serviced or the locomotive was being changed. It was the popularity of these restaurants that gave birth to the famous Canadian Pacific hotels, still flourishing today.

As Macdonald had predicted, the railway carried droves of settlers out to the now accessible west. Special 'land seeker' tickets were offered at reduced rates to encourage people to go and investigate areas under development. By the end of the railway's first decade of operation it had changed the lives of thousands of Canadians and, in turn, had changed the face of Canada itself.

Into the 20th century: CNR and VIA Rail

Consult the annals of Canada for the past fifty years at random and whatever party may be in power, what do you find? The government is building a railway, buying a railway, selling a railway or blocking a railway. **Paul Lamarche**, Speech in Montreal, 1917

The CPR proved to be an enormous financial success. Not only did it operate a highly profitable railway service: it also established a national telegraph network, an express parcel service and it branched out into steamships, hotels and real estate. Entrepreneurs clamoured to emulate the company's achievements and the early 20th century saw a rapid and undisciplined growth in railway building, all of which finally led to the birth of the CPR's present-day competitor: the Canadian National Railways system.

TWO MORE TRANSCONTINENTAL LINES

The boom years of the first decade of the 20th century brought thousands of settlers flooding out west to make their fortunes. It was felt that the country needed a second transcontinental line and two companies eagerly put themselves forward for the task. Somewhat recklessly, the Liberal government, in power under Wilfrid Laurier, gave charters to both companies: the Canadian Northern Railway and the Grand Trunk Pacific.

The Canadian Northern Railway

This young company operated a series of railway lines along the northern prairies. The entrepreneurial owners planned to extend the prairie route to the Pacific via the Yellowhead pass in the Rockies, Sandford Fleming's original choice for the first transcontinental. The line would go down to Kamloops where it would meet

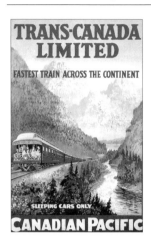

1920s poster advertising Canadian
Pacific's Trans-Canada service
CANADIAN PACIFIC/GY KAUFFMAN (1924)

the tracks of the CPR. From there it would
follow the course of the CPR down the Fraser
Canyon, always on the opposite bank since
there was room for only one track on one
side. Building proceeded and the last spike
was driven on 23 January 1915.

The Grand Trunk Pacific

The Grand Trunk was one of Canada's oldest
railway companies with a well established
network in eastern Canada. The epitome of
prudence and circumspection, the Grand
Trunk wasn't ordinarily given to taking risks
but its new general manager, Charles Hays,
was convinced that the company needed to
expand westwards to capture a share of the
Pacific market. His new line would also follow a northern prairie route, taking the
Yellowhead pass through the Rockies. From
here, however, it would part company with
the Canadian Northern and travel north-west
up to the new coastal town of Prince Rupert.
This was the closest Canadian port to Asia, and Hays envisioned it as the port of
the future, the key to the Grand Trunk's success.

Sadly, Hays was never to see the line reach this terminus. Following a trip
to London to raise more funds for the project, he returned in April 1912 aboard
the ill-fated *SS Titanic* and drowned with the sinking ship. Two years later in
April 1914 the last spike was driven in the Grand Trunk Pacific railway.

Failure

Canada had overstretched itself. There was nowhere near sufficient traffic to
sustain three transcontinental lines. A world-wide depression was having dire
effects on the economy, which grew steadily worse with the outbreak of World
War I. The two new lines were dead losses. And they weren't the only ones.
Canada's railways had by now got completely out of hand – there were about
two hundred companies operating a chaotic network of profitless lines.

In 1916 a royal commission investigating the railway crisis concluded that
the private companies should be taken over and reorganized by the government.
This is exactly what happened in 1923 when all the railways, with the notable
exception of the CPR, were combined to form the publicly owned Canadian
National Railways (CNR) system.

THE CNR TAKES OVER

Railways overhauled

The CNR lost no time in trimming down, shaking up and integrating the sprawl-
ing rail lines it had inherited. As a result of innovative restructuring and tight

management the chaos was eliminated and the CNR emerged as a highly efficient business. Like its competitor, the CPR, the new railway system carried both passengers and freight across its transcontinental lines. It also followed the CPR's example by building a series of grand railway hotels in major cities along the line.

Decline in passenger travel

As the railways advanced further into the 20th century the volume of passenger traffic steadily decreased, particularly after World War II. Motor cars were taking over as the primary mode of transport and highways were constructed right across the nation. Air travel, too, became increasingly affordable and cut travelling time down to a minimum. In an effort to win back passengers, both railways launched faster, spruced-up services in 1955: *The Canadian* was introduced by the CPR and 'the Super Transcontinental' by the CNR. Nonetheless, the volume of passenger traffic remained low and the CPR decided to concentrate on its freight operations, leaving the CNR to handle the bulk of Canada's passenger service.

Formation of VIA Rail

The completion of the Trans-Canada Highway in 1962 dealt a crippling blow to rail traffic. By the 1970s the situation had become dire and in 1976 a government report concluded that passenger traffic was set to decrease even further. In response, the government decided to discontinue non-essential rail services and place the remaining passenger lines in the hands of a new government-owned body: VIA Rail Canada. VIA would operate the passenger service, leasing CPR and CNR tracks while these companies focused on freight transportation.

Southern route abandoned

For some years VIA ran *The Canadian* across the southern and northern routes through the Rockies. In 1988 it introduced *The Rocky Mountaineer*, a daylight-only train ride through the mountains. However, the experiment proved a failure and a year after its launch the government decided to privatize this route. *The Rocky Mountaineer* was subsequently taken over by The Great Canadian Railtour Company Ltd who have succeeded in turning the route into a highly profitable tourist attraction. Meanwhile the southern (and more historic) route via Calgary and Banff was abandoned by VIA Rail in 1989 leaving the northern route, via Edmonton and Jasper, as the only remaining transcontinental passenger line.

The future

Faced with ever shrinking government subsidies and the continual pressure to cut costs, a question mark hangs over the future of some of VIA's less profitable lines. You may hear rumours, for instance, about the supposedly imminent discontinuation of *The Hudson Bay* route to Churchill or *The Skeena* route to Prince Rupert. Even aboard *The Canadian*, fellow travellers may tell you they've heard the transcontinental line is soon to be terminated – and many people outside Canada think it's already stopped running! But behind the gossip no one knows for sure what the future holds for passenger rail service in Canada. One can only hope that what is truly a first-class service through one of the most beautiful countries in the world will be able to withstand the onslaught of declining passenger traffic and cruise through the 21st century intact.

TRANS-CANADA RAILWAY

Certainly No Rush
Canada's rail lines earned themselves a variety of nicknames over the years, some affectionate, some definitely not. A few of the most widely used were:

- **Atlantic, Quebec and Western**: All Queer and Wobbly
- **Canadian National Railways**: Certainly No Rush
- **Canadian Pacific Railway**: Can't Pay Rent;
  Can't Promise Returns; Chinese Pacific Railway
- **Grand Trunk Pacific**: Get There Perhaps
- **Grand Trunk Railway**: The Big Suitcase,
  The Leaky Roof
- **Hudson Bay**: The Muskeg Special
- **Niagara, St Catharines and Toronto**: Naturally Slow
  and Tiresome; Never Starts on Time
- **Pacific Great Eastern**: Please Go Easy; Prince George
  Eventually, Past God's Endurance
- **Quebec, Montreal and Southern**: Quel Maudit Service

The lines today

If you take the train right across Canada you'll notice that different sections of the route use different types of train and offer slightly different services. By far the longest through train is VIA's flagship, *The Canadian* – the tri-weekly transcontinental between Toronto and Vancouver.

The other routes covered by this book are *The Ocean* (Halifax to Montreal), *The Corridor* (Montreal to Toronto), *The Hudson Bay* (Winnipeg to Churchill), *The Skeena* (Jasper to Prince Rupert) and the privately run *Rocky Mountaineer* (Vancouver to Jasper or Banff/Calgary, and Whistler to Jasper) and *The Whistler Mountaineer* (Vancouver to Whistler).

THE CANADIAN

Renovation

The Canadian was first introduced by the CPR in 1955. At that time the stream-lined, stainless-steel trains, designed and built in America, were considered ultra modern, representing the latest in railway technology. Thirty-seven years later VIA reinvented *The Canadian*, this time marketing its nostalgic appeal, elegant appearance and the luxurious comforts of old-style, long-distance rail travel.

Before launching a new service aboard *The Canadian*, VIA carried out a massive renovation project on the 190 trains. Steam heating was converted to electric; new wiring and lighting were installed; air conditioning was introduced; showers were fitted in each sleeping car; ventilation was improved; mechanical components such as brakes and trucks were completely overhauled and the interiors were recarpeted and reupholstered throughout. The total cost of the project was over $200 million.

Economy or Silver & Blue

There are two ways of travelling on *The Canadian*: in economy class or in Silver & Blue. In **economy** class you get reclining seats (where you sleep overnight) with pull-down trays, overhead lights and leg rests. The seating seems to have been designed with your average basketball player in mind: the leg room is very generous. You also have access to a panoramic dome car (see p65), though competition for space there is fierce. **Silver & Blue** is for passengers travelling in sleeping cars and is much more luxurious than economy class. This section has its own dome car and lounges and passengers have exclusive use of the dining cars.

Staff on the train

VIA's on-board staff are almost without exception helpful, efficient and friendly. They also tend to be very knowledgeable about the train and the places it takes you through, the older people who've clearly worked on the railway for many years being particularly interesting. Don't feel shy about asking them questions – they're usually more than happy to talk about anything to do with the journey. During the peak season, however, *The Canadian* gets packed out and things can get rather hectic, which leaves the staff with little time to sit around and chat.

Boss of the train is the **conductor**. He will usually introduce himself (I've yet to come across a female conductor) to economy-class passengers at the beginning of a trip and will explain the layout of the train, the facilities on board and give a brief description of the highlights of the scenery or towns you'll pass through. Next in line are the **service managers** and the **service coordinators**, the latter working mainly in the sleeping cars, where they'll see passengers to their seats and explain the facilities and service.

The staff you'll meet most, whether in economy or Silver & Blue, are the **service attendants** who generally run around making sure everything's okay. The staff are attentive in both sections of the trains but Silver & Blue passengers are particularly well looked after, with drinks and snacks brought to their seats as and when they please.

Bathrooms

Each sleeping car has its own piping hot shower but these are not available to economy-class passengers, who have to make do with the wash basins. You might expect this part of the train to get a bit whiffy by the third day but this rarely seems to be the case. The passengers seem happy to improvise with the basin – or else the air conditioning is extremely effective.

Eating and drinking

If you're travelling in **economy class** during the peak season (1 June–21 October) you'll be feeding yourself at the Skyline Café which serves light snacks you can take back to your seats (sandwiches, crisps, and the ubiquitous Oh Henry bars) or warm meals you can eat at the tables (burgers, fries, pizza etc). Alcohol is served here, as well as in the Skyline Bar. You can't, however, take your booze back to your seat: you must drink it where you bought it. Outside the peak season, economy-class passengers also have access to the dining car, where all meals must be paid for as you go along.

Over in **Silver & Blue** your meals are included in the price of your ticket and during the peak season you have exclusive use of the **dining car** with its crisp linen tablecloths and efficient service. You're given a choice of three sittings which are rarely on time in the busy summer months. The food is usually very good: typical evening fare might be soup, followed by salmon steak with potatoes and vegetables, followed by (invariably sickly) pastries or gateaux.

Sleeping accommodation

There are four types of sleeping accommodation available to **Silver & Blue** passengers.

● **Berths** These are wide double seats facing each other which convert to bunk beds at night. It's an open section of the train and people will be wandering up and down the carriage all day on their way to the dome or the dining car. You do get a bit of privacy at night time, however, when the bunks are enclosed by heavy curtains. There's always a toilet close by.

At night the upper berths are folded down

● **Single bedroom** These ingenious little one-person rooms contain a private loo (doubles up as a leg rest) and your own corner sink and mirror.

You sleep on a pull-out bed which slots into position on top of your seat and the toilet. If you need the loo in the night it can be a little tricky sliding back the bed to get to it quickly; it is advisable to practise this handy manoeuvre before going to sleep.

● **Double bedroom** These private rooms contain two armchairs by day and pulldown bunks by night.

Unlike the single bedrooms and the berths, these beds lie along the width instead of the length of the train which apparently induces a pleasant rocking or cradling sensation as the train chugs along.

Each bedroom is equipped with its own washbasin, fold-out table and a private loo in an adjoining little room.

Service attendants make up the bunks which are enclosed by curtains

● **Drawing room** Like the bedrooms but for three people. They are the most spacious private compartments on the train.

Bunks are comfortable and wellequipped with reading lights and pockets for your belongings

(Opposite) Top: VIA's flagship, the Canadian, takes a rest at Edmonton station before continuing to Vancouver. (Photo © Jim Manthorpe). **Bottom**: Lunch aboard the Ocean, en route from Halifax to Montreal. **(Overleaf)**: Some Canadian wildlife.

WILDLIFE FROM THE TRAIN

You know it's out there but it's doing its damnedest to hide from you. Still, the vigilant observer should be rewarded with a few sightings – here's a rough guide to what to look out for and where:

● **Ocean** Tantramar Marshes near Amherst: Canada geese, marsh hawks, black ducks, blue-winged teal; around Mont-Joli: moose and deer.

● **Canadian** Whiteshell Provincial Park (around Rice Lake): black bear, deer, moose, coyotes and beavers; Wainwright: peregrine falcons (breeding ground nearby); near Viking: elk, coyote, ruffed grouse; Wabamun Lake (near Edmonton): moose, beaver, white-tailed deer; Rocky Mountains: grizzly and black bear, moose, elk, caribou; mountain goats, bighorn sheep; Coast Mountains: osprey, bald eagles, bears.

● **Skeena** Rocky Mountains: (see above); Endako to Smithers: moose; Pacific: bears; Skeena Valley: many bald eagles.

● **Hudson Bay** Wildcat Hills Wilderness Area near Hudson Bay (SK): bear, lynx, wolves, deer; Cormorant Lake, near The Pas: geese, teal, crow-ducks, other waterfowl; approaching Churchill: arctic ptarmigan, snow geese, arctic fox, caribou.

● **Rocky Mountaineer & Whistler Mountaineer** Grizzly and black bear, moose, elk, caribou, mountain goats, bighorn sheep, osprey, bald eagles.

Above: Polar bear © Manitoba Tourism.
Opposite page: (clockwise from top): Rocky Mountain goats © Tourism BC; Elk, Banff National Park © Jim Manthorpe; Mountain sheep © Tourism BC; Moose, near Jasper © Jim Manthorpe; Brown bear © Jim Manthorpe; Mountain sheep; Chipmunk © Melissa Graham.

Breakfast is hearty – usually toast, bacon and eggs, or pancakes with maple syrup – and lunch will be something like a burger, or fried chicken. The menu always includes vegetarian options.

The dining car also has a good range of alcohol on sale which you'll be billed for at the end of your meal. Be warned that the dining-car experience can be a little manic in the middle of peak season as the harassed staff work flat out to serve three sittings of three meals a day to hundreds of hungry people.

In Silver & Blue you can also help yourself to complimentary tea and coffee in the Park Car (at the very back of the train), or get a service attendant to bring a cup to your seat.

Note that smoking is not permitted on any of VIA's trains.

The dome cars
The glass-roofed, panoramic observation domes are probably the most famous feature of *The Canadian*. There's one in the sleeping-car section and one in the economy-class section, and seats are at a premium in both.

Passengers tend to treat the dome the way holidaymakers treat pool-side sun loungers: they get there early, they stake their claim and they stay there. They do get hungry, though, so you can usually find a free seat at mealtimes and in the early morning or late evening. The best time to sit in the dome is at dawn. No one's around, the only sound is the movement of the train and Canada's vast, wide open space is at its most haunting.

Life on the train
If you're travelling in economy class you'll doubtless find yourself surrounded by a young and cosmopolitan crowd. Fellow travellers are often backpacking or hostelling and there are a lot of Europeans on board in the summer months. Strangers strike up conversations quite easily and meeting new people is all part of the enjoyment of the trip. Between scanning the horizon for bears you can stretch your legs by wandering to and from the café or hover around the dome car in the hope that someone will offer you their seat.

Silver & Blue passengers are a particularly convivial lot. The service is inevitably patronized by slightly older and wealthier travellers who all appear (when thrown together three times a day in the dining car) to get on extremely well. There is a shared preoccupation with nocturnal comforts. Conversations at breakfast tend to focus on the previous night's sleep, and conversations at dinner on the impending night's sleep.

Silver & Bluers may also pursue a social life in the bullet lounge or the mural lounge, where they can discuss the merits of the specially commissioned artwork on display. The original murals, painted by artists from the Group of Seven (see p121), are now on show in a museum in Ottawa. There's also an activity car where movies are shown in the evenings and, if you're lucky, there may be a wine-tasting session, concentrating on Canadian wines from southern Ontario.

TRANS-CANADA RAILWAY

(**Opposite**) The highlight of Canadian rail travel is a journey through the Rocky Mountains, which you can experience on both VIA's Canadian (top) and the Rocky Mountaineer (bottom).

> **Romance by Rail**
> Between November and April, when most of Canada is covered by a deep layer of snow, you can experience a winter rail journey in true style with VIA's 'Romance by Rail' package on the Canadian. Two bedrooms are joined together so that instead of sleeping in bunk beds, couples can sleep in a double bed, beneath a cosy down duvet instead of the usual grey blankets. Fresh flowers and a bottle of chilled sparkling wine in each room add to the sense of luxury; extra pampering is offered by way of breakfast in bed. This is a fabulous way to travel, particularly the leg between Jasper and Vancouver, where the Rocky Mountains are quite dazzling, enveloped in snow and ice. See p15 for fares – note that these are per couple, not per person.

THE OTHER TRAINS

The Ocean

Between Halifax and Montreal you'll most likely travel aboard the same stainless-steel trains as *The Canadian*, though some services are on modern 'Renaissance' trains – check before booking if you'd like to travel old-style. Again, you can travel either in economy class or in sleeping cars, though here you have a choice of two types of sleeper class. Comfort Sleeper Class (available year-round) is pretty much like Silver & Blue on *The Canadian*, though your meals are not included in the price of the ticket. Easterly Class is a new peak-season tourist service, including on-board commentary from guides, exclusive access to some areas of the train and priority access to the dining car (meals included in the ticket).

The train never gets as hectically busy as *The Canadian* and the $19^1/_2$-hour journey proceeds at a leisurely, relaxed pace.

The Corridor

Moving on from Montreal to Toronto you'll take the aptly titled 'Corridor' route. The LRC (light, rapid and comfortable) trains operating along *The Corridor* carry the highest volume of passenger traffic in Canada. The trains are sleek, modern and very fast – downtown Montreal to downtown Toronto takes just four hours. The train offers First Class travel, known as VIA 1, or economy class. VIA 1 is super luxurious: you get to sit in a posh lounge before boarding; delicious three-course meals are served to you at your seat and you're plied with wine or liqueurs during and after each meal.

Economy class has the usual roomy seats and the attendants periodically bring round refreshments for which you have to pay. The journey is more functional than recreational and you're not likely to walk around the train meeting people. It gets you from A to B good and fast but it's probably the least memorable train ride you'll take in Canada.

The Skeena

The 21-hour *Skeena* service from Jasper to Prince Rupert, completed in 1914 by the Grand Trunk Pacific Railway, is a two-day daylight-only journey, in direct competition with the privately operated *Rocky Mountaineer* (see p68). *The*

Skeena is arguably the most beautiful rail journey in Canada, taking you through the heart of the Rocky Mountains and ending in the misty, deep-green fjordland of north-west British Columbia.

Passengers spend a night in Prince George en route and must arrange accommodation there themselves (you can call VIA for assistance with hotel bookings: ☎ 250-562-3700 for Prince George and ☎ 250-624-5637 for Prince Rupert. We also give some suggestions on p216 and p220).

The trains are the same stainless-steel ones used by *The Canadian*. **Economy class** is available year-round, and from mid-May to mid-October there's the extra choice of **Totem class**, which includes all meals served at your seat and offers exclusive use of the Park Car at the back of the train, featuring the Bullet Lounge (with wrap-around windows) and an observation dome above. **Totem Deluxe** class goes one step further, including reserved seats in the Panorama Dome Car.

Economy-class passengers do not have access to an observation dome during this peak season, but from 18 October to 13 May they can use the Bullet Lounge.

The Hudson Bay

The train that takes you on the 1000-mile journey up to Churchill has rather gone to seed. Operated by VIA, it's as old as *The Canadian* but lacks its elegance and expensive renovations. All the same it has a charm and character all of its own and travelling aboard *The Hudson Bay* is a magical railway experience.

For a start, there'll be very few of you on the train unless you go in the middle of the polar bear season. This creates a camaraderie among the passengers and by the second night you may find yourself playing poker, drinking whisky, swapping spurious anecdotes, telling obscene jokes and singing Abba songs.

Life on the train gets particularly interesting north of The Pas as you're joined by Cree and Chepewyan natives, or wizened fishermen and trappers. For once you're travelling not only with fellow tourists or elderly Canadians but face to face with an entirely different culture. The railway provides a vital link for the small communities along this northern stretch of the route.

The crew on *The Hudson Bay* is uniformly relaxed and friendly and, to tell the truth, a little on the eccentric side. This is no doubt due to the fact that most of them have been working this lonely line for many, many years. They know the route inside out, back to front; they will happily tell you everything they know about the land you're travelling through and will point out osprey, geese, teal and ducks, giving you the names of all the wild flowers, trees and lakes that you're passing. In winter it's also worth keeping an eye out of the window even when it's dark, as this is the place to catch the spectacular northern lights.

The Canadian gets a wash-down during its 70-minute break at Jasper station
PHOTO © MELISSA GRAHAM

TRANS-CANADA RAILWAY

The Rocky Mountaineer and The Whistler Mountaineer

In 1989, the Armstrong Group took over *The Rocky Mountaineer* from VIA Rail and launched Rocky Mountaineer Railtours (now Rocky Mountaineer Vacations). It subsequently (and with some justification) dubbed its daylight-only routes as 'the most spectacular train trips in the world', becoming a roaring success.

The flagship **Rocky Mountaineer** train travels along three differing routes: the **Kicking Horse** route from Vancouver to Banff/Calgary; the **Yellowhead** route from Vancouver to Jasper; and the newly launched **Fraser Discovery** route from Whistler to Jasper. All of these are two-day trips, with overnight hotel stops included in the package. In addition, the company has recently introduced a new service, *The Whistler Mountaineer*, which travels on the old BC Railway lines from Vancouver to Whistler (a three-hour trip). All train rides can be taken in either an eastbound or westbound direction.

There are two ways of travelling on *The Rocky Mountaineer*: Red Leaf or Gold Leaf service. Gold Leaf passengers travel in an ultra-luxurious dome car – and pay $400 extra for the privilege. The dome area seats 74 people who are assigned seating there for the whole of the journey. Downstairs there's an open-air observation platform and a dining area which serves hot gourmet meals. Accommodation is provided for the overnight stop at Kamloops.

At either end of the dome car are the ordinary coaches where you'll be if you're travelling Red Leaf. These are nowhere near as stylish as VIA's stain-less-steel fleet and you might be disappointed by the absence of a dining car or observation dome if you've already taken *The Canadian*, although there are complimentary snacks.

The Rocky Mountaineer, however, excels in other ways, primarily with their onboard service attendants. Each carriage has its own attendant who (ingenious recruitment policies ensure) will almost certainly be warm, outgoing and charis-matic, inspiring instant devotion among the passengers. His or her duties include serving you breakfast, lunch, snacks and soft drinks at your seat (included in the price of the package) and providing you with commentary about the route. This is one of the highlights of the trip: the attendants have obviously been required to learn large volumes of information by heart, as their knowledge of the histo-ry of the railway and the landscape you pass through is encyclopaedic. They also do a good line in amusing anecdotes and corny jokes. Our attendant told us the railway workers constructing the line from Kamloops to Revelstoke were so fed up with the local fare – moose for breakfast, moose for dinner, moose for tea – that they expressed their frustration in the name they chose for the next station we were to pass. It was Sicamous. One attendant is also known to switch out the lights and recite Shakespeare through the five-mile Spiral Tunnels.

The Rocky Mountaineer is essentially group travel and the service attendants encourage everyone to join in, getting people to look out for mile markers or shout out to the others if they see any wildlife. This makes for a highly enjoyable atmos-phere (unless you're averse to group travel), though the real draw is, of course, the magnificent scenery and the luxury of travelling through it all in daylight.

Halifax

I am neither a prophet, nor the son of a prophet, yet...I believe that many in this room shall live to hear the whistle of the steam engine in the passes of the Rocky Mountains and to make the journey from Halifax to the Pacific in five or six days.

Joseph Howe, speech in Halifax, 15 May 1851

Halifax, the hub of the Maritime Provinces (New Brunswick, Nova Scotia and Prince Edward Island), is exactly as you'd expect it to be: bustling, lively streets clustered around the waterfront; brightly painted clapboard houses; fish markets; quayside bars; the smell of salt in the air; old-fashioned charm. It's the capital of Nova Scotia and is located on the second-largest natural harbour in the world. The downtown core is extremely compact and all the interesting parts are within easy walking distance of each other.

Being one of the older Canadian cities, Halifax has taken enormous care to preserve its colonial heritage and you'll see some fine old buildings dotted around the place. It does tend to overdo the history thing though, and just about every building over 80 years old seems to have a plaque on it. All the same, Halifax is an excellent starting point for a trip across Canada (it somehow feels like the proper place to begin) and is well worth a couple of days' visit.

HISTORY

The Micmacs

The first people to live here were the Micmac Indians who named the settlement 'Chebucto' meaning 'Great long harbour'. Their fishing and hunting communities proliferated throughout the region until contact with European fishermen in the early 16th century exposed them to new diseases which seriously depleted their numbers. These fishermen came over to take advantage of the area's prodigious supplies of cod, discovered by the Italian sailor John Cabot in 1497.

Britain and France vie for power

The French staked the first European claim to the area in 1605 when they founded Port Royal on the Bay of Fundy. Britain was keen to get in on the act and attempted to establish its own colony nearby. In 1621 the area occupied by the French, known as Acadie, was claimed for the British Crown and renamed Nova Scotia ('New Scotland'). The rival claims dragged on until 1713 when the Treaty of Utrecht handed over the mainland Maritimes to Britain, forcing France to shift its power base to Louisbourg on Cape Breton Island.

Garrison town established

Britain continued to feel threatened by the French presence at Louisbourg, so in 1749 Edward Cornwallis was sent over with 2500 settlers to found a garrison town by the harbour to protect the New England colonies. They named it Halifax, after the second Earl of Halifax, and built a fort at the top of the town's hill.

The Royals in Halifax

For many years Halifax provided a home to the two wayward sons of King George III, who were practically kicked out of Britain by their frustrated father. The youngest, Edward (the future father of Queen Victoria), served as the commander of the Nova Scotia forces for six years. He was notorious for his obsession with discipline and punctuality. Modern-day Haligonians can still keep an eye on the time by the great clock tower standing on the hillside – a gift from Prince Edward to the city.

Halifax today

The city's importance as a military and naval base continued well into the 20th century. Halifax also emerged as the industrial, commercial and educational centre of the Maritime Provinces, boasting one of Canada's busiest ports (ice-free all year) and no fewer than five universities, giving the place a youthful, vibrant atmosphere. The current population of around 370,000 is made up of over a hundred different ethnic groups.

Halifax is also a very prosperous city, a fact reflected in the glittering high-rise blocks springing up around town, and the money poured into renovating its historic waterfront buildings. However, while Halifax has gone from strength to strength in recent decades, it suffered a horrific tragedy in the early part of the 20th century – for more details see p79.

ARRIVING IN HALIFAX

By air

Flights into or out of Halifax touch down at Halifax International Airport, about 35km out of town, where you'll find several ATMs and a well-stocked **tourist information** desk (open daily 9am–9pm).

From the airport, the **Airbus** leaves for the town centre every 30 or 40 minutes, stopping at all the major hotels in Halifax. It runs daily from 6am to 1am

---

❏ **Halifax online**

💻 **www.halifaxinfo.com** Halifax Regional Municipality's website, with details on city sights, accommodation and practical visitor information.

💻 **http://novascotia.com** 'Virtual Nova Scotia' site, put together by the Government of Nova Scotia, with travel information on the whole province.

💻 **www.where.ca/halifax** Another useful website providing information about the city. *Where* is also available from many hotels and tourism offices in magazine format.

and tickets cost $16 for a single or $28 for an open return. A **taxi** into town costs $53. There are also several car-hire companies at the airport.

By rail
The train station is at the south end of Halifax, adjoined to the Westin Nova Scotian Hotel, about a 15-minute walk from downtown. The No 9 and 7 buses stop just outside the station about once every 30 minutes and will take you into the city centre (as will the No 35, less frequently). To get back to the station, the best place to catch a bus is on Barrington St.

GETTING AROUND

Halifax is a very manageable size and the best way to get to most places is on **foot**. If you do need to go a little further afield, the **bus** network (Metro Transit) is very efficient. There's a flat fare of $2 per journey and you have to pay with the exact money. There's also a regular **ferry** service ($2; every 15 or 30 minutes) across the harbour to the neighbouring town of Dartmouth, which makes a pleasant excursion and gives great views of Halifax's skyline.

Another good way of getting out of downtown, particularly for a jaunt to Point Pleasant Park, is by **bike**. These can be rented from Freewheeling Adventures (☎ 902-857-3600 or 1-800-672-0775, 🖥 www.freewheeling.ca; $25 per day, including bike helmet and lock), which is based outside Halifax but will usually deliver bikes to your hotel. They also offer organized bike tours around Nova Scotia – see their website for more details.

ORIENTATION

You can't get lost in Halifax. The city centre is situated on a hillside. At the top, you've got the **citadel**, at the bottom you've got the **waterfront** and in between are about six streets running parallel to the water's edge. Right in the centre of all this is the **Grand Parade**, the city's main square, home to the City Hall and St Paul's Church.

SERVICES

Tourist information
There are several tourist information centres around town. The most centrally located is the **Waterfront Visitor Centre** (☎ 902-424-4248), in a glass pavilion directly behind the Maritime Museum. Its opening hours are: June to September daily 8.30am–8pm; October, November and May daily 8.30am–4.30pm; December to April Wednesday–Sunday 8.30am–4.30pm.

Money
There are ATMs all over the place, from hotel lobbies to shopping malls, with a big concentration on Spring Garden Rd. Most banks offer currency exchange facilities, including the Royal Bank at 5161 George St, the Bank of Montreal at 5151 George St and the Bank of Nova Scotia at 1709 Hollis St.

Town plan key

⇧	Place to stay	⊞	Museum	☺	Bus stop
○	Place to eat	✝	Church / Cathedral	⊸○⊸	Metro
⊠	Post Office	📖	Library / Bookshop	⛴	Ferry
ⓘ	Tourist Information	✍	Internet	●	Other

Consulates

Austria (☎ 902-429-8200) Suite 710, 1718 Argyle St
Belgium (☎ 902-468-1030) 90 Bluewater Rd, Dartmouth
Denmark (☎ 902-429-5680) 1525 Birmingham St
Germany (☎ 902-420-1599) Suite 1100, 1959 Upper Water St
Italy (☎ 902-492-3934) 7th Floor, 1474 Argyle St
Netherlands (☎ 902-422-1485) 2000 Barrington St
Norway (☎ 902-468-1330) Suite 206, 11 Morris Dr
Sweden (☎ 902-491-1150) 9th Floor, 5151 George St
USA (☎ 902-429-2480) 1969 Upper Water St

Post, internet and laundry

Halifax's central **post office** is at 1680 Bedford Row. **Internet access** is available at a little café hidden away upstairs in Paperchase, a newsagent's store on Blowers St, just up from Barrington. The staff are helpful, the couches comfy and you can feast on home-baked treats and smoothies whilst you surf the net for $8 an hour.

The most central **laundries** in town are the Spin and Tumble Laundromat at 1022 Barrington St, which is open daily from 8am–9pm (☎ 902-422-8099) and Kwik Wash Laundromat at 5506 Clyde St, open 9am–8pm Monday to Friday, 9am–6pm Saturdays and 11am–6pm on Sundays (☎ 902-429-2023).

WHERE TO STAY

There's a lot of accommodation in Halifax, the vast majority of it upmarket and of a high standard. Mid-range options are much thinner on the ground but there's a reasonable choice of budget rooms. Despite the large number of hotels, it's not uncommon for the town to get booked out when events or big conferences are taking place, so it might be worth booking in advance. That said, booking on or just before the day often gets you a big discount in the more expensive hotels.

❏ Accommodation prices quoted in this book are for **high season** (normally May or June to September). In low season many hotels offer substantial discounts.

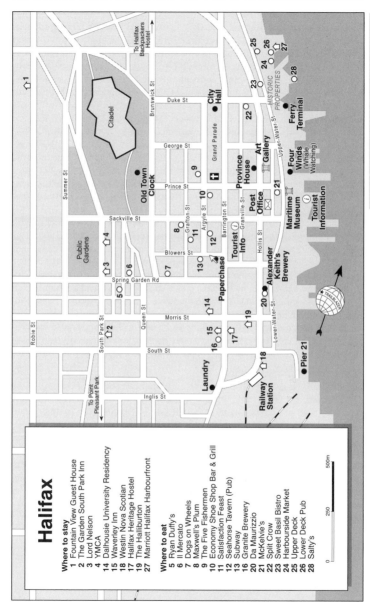

Halifax

Where to stay
1 Fountain View Guest House
2 The Garden South Park Inn
3 Lord Nelson
4 YMCA
14 Dalhousie University Residency
15 Waverley Inn
18 Westin Nova Scotian
17 Halifax Heritage Hostel
19 The Haliburton
27 Marriott Halifax Harbourfront

Where to eat
5 Ryan Duffy's
6 Il Mercato
7 Dogs on Wheels
8 Maxwell's Plum
9 The Five Fishermen
10 Economy Shoe Shop Bar & Grill
11 Satisfaction Feast
12 Seahorse Tavern (Pub)
13 Subway
16 Granite Brewery
20 Da Maurizzio
21 McKelvie's
22 Split Crow
23 Sweet Basil Bistro
24 Harbourside Market
25 Upper Deck
26 Lower Deck Pub
28 Salty's

0   250   500m

Budget accommodation

Part of the Hostelling International (HI) network, the **Halifax Heritage House Hostel** (☎ 902-422-3863, 🖳 www.hihostels.ca), 1253 Barrington St, is a dream hostel. It's in the middle of town in a beautiful Georgian building, has a well-equipped kitchen, a big common room, a TV, library and shop and is spotlessly clean throughout. What's more it's very cheap – dorm beds are $20 for members, $25 for non-members, with private rooms at $50. Note that sleeping bags are not allowed but bed linen is provided and is included in the price. There are 75 beds but with standards like this they get snapped up quickly so book in advance.

Between mid-May and late August, **Dalhousie University Residency** (☎ 902-494-8840, 🖳 www.dal.ca/confserv) offers small, neat rooms in several halls of residence. The centrally located O'Brien Hall, at the corner of Barrington and Morris, is currently closed for refurbishment (reopening 2008) but Gerard Hall is just a block further north at 5303 Morris St. Rooms are $40.51 a single ($26.44 students) and $63.92 a double ($48.71 for students), and include towels and bed linen.

Up near the citadel at 1565 South Park St, the **YMCA** (☎ 902-423-9622, 🖳 www.ymcahrm.ns.ca) has excellent facilities (café, fitness centre, pool) and although its 31 single rooms ($40 plus tax) are spartan and a bit bleak, they are very clean. The residence is for students only between September and May but provides mixed-sex accommodation to tourists during the summer months, with separate male and female bathrooms, plus a common room and kitchen.

About 15 minutes' walk from downtown at 2193 Gottingen St is **Halifax Backpackers Hostel** (☎ 902-431-3170, 🖳 www.halifaxbackpackers.com). The location is not great and those travelling alone may feel uncomfortable wandering around the area on foot but the hostel itself is young, friendly and cheap with dorm beds from $21, private rooms for $57.50 and family rooms for $65.

Mid-range accommodation

An affordable mid-range choice is the clean and comfortable **Fountain View Guest House** (☎ 902-422-4169, 🖳 www.browser.to/fountainviewguesthouse), on a busy road behind the citadel at 2138 Robie St. Doubles here (with separate bathrooms) cost from $34, single rooms from $25 and family rooms from $60.

Moving up in price, **The Garden South Park Inn** (☎ 902-492-8577, 🖳 www.gardeninn.ns.ca) at 1263 South Park St is a pink clapboard house with 23 spotless en-suite rooms ($109–169, breakfast included) all with TV, phone, wireless internet and cheerful floral décor. Slightly more expensive, the charming **Waverley Inn** (☎ 902-423-9346, 🖳 www.waverleyinn.com) at 1266 Barrington St is crammed with antiques, gilt mirrors, and fabulous old mahogany beds. The exquisite lobby and hallways boast as much character as the bedrooms themselves. Double rooms (all en suite) cost from $125 to $190, with breakfast included.

❏ **Room reservation service**

The Nova Scotia tourist board operates a room reservation hotline covering the whole province: ☎ 1-800-565-0000 from North America, or ☎ 902-425-5781 from elsewhere.

Upmarket hotels

Halifax is well endowed with top-range hotels, most of them of a very high standard. For rail travellers, the most obvious choice is the luxurious *Westin Nova Scotian* (☎ 902-421-1000, 🖳 www.westin.ns.ca), built in 1930 by Canadian National Railways, right next to the train station at 1181 Hollis St. The hotel originally contained a special section with living quarters for CNR staff and its vast kitchen prepared all the food for the trains as well as offering laundry facilities for the linen used on the trains. Today it's independently owned but remains a romantic and stylish symbol of the town's railway heritage with a trendy cocktail bar near the lobby. One of the highlights of a stay here are the so-called 'Heavenly Beds' in all 297 rooms, which amply deserve their name. Rates range from $139 up to $275.

More centrally located, right next to the Historic Properties at 1919 Upper Water St, the *Marriott Halifax Harbourfront* (☎ 902-421-1700, 🖳 www.marriott.com) boasts fantastic harbour views and some nice art deco touches – and for those who fancy a flutter, links with Casino Nova Scotia through an indoor walkway. Rack rates here are anywhere from $199 to $425.

For a little more character try *The Halliburton* (☎ 902-420-0658, 🖳 www.thehalliburton.com) at 5184 Morris St, which boasts immaculate, spacious rooms ($190–$350) and a central location. It's very charming, and also has a pretty courtyard garden. Overlooking the Public Gardens at 1515 South Park St is the *Lord Nelson* (☎ 902-423-6331, 🖳 www.lordnelsonhotel.com), built in 1928 and still preserving the high ceilings, oak panelling and shining brass lifts of its entrance lobby. The rooms, which have recently been refurbished to a high standard, cost from $199, with special rates starting at $159.

WHERE TO EAT

There are dozens of places to eat in Halifax, many of them concentrated around the waterfront or along Spring Garden Rd.

The local speciality is, of course, fish and seafood, particularly Atlantic salmon, crab, scallops and lobster – the quality is generally excellent and the prices usually moderate, with main courses from around $15 in many places. Make the most of the ocean's delicacies while you can – you've got over 6000km to go before you'll get seafood this fresh again.

Where, a free weekly publication available in the tourist office and hotels, has a restaurant listings section with a run-down of each place's food and atmosphere.

Budget food

The classic cheap eat in Halifax is *Dogs on Wheels*, a burger and hotdog van outside the public library on Spring Garden Rd. Nearby, on the corner of Argyle and Blowers St, *Subway* is good for takeaway sandwiches and baguettes and offers well-priced meal deals. For a few dollars more you can get a cheap lunch (around the $10 mark) at many of the city's pubs, including the always-lively *Split Crow* on the corner of Granville and Duke, with a pleasant outdoor veranda and a selection of local beers on tap. The dimly lit basement bar *Seahorse*

Tavern at 1665 Argyle St caters for a young clientele, with a good lunch menu at very affordable prices. Further south at 1662 Barrington St is *The Granite Brewery*, which offers a great pub atmosphere, a decent menu and a fine selection of ales, many of them brewed on-site.

Another pub renowned for its beer is the intriguingly named *Maxwell's Plum*, at 1600 Grafton St. It boasts 160 beers from around the world, including 60 on tap, and you can get a steak for under $10.

Perhaps the most atmospheric place to head for a cheap bite is *Harbourside Market* in the Historic Properties, which houses colourful fresh-produce market stalls alongside cafés, pizzerias and other snack outlets in a beautiful converted warehouse, with outdoor seating by the water's edge. Also in the Historic Properties, the *Lower Deck Beer Market*, which sits upstairs from the very popular *Lower Deck pub*, has a nice selection of beers on tap, friendly staff and a good-value lunch menu, including soup and sandwiches – make the most of the fantastic harbour views by taking a table by the window.

Halifax has a number of inexpensive vegetarian restaurants, including *Satisfaction Feast* at 1581 Grafton St, which offers nutritious wraps, hot sandwiches and great salads at very affordable prices (under $12).

Mid-range and upmarket restaurants

Halifax has several excellent, moderately priced bistros including *Il Mercato* at 5650 Spring Garden Rd, offering a contemporary fusion of Italian cuisine and seafood from the Maritimes. *Sweet Basil Bistro*, at 1866 Upper Water St, is another good choice, with a super location within the Historic Properties and an outdoor patio. Its menu features fish, veal and homemade pasta dishes, imaginative salads and incredible desserts, with lunch dishes between $12 and $15 and dinner main courses from $15 to $25. Charming by day, romantic by night, the eccentrically named *Economy Shoe Shop Bar & Grill*, a pavement café at 1663 Argyle St, is a local treasure. The décor alone is worth a visit, with its three distinctly different dining areas which contrast candlelit nooks and twinkling fairy lights with funky artwork and indoor shrubbery. Soak up the ambience over mouthwatering snacks and meals, including the best nachos in town.

For more traditional fish and seafood, try *McKelvie's*, a large, busy restaurant housed in a former fire station at 1680 Lower Water St (try the excellent crab and leek bisque), or the popular, buzzing *Salty's* on the waterfront, offering first-rate lobster, an outdoor patio and harbour views. Close by, in Privateer's Warehouse, *The Upper Deck* is another perennial favourite, with starched linen tablecloths, candles at the table and a romantic atmosphere. Over at 1740 Argyle St, the elegant *The Five Fishermen* is famous for its eat-as-much-as-you-can mussel bar and generally delicious seafood (reservations advised on ☎ 902-422-4421). If you aren't sure how to tackle a lobster this is the place to head: the friendly staff will provide you with a step-by-step guide, diagrams included.

If all this fish and seafood is proving a bit much, head for *Ryan Duffy's* at 5640 Spring Garden Rd for the best steak in Halifax – wheeled out, cut and weighed in front of you, before being cooked to perfection. Finally, if you fancy a splurge, the renovated old Brewery Market, on Lower Water St, contains one of the city's best (and most expensive) restaurants: *Da Maurizzio*, where superb homemade pasta is served to a background of Italian opera in a beautiful dining room crammed with Italian reproductions.

NIGHTLIFE

With more pubs per head than any other city in Canada and enormous numbers of students, Halifax boasts a lively nightlife scene. In summer, the most enjoyable and popular of the pubs are those with rooftop decks, including *The Thirsty Duck* at 5472 Spring Garden Rd, near the corner of Queen, and *Your Father's Moustache*, a couple of blocks away at No 5686 on the same street, which houses a popular blues set on Saturday afternoons.

Many other pubs also offer live-music slots, from jazz and blues through to fiddle tunes and rock; check out the free weekly listings paper, *The Coast*, for details (available at the tourist office or online at 🖳 www.thecoast.ca). Regular pub-venues include *The Split Crow*, on the corner of Granville and Duke, *The Lower Deck*, bottom floor of Privateer's Warehouse in the Historic Properties, and *Bearly's House of Blues & Ribs* at 1269 Barrington St, which hosts a lively blues jam on Sunday evenings. For something quieter, try *The Henry House* in the original location of The Granite Brewery, 1222 Barrington St, where you'll find great ales in a handsome old granite building.

Halifax has opened its doors to many Irish immigrants over the years, so it's no surprise that there are a number of lively Irish pubs here, including *O'Carroll's* at 1860 Upper Water St, which boasts an impressive selection of single-malt scotches, and *Pogue Fado Irish Public House* at 1581 Barrington St, featuring traditional Irish décor and live music.

For a spot of dancing, head for *The Liquor Dome*, or 'The Dome' as it's known locally, at 1726-1740 Argyle St, open Wednesday–Sunday until 3.30am. It's something of a Halifax institution and houses several bars under one roof, including *Cheers* (mainly an older crowd), *The Attic* (with live music) and *The Dome* itself, with a largish dance floor.

WHAT TO SEE

Though it boasts a couple of first-rate museums, Halifax is not really about 'sights' so much as strolling around and soaking up the atmosphere. If you're staying in the downtown core, try to fit in a walk out to the residential quarters south of town, towards Point Pleasant Park, where you can admire the fabulous clapboard townhouses and mansions from the early 20th century.

The Citadel

The star-shaped fortress atop the hill (with its entrance on Sackville St) is a good place to start exploring Halifax; there's a superb view from here over the harbour and city and you'll be able to get your bearings and take in the lie of the land. There have been four forts here since 1749; the current one dates from 1856.

From June to October there are 45-minute-long guided tours (daily 9am–5pm; $10.90), featuring the changing of the guard (performed by students dressed up as members of the 78th Highlanders and the Royal Artillery), a visit to the barrack rooms, furnished as they were in the 1860s, and an audio-visual display. During the rest of the year you can wander around the grounds for free (9am–5pm daily). Beware of the eardrum-splitting gun that's fired at the Citadel every day at noon.

Old Town Clock

This rather beautiful clock tower stands just below the Citadel. It was presented to Halifax as a gift by Prince Edward in 1803 – a fitting present, given his legendary obsession with punctuality.

St Paul's Church

You'll walk past this pretty, white-timbered church many a time while wandering around Halifax. It's right in the centre of town, at the south end of the Grand Parade on Argyle St. Opened in 1750, it is the oldest building in Halifax and the oldest Anglican church in Canada.

It's open to visitors daily, 9am–6pm in summer and 9am–4.30pm in winter; walking-tour leaflets are available by the entrance, pointing out the church's most important features. Notice the Royal Pew, reserved specifically for Her Majesty the Queen or any representatives sent to Halifax on her behalf. Look out, too, for the piece of metal embedded in the north wall above the door; it's a bit of the *Mont Blanc* that exploded in Halifax harbour over $3^1/_2$km away in 1917 (see opposite).

Halifax City Hall

Across from St Paul's Church at the other end of the Grand Parade is Halifax's Victorian City Hall. Visitors are welcome to wander in and take a look around the building.

Province House

Charles Dickens visited Province House in 1842 and said 'it was like looking at Westminster through the wrong end of the telescope'. Presumably he was referring to the business conducted inside and not the building, which is Georgian, sandstone and delicately understated. Built in 1819, it is Canada's oldest seat of government. It's a stone's throw from the Grand Parade, down George St, and is open to the public Monday to Friday 9am–5pm and weekends 10am–4pm from mid-June to mid-September; and Monday to Friday only, 9am–4pm for the rest of the year. Guided tours of roughly 15 minutes are available and entrance is free.

Art Gallery of Nova Scotia

Opposite Province House at 1723 Hollis St, the Art Gallery of Nova Scotia (open daily 10am–5pm, with late opening on Thursday until 9pm; entrance $12 adults; $3 students) houses a substantial collection of Nova Scotian, Canadian and some international art, spread over eight floors in two adjacent buildings.

In the **north gallery**, the ground level contains some arresting works by **contemporary Canadian** artists, including Tom Forrestall's *Island in the Ice*, showing enormous chunks of ice breaking up around a tiny island with a lighthouse and a fragile-looking home, and Jean Paul Lemieux's *The Explorer*, a menacing close-up of a man wearing a dark coat and sunglasses on a snowy plain. In contrast, William Kuralek's series of Eskimo scenes are light and celebratory, particularly those of children playing. One of the gallery's highlights is the **folk art** on level 2, displaying works by local, untrained artists including Francis Silver's delightful scenes painted on the wooden planks of a carriage house, and many life-size, brightly painted carvings by other Nova Scotian craftsmen. Other works in this gallery include numerous **landscapes** (level 3), both Canadian and international, and a roomful of beautiful **religious carvings** (level 4) from the 15th century onwards.

Over in the **south gallery**, the main attraction is the tiny wooden house that belonged to **Maud Lewis**, the Nova Scotian folk artist who became a household name in Canada before her death in 1970. Transported in its entirety to the museum, every available surface has been painted with bright, cheerful flowers, making it look like an oversized doll's house. Many of Lewis's paintings – landscapes and country scenes – are on display alongside and there's some charming footage of the artist herself, which explores her background and passion for art.

Historic Properties

Down by the waterfront is a collection of beautifully renovated wharves and warehouses, known as the Historic Properties. The oldest is Privateers' Warehouse, built in local granite and ironstone in 1813 (the Privateers were the British Crown's licensed pirates). The area, which had been falling into a state of dereliction following years of disuse, has been successfully transformed into an attractive collection of shops, pubs, eating places and artists' studios. It's a lively place to linger on a sunny day or for an evening stroll, after dinner, when the whole area is lit up.

Alexander Keith's Nova Scotia Brewery

In 1820, the young Scottish immigrant Alexander Keith established his humble brewery at 1496 Lower Water St. Little did he know that over 180 years later

---

The Halifax explosion

On the morning of 6 December 1917 two ships collided in Halifax harbour. One of them, the French *Mont Blanc*, was carrying relief supplies for the war: 2300 tonnes of pitric acid, 10 tonnes of gun cotton, 35 tonnes of benzol and 200 tonnes of TNT. The result was the biggest man-made explosion the world had ever seen.

Before she exploded the ship drifted to one of Halifax's piers and burned away for 20 minutes. This left plenty of time for crowds to gather round and watch the spectacle. When the big bang came more than 1900 people were killed instantly. Of the survivors, many were horrifically maimed – 25 limbs were later amputated and more than 250 eyes had to be removed. The force of the blast razed half the city to the ground, leaving thousands of Haligonians homeless. Incredibly, all but one of the men aboard the *Mont Blanc* survived the disaster, having rowed to shore in the right direction.

This tragic accident proved to be a precursor to atomic warfare; Oppenheimer studied the effects of the Halifax explosion while developing America's bombs for Hiroshima and Nagasaki.

his name would be associated with the oldest working brewery in North America. The brewery offers fun, highly interactive tours led by actors in period costume, who shed fascinating light not just on the beer-making process but also on life in 19th-century Halifax. The tour ends up at the Stag's Head Tavern, within the brewery, where you can sample Keith's finest ales. From June to October it's open Monday to Saturday 11am–8pm and Sundays noon–4pm, with restricted opening hours for the rest of the year. Entrance is $15; you'll find more details on 🖳 www.keiths.ca.

The Maritime Museum of the Atlantic

Down by the water's edge at 1675 Lower Water St, this museum has some good displays depicting the maritime history of the region. Particularly fascinating is the section on the *Titanic*, featuring some salvaged items, a recreation of first-, second- and third-class cabins and a 3-D 'virtual tour' of the ship. When this unfortunate ship sank on 15 April 1912, a huge rescue operation got underway from Halifax. Two hundred and nine bodies were recovered and brought to the city, and embalmers were enlisted from all over the Maritimes to cope with the work. About 55 bodies were claimed; the rest were buried in unnumbered graves. The privileges of first-class travel were upheld even in the face of death: the bodies of ordinary passengers were simply tagged before being brought into Halifax; the bodies of first-class passengers were immediately embalmed and laid in coffins. The museum's other highlights include a massive octagonal lens from an 18th-century lighthouse; a roomful of small wooden boats (including Queen Victoria's royal barge); casefuls of beautiful 19th-century sextants, clocks, figureheads and anchors – and a very vocal resident parrot named Merlin.

The museum is open daily 9.30am–5.30pm, with late opening until 8pm on Tuesdays; in winter (mid-October to end May) it's closed on Monday and does not open until 1pm on Sunday. Entrance is $8 in summer, $4 in winter and free on Tuesday nights between 5.30pm and 8pm. The museum also gives regular Tuesday-evening talks at 7.30pm.

Pier 21

Directly behind the train station on the harbourfront, Pier 21 is one of Halifax's most engaging attractions. Between 1928 and 1971, the pier was the entry point and immigration clearing post for over a million arrivals from Europe, most of whom boarded trains to other parts of Canada. Designated a national historic site,

---

🚂 Whale-watching

There are a number of outfits on the waterfront near the Maritime Museum offering boat, and more specifically, whale-watching trips (from June to October). One of the best deals is the Maritime Experience Tour with **Four Winds Charters** (☎ 902-492-0022 or toll-free on ☎ 1-877-274-8421, 🖳 www.fourwindscharters.com) who, for $25, offer $2^{1}/_{2}$-hour trips in search of minke, humpback and blue whales with stories of shipwrecks and pirates to entertain along the way.

the building now provides a fascinating and often moving testimony to Canada's immigrants – whose numbers included thousands of refugees, war brides, wartime evacuees and 'home children' from orphanages – with a hall full of evocative black-and-white photographs, information panels, displays of passports, letters, telegrams and other personal effects, and a series of tape recordings of first-hand accounts reflecting the different experiences of immigration.

Rounding it all up is a highly entertaining holographic show depicting some of the typical people that passed through Pier 21, including a Ukrainian farming family, a Canadian soldier returning from World War II, and a couple of hilarious British war brides (with rather dubious cockney accents). The museum celebrates the legacy of those who came to Canada looking for a new life and the incredible journeys taken to reach their destination.

Pier 21 (⌨ www.pier21.ca) is open daily between 9.30am and 5.30pm from May to November, and for the rest of the year Tuesday to Friday 10am–5pm, Saturdays noon to 5pm; entrance costs $8.

Point Pleasant Park

A few miles out of town is the splendid Point Pleasant Park, 186 acres of forestland on the tip of the Halifax peninsula (currently undergoing improvement and restoration work following the damage caused by Hurricane Juan in 2003). The park has a good network of trails and footpaths (much more accessible than in the more famous Stanley Park, in Vancouver) and the shoreline boasts a sandy beach from which you can bathe. Look out for the heather close to the southern shores; it grew from seeds accidentally brought over in the mattresses of the Scottish Highland Regiment and has flourished ever since. Incidentally, Halifax still rents this park from the British Government on a 999-year lease for the bargain rate of one shilling a year.

To get to Point Pleasant Park by public transport, take bus No 9 from Barrington St (around every 20–30 minutes on weekdays, and hourly at 45 minutes past the hour on Saturdays, and on the hour on Sundays).

MOVING ON

By rail

Trains leave Halifax for Montreal daily except Tuesday at 12.35pm. The journey takes 19 hours. The toll-free VIA information number is ☎ 1-888-842-7245.

To get to the rail station from downtown, take the No 9, 7 or 35 bus running south along Barrington St.

By air

The cheapest way of getting to the airport is on the Airbus (☎ 902-873-2091). Tickets are $16 and the bus picks passengers up at all the major downtown hotels. The phone number for Air Canada is ☎ 902-429-7111 or for reservations made within Canada, call toll free on ☎ 1-888-247-2262 .

Quebec City

Nothing struck me as so beautiful and grand as the location of the town of Quebec, which could not be better situated even were it to become, in some future time, the capital of a great Empire.   **Frontenac**, in a letter, 1672

Quebec City, spilling down Cap Diamant's slopes onto the banks of the St Lawrence, is surely one of the most picturesque cities in North America and is the only one to be listed as a UNESCO World Heritage Site. Inside the old quarter, Quebec's much-vaunted European flavour exceeds expectations: its narrow, cobblestoned streets are lined with 17th- and 18th-century houses; 95% of the population is of French ancestry and many inhabitants speak English with a strong French accent (and some not at all). It's all wonderfully exotic and more than a little disorientating.

It would be a great shame not to visit Quebec City while in Eastern Canada but two or three days should be enough to savour its charms before moving on. This is, after all, a city that makes a living out of its history and after a while you can begin to feel that you're trapped in a little time bubble.

HISTORY

Cartier lands at Stadacona
Quebec City is the oldest European settlement in Canada though it was, of course, inhabited long before Jacques Cartier first landed on the site in 1535. It was then the location of an Iroquois village named Stadacona, presided over by Chief Donnacona. After spending the winter there, Cartier and his men abducted Donnacona and some Iroquois, and took them back to France. All of the natives except one girl died within a few years of arriving in Europe.

Permanent French base established
It wasn't until 1608 that a permanent European base was established, not by Cartier but by Samuel de Champlain, who founded a fur-trading post at the foot of Cap Diamant and named it Quebec. By this time the settlement at Stadacona had vanished, and there was no trace of the Iroquois. Seven years later the first Récollet missionaries arrived, followed by the Jesuits in 1625. The new colony, however, provoked the jealousy and hostility of the British, who blockaded it until it surrendered in 1629. Britain held on to the settlement for just three years before the territory was returned to France in 1632.

Expansion
Back in the hands of the French, the settlement began to expand rapidly as more settlers came out and a church, a school and a hospital were built. It wasn't long before the economy, which revolved around the fur trade, began to diversify: leather manufacturing, shipbuilding and logging were all initiated in the latter

half of the 17th century. Foreign aggression continued to disturb the city's peace, however, and in 1690 Quebec was unsuccessfully attacked by troops from New England. It was at this point that the city's fortifications began to be built.

Battle on the Plains of Abraham

In 1759 the British were back to launch a massive assault on the city, with the aid of 76 warships, 9000 soldiers, 10,000 fire bombs and 40,000 cannon balls. Quebec, under the command of the Marquis de Montcalm, held out for three months before the British – under General Wolfe – managed to land on the western side of Cap Diamant during the night. Taken by surprise, Montcalm's forces were defeated in a battle lasting less than half an hour. Both Wolfe and Montcalm were killed and Quebec fell to the British. The battle marked the beginning of the end of New France, which was handed over to Britain in its entirety in 1763.

Quebec under the British

The city's French-speaking community of 8000 people suddenly found itself under the rule of an English governor. Despite fears of enforced anglicization, the Quebec Act of 1774 guaranteed the protection of the Catholic religion and the French language. Apart from an unsuccessful attempt by the Americans to take the city in 1775, Quebec was allowed to develop undisturbed over the next century. The mainstays of its economy were logging and shipbuilding and it continued to be an important port right through to the 1950s when the St Lawrence was artificially widened to allow ships to reach Montreal.

Quebec today

Largely ignored in favour of Montreal by the immigrant Irish and Scottish merchants at the turn of the 20th century, Quebec City has remained almost completely Francophone. The city, which is the capital of the Province of Quebec, is an important administrative and educational centre and has spread out well beyond the confines of the old quarters. Today the metropolitan area of Quebec has a population of 717,600.

For most visitors, however, the most visible face of Quebec is that of its narrow streets and old-world charm that draws thousands of tourists here each year. Nonetheless, Quebec does not pander indiscriminately to tourists and its people often seem refreshingly detached from the predominantly English-speaking, camera-clicking crowds wandering through their streets. As for the future, the Quebecois are already planning for 3 July, 2008, when the city celebrates its 400th anniversary.

❏ **Quebec City online**

🖳 **www.quebecregion.com** Put together by the Greater Quebec Area Tourism and Convention Bureau, this is a very useful website on the city.

🖳 **www.bonjour-quebec.com** Tourisme Québec's site, with information on the whole province. Emails can be sent to 🖳 info@tourisme.gouv.qc.ca.

CITY GUIDES & PLANS

CITY GUIDES & PLANS

ARRIVING IN QUEBEC CITY

By train
Since the land where *The Ocean* used to pull in has been sold to property developers, trains from Halifax now arrive at **Charny**, a small town 26km outside Quebec City. From Charny, a small minibus ($9.90) takes passengers to the **Gare du Palais**, the beautiful old train station in Quebec's Basse-Ville. From here, unless you're prepared to hike up the steep streets to the Haute-Ville where you'll probably be sleeping, the only way up is by taxi (roughly $5 to the top of the Haute-Ville); there are usually a few around the train station but if none appears, call one of the taxi companies listed below.

By air
Serving mainly domestic flights, Jean-Lesage Airport is 20km outside the city. It's connected to downtown by an airport shuttle bus (around $8), or taxi (fixed rate of $30).

GETTING AROUND

Vieux-Québec is entirely navigable **on foot**. The only reason you might need to take a bus is to avoid the walk to the Musée du Québec or if you want to get out of town to the Montmorency Falls.

The **bus** service is run by the Société de Transport de la Communité Urbain de Québec, otherwise known as STCUQ (☎ 418-627-2511). The main point for catching buses is at Place d'Youville, near Porte Saint-Jean.

There are several **taxi** ranks dotted around town, or you can call one from Taxi Co-op Quebec (☎ 418-525-5191) or Taxi Quebec (☎ 418-522-2001).

Finally, you can hire **bicycles** at Vélo Passe-Sport Plein Air at 6 rue du cul-de-sac (☎ 418-694-001, 🖳 www.velopasse-sport.com).

ORIENTATION

Quebec City is very small and you'll have no problem finding your way around. Most visitors are here to see Vieux Québec which is divided between the **Basse-Ville** (or Lower Town) at the foot of Cap Diamant and the **Haute-Ville** (or Upper Town) perched on the top of Cap Diamant. There are steps leading from Place Royale in the Basse-Ville to the terrace beside Château Frontenac in the Haute-Ville. There's also a funicular to and from the same places. Haute-Ville is where you'll probably spend most of your time and it's where almost all the accommodation is located. Part of the Haute-Ville is surrounded by the old city walls. Quebec is, incidentally, the continent's only walled city north of Mexico.

SERVICES

Tourist information
There are two tourist information centres. The most centrally located is the large **Centre Infotouriste de Québec** at 12 rue Sainte-Anne, just across from Château

Frontenac, where you can pick up information about the whole region and book accommodation. It's open daily 8.30am–7.30pm between late June and early September, and 9am–5pm for the rest of the year. The other, focusing more on the city, is the **Bureau d'Information Touristique du Vieux-Québec** (☎ 418-641-6290) at 835 ave Wilfred-Laurier, just off Grande Allée Est and near the Drill Hall; it is open daily 8.30am–7.30pm from late June to early September, and from Monday to Saturday 9am–5pm, Sunday 10am–4pm during the rest of the year.

Money
The conveniently located Caisse Populaire Desjardins du Vieux-Quebec, at 19 rue des Jardins, changes travellers' cheques between 9am and 6pm daily in summer and from 10am to 3pm for the rest of the year; it also has a 24-hour ATM. Other banks include the Royal Bank of Canada at 888 rue Saint-Jean and the National Bank of Canada at 1199 rue Saint-Jean.

Consulates
Finland (☎ 418-683-3000) Suite 200, 801 chemin Saint-Louis
France (☎ 418-688-3820) 1110 ave des Laurentides
Italy (☎ 418-529-9801) 3876 Pollack St
Netherlands (☎ 418-525-8171) 174 Grande Allée
Norway (☎ 418-525-8171) 2 Nouvelle France, Wolves Crove, PO Box 40
Switzerland (☎ 418-623-9864) 3293 1ère ave
USA (☎ 418-692-2095) 2 Place Terrasse Dufferin

Post, internet and laundry
The main **post office** is at 300 rue Saint-Paul. The city has a number of **internet cafés**: opposite each other on Place d'Youville are Al Van Houtte, with eight terminals, and Café du Tribunal, with two, both charging $6 per hour. There's another terminal at the TIC at 12 rue St Anne, while just around the corner at 5 rue du Fort there's a free terminal in the sub-post office.

The most conveniently located **laundry** is the Buanderie du Vieux-Quebec at 41 rue Saint-Louis. Alternatively, there's the rather dated Lavoir St-Ursule at 17b, Rue St-Ursule, just off Rue St Jean, where all the signs and instructions are in French, and although the washing machines are fairly standard, the dryers appear to be a few decades old – you can actually catch a glimpse of flames as the gas heaters dry your clothing!

WHERE TO STAY

Surprisingly for such a popular tourist destination, accommodation in Quebec City is very reasonably priced and most of it is located right in the heart of the old town.

> ❏ Accommodation prices quoted in this book are for **high season** (normally May or June to September). In low season many hotels offer substantial discounts.

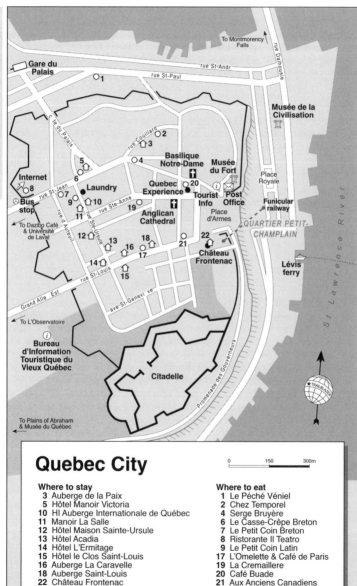

Quebec City

0   150   300m

Where to stay

3 Auberge de la Paix
5 Hôtel Manoir Victoria
10 HI Auberge Internationale de Québec
11 Manoir La Salle
12 Hôtel Maison Sainte-Ursule
13 Hôtel Acadia
14 Hôtel L'Ermitage
15 Hôtel le Clos Saint-Louis
16 Auberge La Caravelle
18 Auberge Saint-Louis
22 Château Frontenac

Where to eat

1 Le Péché Véniel
2 Chez Temporel
4 Serge Bruyère
6 Le Casse-Crêpe Breton
7 Le Petit Coin Breton
8 Ristorante Il Teatro
9 Le Petit Coin Latin
17 L'Omelette & Café de Paris
19 La Cremaillere
20 Café Buade
21 Aux Anciens Canadiens

Budget accommodation

The best choice is the bright, attractive *Auberge de la Paix* (☎ 418-694-0735, 🖳 www.aubergedelapaix.com), 31 rue Couillard, in a beautiful old house with a garden; the beds are in small dormitories and the rate ($20, or $23 per person with bedding) includes breakfast. The hostel also offers a small number of rooms with beds for 2, 3 and 4 people at the same rate but, unlike dormitory beds in larger rooms, they cannot be booked in advance. The *HI Auberge Internationale de Québec* (☎ 418-694-0755, 🖳 www.aubergeinternationalede quebec.com) at 19 rue Sainte-Ursule is also very popular and tends to get packed out. Its dorm beds are $26 for members and $30 for non-members, while its private rooms start at $69. The staff are really friendly and there's a nice, bustling atmosphere. Both Auberge de la Paix and HI Auberge Internationale de Quebec are well located in the heart of the old town.

The *Université de Laval* (🖳 www.sres.ulaval.ca) has good private rooms with shared bath: singles cost $30.20 for students and $36.46 for non-students, with doubles at $42.16 and $47.86, respectively. The only downside is that it's around a ten-minute bus ride from the centre (take bus No 3, 7, 800 or 801 from Place d'Youville).

Mid-range hotels

This is where the real bargains are to be found. Many of the city's old residences have been converted to small inns or guesthouses, usually containing about 10 to 15 rooms of varying sizes and prices. One of the cheapest options is friendly *Manoir La Salle* (☎ 418-692-9953) at 18 rue Sainte-Ursule where you'll find a variety of simple, spacious rooms (some with shared bathrooms) from $45.50.

Another good choice, at No 40 on the same street, is *Hôtel Maison Sainte-Ursule* (☎ 418-694-9794, 🖳 www.quebecweb.com/maisonste-ursule), with 15 cheerful rooms, a friendly owner and an entertaining, bilingual cockatoo. Eight of the rooms are in the original old house, which in 1786 was only the second to be built on the rue Sainte-Ursule; the remaining newer rooms overlook a pleasant garden area. Rates here range from $49 to $119 depending on the type of room and bathroom facilities. Almost opposite, at No 43, *Hôtel Acadia* (☎ 418-694-0280, 🖳 www.hotelacadia.com) has 41 lovely rooms with period features; singles cost from $85 and doubles from $125. The hotel also has a massage parlour and a brand-new outdoor spa is due to open soon. Owned by the same company, the *Hôtel L'Ermitage* (☎ 418-694-0968, 🖳 www.hotellermitage.com) is further along rue St-Ursule at number 60 and is a lot smaller than its sister hotel, with only ten rooms. It does, however, offer the same facilities as larger hotels, such as internet connection and cable TV; doubles range from $109 to $149.

Another street with a concentration of hotels is rue Saint-Louis where at No 68 you'll find *Auberge La Caravelle* (☎ 418-694-9022, 🖳 www.quebecweb. com/lacaravelle); the bare stone walls of the bedrooms here date back to 1814. Rooms cost $109–189 and dinner, bed and breakfast packages are available. *Auberge Saint-Louis* (☎ 418-692-2424, 🖳 aubergestlouis@videotron.ca) at No 48 has far less character but it's clean and fine, with doubles starting at $89 for two people with a full breakfast included.

Upmarket hotels

You can't get much more upmarket than the *Château Frontenac* (☎ 418-692-3861, 🖥 www.fairmont.com). If you feel like indulging your fantasy of staying in a glamorous hotel, this is the place to do it. Everything is swimming in luxury, from the vast entrance lobby with its shining brass elevators to the sumptuous marble bathrooms. Some of the guests, however, look rather out of place in their trainers and jeans: it's the kind of establishment where you'd expect everyone to wear evening dress at the very least. Breakfast is served in an elegant restaurant overlooking the Château grounds (and note that the Eggs Benedict are not to be missed). As you might expect, a night at the Château does not come cheap, with standard high season doubles starting at $399, but it's worth calling ahead to check if there are any discounted rates available.

If there's no room at the Château, you could try the elegant *Hôtel Manoir Victoria* (☎ 418-692-1030, 🖥 www.manoir-victoria.com) at 44 côte du Palais. This 4-star hotel juxtaposes old with new, its handsome original architecture complemented by some impressive modern touches, such as the water feature in the lobby. The hotel boasts the only pool within the walled area of Quebec City and offers a brand new spa. The spacious rooms are from $155 to $205.

For something smaller and more intimate, head for the splendid *Hôtel le Clos Saint-Louis* (☎ 418-694-1311, 🖥 www.clossaintlouis.com) on 69, Rue Saint Louis, where many of the 18 deluxe rooms boast antique beds, high ceilings and fireplaces. The lounge is a pleasure to relax in with its elegant décor and exquisite furniture and the hotel manager is very friendly. Doubles are from $195 in high season.

WHERE TO EAT

The narrow streets of the old town are jam-packed with pavement cafés, bistros, crêperies and restaurants which, although directed mainly at tourists, are irresistibly appealing and atmospheric. As with the city's architecture, the food is disconcertingly French, with staples like *steak-frites*, *moules marinières* and *salade niçoise* featuring on many menus. Moreover, the quality is generally good and the prices fairly reasonable.

Budget food

An excellent choice for a cheap lunch is the always-packed *Le Casse-Crêpe Breton*, 1136 rue Saint-Jean, which features a huge selection of crêpes (including the option to design your own) at unbeatable prices, cooked in front of you on a big hotplate. Another place to head for is *L'Omelette* at 66 rue Saint-Louis which, besides its 12 trademark omelettes, offers a wide variety of inexpensive breakfasts, salads, soups, lunches, pizzas and cakes in a cheerful, sunny dining room with polished wooden floors and high ceilings. The restaurant opens at 7am with some great breakfast specials so get there early to grab a window seat and watch the world go by.

Well worth the 10-minute walk from the old town is the quirky little *Dazibo Café*, 526 rue St Jean (closed Mondays), whose authentic full Irish breakfasts, served between 11am and 3pm, are highly regarded locally. *Le Petit Coin Latin*, at No 8½ (!) rue Sainte-Ursule, is a cosy establishment known for its hearty breakfasts (try a delicious 'omelette garni' to start the day off well) and simple, filling lunches and there's a pleasant terrace out the back.

Finally, if all this French fare is proving a bit too much, head to *Café Buade* on Rue de Buade, opposite the Basilica, with its comfy booths and American diner-style atmosphere, where you can fill up on tasty omelettes and a selection of hearty breakfast dishes.

Mid-range and upmarket restaurants

Probably the most popular restaurant in Quebec, *Serge Bruyère* at 1200 Rue St Jean combines an excellent-value bistro on the ground floor, where you can eat unfussy, well-cooked basics likes moules and steak on a lively outdoor terrace for around $15, with a top-notch fine-dining restaurant upstairs offering outstanding, elaborately prepared French dishes (count on at least $50 a head for a full meal).

Tucked away at 25 rue Couillard, *Chez Temporel* is a mellow café-restaurant serving crisp salads, baguette sandwiches and light meals; it's got a relaxed, friendly atmosphere and is the sort of place where locals read their newspapers over a long, leisurely coffee.

Another place popular with locals is *Le Péché Véniel*, an easy five-minute walk from the centre at 233 rue Saint-Paul: it's an attractively decorated bistro with an outdoor terrace, serving typical fish, seafood and meat dishes (the moules are delicious) at mid-range prices to a loyal bunch of regulars. Back in the upper town, *Le Petit Coin Breton* at 1029 rue Saint-Jean, although unashamedly aimed at tourists (forcing its waiters to wear slightly ridiculous Breton costumes), serves a very decent range of sweet and savoury crêpes at affordable prices.

In a lively location at Place d'Youville, *Ristorante Il Teatro* offers good Italian food (main courses between $14 and $19) and a sheltered outdoor patio where you can overlook the bustling square whatever the weather.

Next door to L'Omelette on Rue Saint-Louis, *Café de Paris* provides a nice, candlelit environment in which to enjoy a variety of veal, fish and steak dishes. At the upmarket end of the scale, in a charming whitewashed building with a bright red roof, *Aux Anciens Canadiens* takes its name from the novel written by Philippe-Aubert de Gaspé who lived here during the early 19th century. Located at 34 rue Saint-Louis, this old-fashioned restaurant specializes in traditional Quebec cuisine, such as game and rich meat, and has a reputation for excellent food. Another upscale choice is *La Cremaillere*, at 73 rue Sainte-Anne, with specialities such as milk-fed veal, and a wine cellar stocked with fine Italian wines.

NIGHTLIFE

The city really comes alive at night and you'll find any number of pubs, bars and late-night cafés around town, with a concentration in rue Saint-Jean and

Grande Allée Est, outside the city walls, where trendy young locals hang out after work and at weekends. A couple to look out for are *Le Pub St Alexandre* at 1087 rue St Jean, a slightly formulaic pseudo-English pub but with some good live folk music, and *Sacrilege* at 447 rue St Jean, a popular place for locals drawn here by some well-known local musicians. Down in the Quartier du Petit Champlain, *Le Pape Georges* at 8 rue Cul-de-sac is a dark and cosy little bar with live blues and folk.

Quebec City is famous for its **boîtes à chansons**, which should most definitely be sampled while you're here. They're basically intimate, smoky bars where earnest balladeers strum their guitars and sing their hearts out to an enthusiastic young crowd who seem to know all the words and delight in singing along. They're usually free and have a friendly, unthreatening atmosphere; they're liveliest on Friday and Saturday nights but don't really get going until around 11pm. Two of the best boîtes à chansons are *Chez Son Père* at 24 rue Stanislas and *Les Voûtes de Napoléon* at 680A Grande Allée Est.

WHAT TO SEE

Haute Ville
● **Château Frontenac** More than a hotel, the towering château has become the symbol of Quebec and is probably the most photographed building in Canada. It was commissioned for the CPR by Van Horne in 1893 and was designed by an eminent American architect, Bruce Price.

Château Frontenac
PHOTO © JIM MANTHORPE

Guided tours ($8; 🖥 www.tours chateau.ca) around the hotel's magnificent interior leave on the hour (daily 10am–6pm May to October, weekends 12–5pm November to April), and last around 50 minutes.

● **Terrasse Dufferin** Next to Château Frontenac is this long boardwalk skirting the edge of Cap Diamant. The views from here – over the St Lawrence, the Basse-Ville, the Laurentian mountains and even the foothills of the US Appalachians – are absolutely stunning, especially at sunset. The Terrasse extends into the **Promenade des Gouverneurs** which climbs to the Citadelle and continues to the Plains of Abraham.

● **Citadelle** This massive star-shaped fortress was built over a 30-year period (1820–50) by the British. Contained within its wide dykes and thick, squat walls are 25 buildings, including the Governor-General's summer residence, the officers' mess and a military museum. Still used as the headquarters of the Royal 22nd Regiment, it is the oldest occupied North American fort and has its own mascot, a regimental goat named Batisse.

Entrance to the Citadelle costs $8 for adults; once inside you can take a 45-minute guided tour, watch the Changing of the Guard (mid-June to August, 10am) or the Ceremony of the Retreat (July to August, 7pm on Friday nights). The grounds are open to the public on a daily basis (9am–5pm between May and June, 9am–6pm from July to early September); you'll find further details at 🖳 www.lacitadelle.qc.ca.

● **Plains of Abraham** It's hard to believe that this undulating parkland was the scene of the violent confrontation between Wolfe and Montcalm in 1759 (see p83), an episode that changed the course of Canadian history. Today it's a favourite area for picnickers and joggers and only a few monuments, plaques and information boards bear testimony to the famous battle played out on these fields.

● **Musée National des Beaux-Arts du Québec** Situated at the far end of the Plains of Abraham, this museum contains the biggest and best collection of Quebec art, covering a period of about three hundred years. Works range from 17th-century religious painting through to the latest movements in contemporary art and includes sculpture, photography and decorative art. It's also in the process of receiving the compelling collection of Inuit art from the Musée National d'Art Inuit Brousseau, which is soon to close. The Musée National des Beaux-Arts (🖳 www.mnba.qc.ca) opens daily 10am–6pm (Wednesdays until 9pm) from June to August, or Tuesday to Sunday 10am–5pm (Wednesdays until 9pm) for the rest of the year. The entrance price is $10.

● **Musée du Fort** This tiny museum (which hasn't changed much since it opened in 1965) is loads of fun. Visitors are seated in front of a huge plastic model of 18th-century Quebec City; the lights are dimmed and a rippling voice, accompanied by atmospheric music and flashing lights, relates the story of the six sieges of the city, including the famous battle in 1759. The show, alternating throughout the day in French and English, lasts about half an hour and costs $7.50; it's worth it just for retro-value and the entertaining interactive quiz which follows the story.

The museum (🖳 www.museedufort.com) is at 10 rue Sainte-Anne. It's open daily 10am–5pm between May and October and during the Christmas holidays, and Thursday to Sunday 11am–4pm for the rest of the year.

● **The Quebec Experience** At the other end of the technical spectrum is this slick 3-D hologram show depicting Quebec's history from the first explorers through to the last few decades. You don your 3-D specs and sit back in a comfy cinema armchair to watch the show, with commentary provided by a hologram of Cartier, who looks so real it's scary. The audio-visual effects are stunning (and occasionally terrifying – the rifle-shot episode for example).The shows alternate in French and English throughout the day at 30-minute intervals. Not to be missed on any account. It's at 8 rue du Trésor; admission is $7.50 and it's open daily 10am–10pm from mid-May to mid-October. The month of May tends to get packed with groups of enthusiastic schoolchildren, so check in advance as shows can get booked up quickly (🖳 www.quebecexperience.com).

CITY GUIDES & PLANS

● **Notre-Dame de Quebec Basilica Cathedral** Notre-Dame is the continent's oldest parish north of Mexico. Work began on the building in 1647 and the first Mass was celebrated in the cathedral in 1650. Sadly, it burnt to the ground in 1922 but has since been rebuilt to the original 17th-century plans. The interior is wonderfully light in tone, with its pale walls, shining gold-leaf altar and sky-blue ceiling.

● **Anglican Cathedral of the Holy Trinity** This church is supposed to be modelled on London (England)'s St Martin's in the Fields (though unfortunately they forgot to build a café in the crypt). There are some interesting features inside such as the benches made of oak imported from the royal forest in Windsor and the rather under-used Royal Seat, reserved exclusively for the use of the British monarch.

● **Grande-Allée Est** Leaving the walled town via rue Saint-Louis, you'll find yourself on the Grand-Allée Est, a lively avenue lined with cafés, restaurants and shops. It has a very modern feel to it and lots of locals come here to enjoy an after-work drink in the bustling pavement cafés. Take a right onto Avenue Cartier and you'll find an abundance of fresh fruit and vegetable stalls as well as fashionable boutiques.

● **L'Observatoire de la Capitale** If you've a head for heights and fancy looking down on Quebec from a different perspective, head for L'Observatoire (🖥 www.observatoirecapitale.org), an observation tower at 1037 rue De La Chevrotière. The lift takes you 221m up to the 31st floor where you can look out over the Laurentian mountains, the St Lawrence River and the whole of the city spread out below you. Entrance is $5; opening hours are daily 10am–5pm from 24 June to mid-October, and Thursdays to Sundays 10am–5pm for the rest of the year.

Basse-Ville

To get to the lower town you can walk down the steps starting at Terrasse Dufferin, or you can take the funicular running next to them ($1.25).

● **Quartier Petit Champlain** This little warren of winding streets full of craft shops and the like is wholly given over to tourism. It's Quebec at its cutest and quaintest.

At the centre of the quartier is **rue du Petit-Champlain**, the city's oldest street (dating from 1685) where you can walk down the charmingly named **Escalier Casse-Cou**; the break-your-neck staircase. Look out too for the **Fresque des Québecois**, an enormous mural covering the entire side of a building in rue Notre Dame that details 400 years of Quebecois history.

● **Place Royale** This is where Quebec City was originally founded back in 1608. The square has been extensively restored over the past few decades and is another example of Quebec's carefully groomed prettiness.

Take a look inside the **Eglise Notre-Dame-des-Victoires** on the southern side of the square; note the curious high altar sculpted to look like a castle. At

1 Place Royale is the **Maison des Vins** which was built in 1689. It is still oper-ated by a vintage wine specialist, and there's free wine tasting for tourists.

● **Musée de la Civilisation** If you have time for just one museum in Quebec, make it the Musée de la Civilisation (🖳 www.mcq.org). The building alone won awards for its architectural excellence and the museum's exhibits are very innovative, particularly in this town that seems so firmly rooted in the past.

The exhibitions are mostly temporary and cover a diverse range of histori-cal, sociological and scientific themes (and even a recent interactive Murder Mystery exhibition). The clever use of space, light and technology makes the museum a pleasure to walk around. It's near to Place Royale at 85 rue Dalhousie and is open daily from late June to early September 9.30am–6.30pm; otherwise Tuesday to Sunday 10am–5pm. Entrance is $8, or free on Tuesdays between November and May.

Montmorency Falls
A few kilometres east of the city are the spectacular Montmorency Falls. At 83m high, they are one and a half times the height of Niagara Falls. You can take a cable car ($6 one-way, $8 for a round-trip) from the foot of the cliffs up to the beginning of the waterfall which you can cross on a rather wobbly bridge. This is the third bridge to be built here; the second one collapsed five days after it was completed in 1855, causing three people to plunge down the falls to their deaths. Nearby is the Manoir Montmorency, a former residence of Edward, Duke of Kent, who was Queen Victoria's father.

You can get the No 50, 53 or 800 bus to the falls from the Haute-Ville at Ave Dufferin. There's also a well-used cycle path from the city out to the falls, which can be reached in about half an hour by bike.

FESTIVALS

● **Carnival de Québec**, early February. Eleven days of freezing madness fea-turing a mass roll in the snow wearing bathing suits, a canoe race across the frozen St Lawrence and the world's largest ice-sculpture competition.
● **Festival d'été**, early July. A ten-day whirl of street parties, concerts, singing, dancing and drinking. Excellent fun.
● **International Jazz and Blues Festival**, last week in June. Concerts all around the city in bars, restaurants, outdoor stages and halls.
● **Saint-Jean-Baptiste Day**, 24 June. Provincial holiday – parades and celebra-tions.
● **Les Médiévales de Québec**, mid-August. A five-day celebration of the Renaissance and Middle Ages. Lots of dressing-up in silly clothes.

MOVING ON

There's a frequent daily train service from Quebec's Gare du Palais to Montreal, just under three hours away. For information on trains from Quebec call ☎ 418-692-3940 (or ☎ 1-888-842-7245).

CITY GUIDES & PLANS

Montreal

This is the first time I was ever in a city where you couldn't throw a brick without breaking a church window.   **Mark Twain**, Speech in Montreal, 1881

Montreal is a delicious, feel-good city. Famous throughout Canada for its party atmosphere, it is positively spilling over with buskers, jazz cellars, wine bars, nightclubs and throngs of beautiful people. It's not an entirely frivolous place, however, and even casual visitors are aware of the complex balance of relationships contained within the city: between the English- and French-speaking inhabitants, for example; between the North American and European influences; and between the claims of Canada and Quebec.

You can see or feel Montreal's contrasts all around: in the architecture, the food, the newspapers, the snatches of conversation you hear on the streets. But far from producing a feeling of tension, it all adds up to a very rich and full-flavoured city that is one of the most appealing and intriguing in North America.

HISTORY

Early settlement
The site of present-day Montreal was first occupied by the Iroquois Indians who called their settlement 'Hochelaga' (meaning 'Place of the beaver'). The first European to arrive was Jacques Cartier who stopped off at the island in 1535 on his way to seek the North-West Passage. He climbed the mountain that rose out of the island's centre, named it Mont Réal and then promptly left. About 70 years passed before the French returned, only to discover that Hochelaga had mysteriously vanished. The site was subsequently chosen as a fur-trading base, erected by Samuel de Champlain in 1611.

French colonists arrive
It wasn't until 1642 that a permanent settlement was established outside the confines of the fur trade. This was created by Paul de Chomedey, the Sieur de Maisonneuve, who brought 53 French colonists out with the intention of converting the natives to Christianity. They built houses, a church and a hospital and named the new community Ville-Marie. By 1672 the population had reached 1200, a figure that began to multiply rapidly during the first half of the 18th century when land grants enticed French settlers out in their droves.

The British take over
In 1756 Europe became engulfed in the Seven Years' War. The fighting spread to the North American colonies, and in 1760 the British took control of Montreal. When the war ended three years later, all of New France was ceded to Britain under the Treaty of Paris. Scottish and Irish immigrants flocked to

Montreal to make their fortunes and it wasn't long before the Brits started nudging the French out of their position in Montreal's business life. All this was briefly interrupted in 1755 when American troops marched in and occupied the city for several months. When they retreated, life in Montreal carried on in much the same way as before.

The French were feeling increasingly frustrated by the disappearance of their power and political representation and in 1837 Louis-Joseph Papineau led an uprising against the British. The rebellion was brutally crushed but resentment, of course, remained strong.

The economic hub of Canada
Following Confederation in 1867, Montreal emerged as the economic, financial and transportation centre of the new dominion. Expansion and rapid industrialization followed and as the city entered the 20th century it was firmly established as Canada's most important metropolis. Prosperity and success endured, culminating in a massive spate of architectural development in the 1960s in preparation for Expo '67 – a colossal affair that brought a staggering 50 million visitors into Montreal.

Unrest breaks out
Meanwhile, resentment within the Francophone community continued to bubble away. Despite being in the majority, they had been manoeuvred into a subordinate, disadvantaged position in most levels of society, and the Anglophones appeared to remain indifferent to this injustice. While movements such as René Lévesque's Parti Québecois began to gather momentum, it was the dramatic action of the extremist FLQ that brought the crisis to a violent head in October 1970.

Following a wave of terrorism, they kidnapped and murdered a Quebec cabinet minister, Pierre Laporte. The assassins were captured and arrested but the shocked government realized that drastic measures would have to be taken to avoid similar explosions of violence. Laws were introduced to protect the French language, and the general 'Frenchification' of Montreal got underway. Many Anglophones felt threatened by what was going on and over 100,000 left the city over the next few years.

Montreal today
The commercial and financial damage brought about by the Anglophone exodus was quickly repaired by a new wave of French-speaking entrepreneurs. Today they control about 60% of Montreal's economy, a balance more acceptable to most Francophones. Montreal is no longer Canada's biggest city – having been overtaken by Toronto in the late 1960s. Nevertheless it continues to be a thriving and affluent metropolis, despite being hit by a recession in the early 1990s.

Secession continues to be the focal issue in Quebec's politics but after the defeat of the 1995 sovereignty referendum it remains to be seen which direction the independence movement will take in the 21st century.

ARRIVING IN MONTREAL

By air

Most international flights arrive at **Montreal-Trudeau Airport** (previously known as Dorval Airport), 22km south-west of the city. From here, L'Aerobus runs a shuttle service to downtown – it's a 20- to 30-minute ride and costs $13 one-way; buses run daily, 7am–2am, every 20 or 30 minutes. In addition, a rail shuttle between the airport and downtown Montreal is currently being constructed. Meanwhile, a taxi from the airport to downtown will cost around $35.

By train

The VIA Rail station is bang in the centre of town, in the large underground complex beneath the Queen Elizabeth Hotel.

GETTING AROUND

Montreal has a good public transport system, although wandering around on foot is probably the most pleasurable way of getting about the city. Its métro was designed by engineers from the Paris métro; stations are signalled by a white arrow on a big blue sign but they're so carefully hidden you may get half way to your destination before you find one. Once underground, it's all very clean, efficient and safe.

There's also an extensive **bus** network which uses the same fare system as the métro. A single ticket costs $2.50; if you ask for *une correspondance* (transfer) you can complete your bus journey by métro or vice versa. Alternatively, you can buy a book of six tickets for $11.25; a one-day pass for $8; or a three-day pass for $16; they're available at métro stations and at the Infotouriste Centre (see opposite) and can be used on both buses and the métro. Public transport starts to wind down at 12.30am, though some buses operate all through the night. There are plenty of **taxis** around town, which can easily be flagged down. To call one, try Co-op on ☎ 514-725-9885 or Diamond ☎ 514-273-6331.

There are a couple of places in Vieux Montréal, down by the port, where you can hire **bikes** and **rollerblades**: Ça Roule (☎ 514-866-0633, 🖳 www.caroulemo ntreal.com), near the corner with rue St-Gabriel at 27 rue de la Commune Est, where bikes can be hired for $30 for a 24-hour period, and also at Vélo Aventure (☎ 514-847-0666) next to the IMAX cinema, where bikes cost $7 an hour or $22 per day; rollerblades cost $9 for the first hour and $4.50 for every additional hour.

ORIENTATION

It comes as a surprise to many visitors when they discover that Montreal sits on an island. The Ile de Montréal is 32km long and 16km wide and is the largest of 234 islands that make up the Hochelaga archipelago in the St Lawrence River. To orientate yourself in the city forget about conventional directions and pay no

---

(Opposite) Christ Church Cathedral (see p106) in Montreal is reflected in the plate glass of its towering neighbour, neatly summing up the contrasts of old and new in this lively city.

attention to the sun's position in the sky: Montreal has its own definitions of north, south, east and west and they make navigation a lot easier. The old port is down in the south; Mont Royal, the extinct volcano known by everyone as 'the mountain', is a few kilometres north. So, the streets between the mountain and the quays are deemed to run from north to south, and the streets crossing them at right angles east to west.

The city is divided into two main areas: downtown Montreal and Vieux Montréal. **Downtown** begins a few blocks south of the mountain and is basically everything within the square formed by rue Sherbrooke in the north, rue St Antoine in the south, blvd St Laurent in the east and ave Atwater in the west. This is the modern, high-rise, high-tech heart of the city. **Vieux Montréal**, down by the port, is where the city's oldest streets were first laid out in 1672. Today it's Montreal's most picturesque, photogenic and tourist-packed quarter.

Finally, a word on street numbers. For east–west streets, 0 is at blvd St Laurent, with numbers increasing as they move east or west from this point. Addresses are suffixed with *est* (east) or *ouest* (west) to designate which side of the boulevard they're on. North–south street numbers start down by the St Lawrence and increase as the streets move north.

SERVICES

Tourist information

There's a large and very efficient **Infotouriste Centre** (☎ 514-873-2015 or 1-800-363-7777) at 1255 Rue Peel, on the corner of Ste-Catherine and Peel streets (about a five-minute walk from the train station). It's open daily, 8.30am –7.30pm June to August and 9am–6pm for the rest of the year. It's stocked with masses of brochures and leaflets and there's an accommodation desk where the staff will ring around to find vacancies for you; it also offers internet access in the basement and a currency exchange desk.

A second, much smaller tourist office is located on the corner of the Place Jacques Cartier in **Vieux Montréal**, open daily 9am–7pm June to August, and 9am–5pm for the rest of the year.

> ❏ **Montreal online**
> 🖥 **www.tourism-montreal.org**
> Tourisme Montréal's very thorough website, focusing on the city.
>
> 🖥 **www.bonjour-quebec.com**
> Tourisme Québec's site is dedicated to the whole province but has some useful pages on Montreal.
>
> 🖥 **www.montrealonline.com**
> Current theatre, cinema, music, nightlife and festival listings and reviews, produced by the *Montreal Gazette*.

Money

There are numerous banks downtown, including several next to the train station. The following charge no commission for foreign exchange: Banque Nationale du Canada at 1001 rue Sainte-Catherine Ouest; Banque Nationale du Canada at 600 rue de la Gauchèterie Ouest; Thomas Cook at 625 blvd René Lévesque Ouest.

(Opposite) The view from Toronto's CN Tower (see p119) is even more impressive at night. At 553m (1816ft) it's the world's tallest free-standing structure. (Photo © Jim Manthorpe).

Consulates

Belgium (☎ 514-849-7394) 999 blvd de Maisonneuve Ouest, suite 850
Britain (☎ 514-866-5863) 1000 rue de la Gauchèterie Ouest, suite 4200
Denmark (☎ 514-877-3060) 1 Place-Ville-Marie, 35th floor
France (☎ 514-878-4385) 1 Place-Ville-Marie, suite 2601
Germany (☎ 514-931-2277) 1250 blvd René Lévesque Ouest, suite 4315
Italy (☎ 514-849-8351) 3489 rue Drummond
Japan (☎ 514-866-3429) 600 rue de la Gauchèterie Ouest, suite 2120
Netherlands (☎ 514-849-4247) 1002 rue Sherbrooke Ouest, suite 2201
Spain (☎ 514-935-5235) 1 Westmount Sq, suite 1456
Sweden (☎ 514-932-7181) 1572 ave Dr Penfield
Switzerland (☎ 514-932-7181) 1572 ave Dr Penfield
USA (☎ 514-398-9695) 1155 rue St-Alexandre

Post, internet and laundry

The main **post office** with its free internet terminal is at 1250 University (one
block north of Place-Ville-Marie). There are several **cyber-cafés** in town; one of
the handiest is at Tip Tours, downstairs from the Infotouriste Centre on Square
Dorchester, where it costs $3.50 to surf the net for 30 minutes. In the old town at
38 rue Notre Dame you'll find three terminals in the Wilson & Lafleur bookshop.

Reasonably central **laundries** include Lavoir Buanderie, 2165 Ste-
Catherine Ouest (métro Atwater), Lavoir du Village, 3686 St-Denis, and Lavoir
St-Laurent, 3632 St-Laurent.

WHERE TO STAY

There are plenty of places to stay in Montreal and you can generally get some
good deals, particularly in the mid-priced range. Be warned, though, that the best
places get snapped up very quickly in July and August and if you're planning on
coming during the Jazz Festival (beginning of July) you should book well ahead.

Budget accommodation

The excellent Hostelling International's *Auberge de la Jeunesse* (☎ 514-843-
3317, 🖳 www.hihostels.ca) is in a beautifully renovated old house on the southern corner of rues Mackay and René Lévesque (1030 rue Mackay). Rooms contain three to ten beds and each one has its own private bathroom; rates are $26
a night for members and $30 for non-members. There are also private doubles,
which cost $65 for members or $75 for non-members. The facilities here are
fantastic with a small café and bar, hairdryers available to borrow and free towels provided. The staff are extremely friendly, especially Chris who runs the tri-
weekly pub crawls on Tuesdays, Thursdays and Sundays – a great way to meet
other travellers and experience Montreal nightlife.

❑ Accommodation prices quoted in this book are for **high season** (normally May or
June to September). In low season many hotels offer substantial discounts.

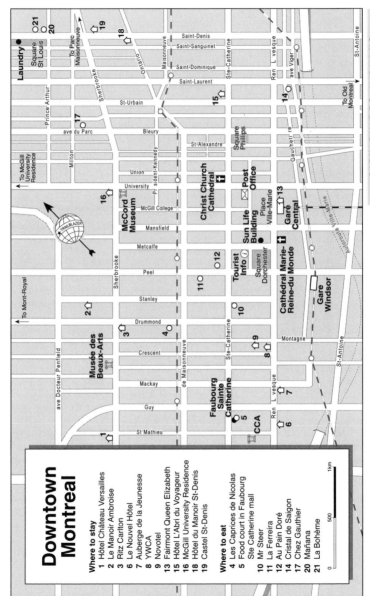

CITY GUIDES & PLANS

Downtown Montreal

Where to stay
1 Hôtel Château Versailles
2 Le Manoir Ambroise
3 Ritz Carlton
6 Le Nouvel Hôtel
7 Auberge de la Jeunesse
9 YWCA
13 Fairmont Queen Elizabeth
15 Hôtel L'Abri du Voyageur
16 McGill University Residence
18 Hôtel du Manoir St-Denis
19 Castel St-Denis

Where to eat
4 Les Caprices de Nicolas
5 Food court in Faubourg
  Ste Catherine mall
10 Mr Steer
11 La Ferreira
12 Au Pain Doré
14 Cristal de Saigon
17 Chez Gauthier
20 Mañana
21 La Bohème

0   500   1km

Also very central, and a short walk from the train station, is the mixed-sex **YWCA** (☎ 514-866-9941, 🖳 www.ydesfemmesmtl.org), 1355 blvd René-Lévesque, where fresh, neat rooms with en-suite bathroom cost $75 for a single and $85 per double (rates are slightly lower if you opt for a room without a private bathroom). The rooms are more typical of a hotel than a youth hostel and the area is remarkably peaceful considering its great location. Available to both men and women, the YWCA offers gym and laundry facilities and a great little café in the lobby.

McGill University Residence (🖳 www.mcgill.ca/residences/summer) offers spartan but clean singles from mid-May to mid-August for around $50 ($46 for students): they're available on the quiet campus of Bishop Mountain Residence at 3935 University (☎ 514-398-6367) and at Royal Victoria College at 3425 University, on the corner with Sherbrooke (☎ 514-398-6378).

Mid-range hotels

At the lower end of the scale, the city's best-value hotel is without doubt *Hôtel L'Abri du Voyageur* (☎ 514-849-2922, 🖳 www.abri-voyageur.ca) at 9 Ste-Catherine Ouest. The rooms are spotless, with scrubbed pine floors, exposed brick walls and high ceilings, and the owners are very welcoming. Double rooms, all with shared bath, cost from $70; advance reservations are highly recommended.

Another great-value choice is *Castel St-Denis* (☎ 514-842-9719, 🖳 www.castelsaintdenis.qc.ca) at 2099 rue St-Denis, run by delightful Mr Imam. The rooms are simple, clean and well priced, starting at $60 for a single and $70 for a double; the Castel is handy for the cafés and restaurants lining this part of St-Denis. A bit further down on the opposite side at No 2006, *Hôtel du Manoir St-Denis* (☎ 514-843-3670, 🖳 www.manoirdenis.com) has 22 small but comfortable double rooms (with fridges) from $58, with continental breakfast included.

For something with a bit more character, try *Le Manoir Ambroise* (☎ 514-288-6922, 🖳 www.manoirambrose.com), a lovely Victorian house converted into a small hotel. The rooms are big and attractively decorated and the guest book is full of enthusiastic comments such as 'C'est fantastique!' It's situated on a tree-lined avenue at the quiet end of rue Stanley (No 3422, at the foot of Mt Royal) and is just a stone's throw from the centre of town. Doubles with a private bathroom start at $85 including breakfast.

Moving up a couple of notches, at 1740 blvd René Lévesque, *Le Nouvel Hôtel and Spa* (☎ 514-931-8841, 🖳 www.lenouvelhotel.com) is a fairly smart hotel; singles start at $149 but there are often offers available so it's best to call ahead or check out the website in advance. The rooms are well-lit, spacious and neat with phone, TV and room service. A similar establishment, though more expensive with doubles from $179, is the *Novotel* (☎ 514-861-6000, 🖳 www.novotel.com), 1180 rue de la Montagne, which has a gym, café and a smart, fresh feel.

For something more intimate, the charming *Hôtel Château Versailles* (☎ 514-933-3611, 🖳 www.versailleshotels.com) stands at 1659 rue Sherbrooke Ouest. A converted Victorian mansion, it combines stylish, elegant décor with lovely old period features and is run to a very high standard. Rooms start at around $149, with discounts available when demand is low. If you'd prefer to stay in

Vieux Montréal, *Auberge Bonsecours* (☎ 514-396-2662, 🖥 www.aubergebo nsecours.com) at 353 rue St-Paul Est is a charming boutique hotel near the Bonsecours Market and the Notre-Dame-de-Bon-Secours Chapel. The hotel combines modern brickwork with renovated stone walls and its seven rooms boast polished, wooden floors and cheerful décor. There's also a great outdoor patio where guests can soak up the atmosphere of Vieux Montréal. Double rooms, with breakfast included, range between $195 and $285.

Upmarket hotels

The classiest joint in town is the glamorous *Ritz Carlton* (☎ 514-842-4212, 🖥 www.ritzcarlton.com/hotels/montreal) at 1228 rue Sherbrooke Ouest. It opened in 1912 and its fantastically opulent interior seems to have changed little since then. An added touch of glamour: it was here that Elizabeth Taylor married Richard Burton in 1964. If its prohibitive prices are beyond your reach (around $325 in high season, $158 in low season), it's worth going in for a drink at the piano bar (or even just a trip to the loos).

If you like the idea of stepping off the train right into your hotel you can do just that at the *Fairmont Queen Elizabeth* (☎ 514-861-3511, 🖥 www.fairm ont.com) which is literally right on top of the station. It's a large, stylish hotel and is always busy with a high-powered international crowd. The hotel's guest list from previous years includes Her Majesty Queen Elizabeth II, Princess Grace of Monaco and Indira Gandhi. John Lennon fans should also note that it was in a suite on the 17th floor that he and Yoko Ono recorded their famous song, *Give Peace a Chance*, in 1969. Standard doubles here cost from $249.

WHERE TO EAT

Montreal is blessed with a wealth of eating establishments ranging from gourmet restaurants to dirt-cheap delis. While it shares the North American obsession with bagels, and although European immigrants have imported interesting specialities (notably smoked meat), the majority of Montreal's restaurants are firmly rooted in the city's French heritage. Many restaurants have a fixed-price *table d'hôte* menu which is considerably cheaper than ordering *à la carte*.

Budget food

For a fine selection of paninis, croissants and mugs of rich coffee, take a seat in *Au Pain Doré*, situated above an excellent little bakery at 1956 rue Peel, and watch the world go by from its large windows overlooking the street. A good place to head for a quick, cheap lunch is the food court spread over two levels of the *Faubourg Sainte Catherine* mall, at 1616 Ste-Catherine Ouest. It's got everything from sandwiches to Thai food or fresh fish, with pleasant seating areas looking out onto the street and attractive fresh-produce stalls on the first floor. A few blocks east at No 1198, *Mr Steer* has been a local institution since 1958, serving good-quality burgers, chicken and steak and daily set lunches at unbeatable prices. It's a great place to escape the hustle and bustle of Rue St-Catherine's busy shops.

CITY GUIDES & PLANS

> ### 🚂 BYOBs
>
> Quebec is the only province in Canada that allows customers to bring their own wine (but not beer or spirits) to certain restaurants, namely those that have been granted a special licence. These restaurants are known as BYOBs (bring your own bottle) and are immensely popular. We've listed a handful of the best below, which all serve typical French bistro food. Most BYOBs are not in the downtown core but in the neighbourhoods just out of the centre.
>
> ● *L'Entrepont* (☎ 514-845-1369) 4622 Avenue de l'Hôtel de Ville (Mont-Royal métro). Elegant décor and an imaginative menu make this an excellent choice. Reservations are advised.
>
> ● *Le P'tit Plateau* (☎ 514-282-6342) 330 rue Marie-Anne Est (Mont-Royal métro). Simple, friendly restaurant with generous portions, an emphasis on fresh produce and many vegetarian options.
>
> ● *Les Héritiers* (☎ 514-528-4953) 5091 rue de Lanaudière (Laurier métro). Delicious salads, meat dishes and lots of rustic style, tucked away in a tiny street between Laurier and St-Joseph.
>
> ● *Les Mauvais Garçons* (☎ 514-524-7989) 4466 rue Marquette (Mont-Royal métro). Simple, honest, traditional bistro food at great prices.
>
> ● *Yoyo* (☎ 514-949-3465) 4720 rue Marquette (Laurier métro). Lively bistro with attractive décor and great food including not-to-be-missed crême brulées.

One area where you're guaranteed to find a cheap meal is Chinatown, packed with tiny restaurants that fill with the local Chinese population. One of the best is *Cristal de Saigon*, hidden away at 1068 blvd St-Laurent, which offers a vast choice of soups and delicious spring rolls among other delights.

There's another concentration of cheap restaurants at the northern end of St-Denis: *Mañana*, at No 3605, is a small, friendly Mexican restaurant serving inexpensive nachos, burritos, ceviche and the like. The dining area is filled with large sombreros and other cheerful accessories and the colourful decorations add to the fun atmosphere of the restaurant. Meanwhile, *La Bohème*, a few doors up at No 3625, is a charming little bistro where you can eat tasty Moroccan and French food for around $10 to $20 a head, (though at the time of writing it was closed for renovations, so check ahead on ☎ 514-286-6659). You'll find plenty more bistros and cafés on St-Denis, particularly between Sherbrooke and Maisonneuve.

Also worth a try is *Gallianos* on rue St-Vincent in the old town, where you can get great Italian dishes for under $20. Alternatively, if you fancy some pub food, head to the corner of rue de Vaudreil and rue St-Paul in Vieux Montréal, where *Les 3 Brasseurs* or 'The 3 Brewers' serves tasty burgers, wraps and a traditional pizza-type dish from Alsace called 'Flamms'. The bar has a lively atmosphere and the restaurant is part of a chain with two other locations in Montreal.

Mid-range and upmarket restaurants

Perhaps Montreal's best-known restaurant, *Claude Postel* (☎ 514-875-5067, 🖥 www.claudepostel.com) is located in a former morgue at 443 Saint-Vincent in Vieux Montréal. A favourite haunt of Montreal's bourgeoisie, this gourmet French restaurant is a little stingy with its portions but the food is superb; count on spending around $50 per person. Chocoholics should note that Claude Postel is also a chocolaterie and prides itself on its exquisite chocolates. You have been warned!

Downtown, *La Ferreira* (☎ 514-848-0988), at 1446 Peel, has a stylish, colourful interior and an outdoor terrace where you can feast on first-rate Portuguese dishes like seafood broth and fresh sardines from around $35 per person. A couple of blocks west at 2072 rue Drummond, *Les Caprices de Nicolas* (☎ 514-282-9790) feels splendidly luxurious and offers an intimate setting in its basement location, with an indoor garden and tasteful artwork adorning the walls. The elaborately prepared French food does not disappoint but it's expensive, with most main courses around $40. Another place for a splurge is the garden restaurant, *Le Jardin du Ritz*, at the Ritz Carlton (☎ 514-842-4212), the very picture of elegance with its crisp, white linen, abundance of flowers, little duck pond and attentive staff. It's best experienced over Sunday brunch or afternoon tea, which features tea made with loose leaves (not tea-bags) and scones with jam and clotted cream.

Arguably the city's best restaurant, *Toqué!* (☎ 514-499-2084), 900 Place Jean-Paul-Riopelle, boasts a buzzing atmosphere, great service and outstanding food (the duck foie gras is amazing), with main courses around $40–45 and a fantastic gourmet menu starting at $101 per person, duck foie gras included. If your budget won't stretch to it, try *Chez Gauthier* (3487 ave du Parc) where you can feast on decent bistro food for around $25 in a pretty, wood-panelled room, or head there on a morning for delicious breakfast dishes priced around $9.

NIGHTLIFE

Montreal's dazzling nightlife scene is concentrated in several different areas, each with its own character and crowd.

Rue Crescent (between Sainte Catherine and Maisonneuve) is an out-and-out party street. Traditionally regarded as the preserve of the Anglos, it's packed with pubs, nightclubs and a dolled-up crowd whose main pursuits seem to be drinking, dancing and attempting to pull. Favourite spots include the *Sir Winston Churchill* at No 1459 and *Thursday's* at No 1449.

The **blvd Saint-Laurent** is considerably more sophisticated (and Francophone) and has some of the most interesting nightspots in town. *Le Balattou* (No 4372) is a steamy, smoky, immensely popular African nightclub, established over 20 years ago, while further down at No 3556 is *Orchid* where a fashionable, lively clientèle come to dance to hip hop and R&B music. Rue Saint-Denis has a more studenty, bohemian feel to it. There are some excellent jazz bars here, including *Les Beaux Esprits* at No 2073.

There's also a thriving gay scene in Montreal, most of it centred in what's known as the **Gay Village**. The core of the village runs along Sainte-Catherine between Saint-Denis and Papineau. One of its most famous clubs is *KOX* at No 1450, which attracts a good number of straights as well as gays.

If you just want a cheap beer and great nachos head to *Carlos and Pepe's*, tucked away at 1420 rue Peel (☎ 514-288-3090) – don't miss the $8 pitcher specials on Sunday and Monday nights.

WHAT TO SEE

Vieux Montréal

Old Montreal with its cobblestoned streets, immaculately restored buildings, churches, boutiques, cafés and restaurants is a magnet for tourists. It contains some of the best examples of 18th-century architecture in North America and, despite the crowds, is completely irresistible. The Infotouriste Centre at the corner of Place Jacques Cartier hands out free walking-tour booklets which give a detailed account of the district's main historic and architectural features. The highlights are as follows:

● **Notre-Dame Basilica** This Gothic Revival extravaganza (🖳 www. basiliquenddm.org) at 110 Notre-Dame Ouest was the biggest religious building in North America when it was completed in 1829. It was designed by James O'Donnell, a New York-Irish architect who was so proud of his work he converted to Catholicism so he could be buried in it. The interior is a dazzling spectacle of gold leaf and stained glass and the main altar is breathtaking. Note also the beautiful vaulted ceiling, and the huge 5772-pipe Casavant organ (remember St-Hyacinthe? See p193). Entrance is $4, which includes an optional 20-minute guided tour.

● **Château Ramezay** More a big house than a château, this is nonetheless a fine old residence. It was built in 1705 for the Governor of Montreal and has

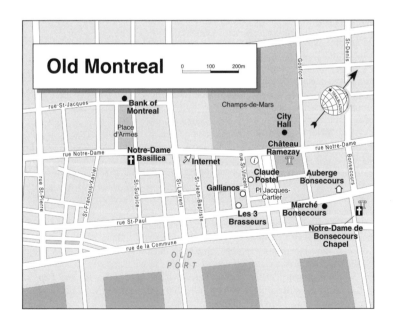

since been used as a furs and spices store for the French West India Company and a base for American revolutionaries trying to get Montreal to join forces with the US. It's now a museum featuring mainly 18th- and 19th-century furniture and costumes, and houses historically themed temporary exhibitions throughout the year. It's located at 280 Notre Dame Est and is open daily 10am–6pm June to September and Tuesday to Sunday 10am–4.30pm for the rest of the year. Entrance is $8; you'll find more information at 🖥 www. chateauramezay.qc.ca.

● **Bank of Montreal** At 119 rue Saint-Jacques stands Canada's oldest banking institution. This is where George Stephen and Donald Smith were directors before leaving to form the CPR Syndicate; the bank continued to be an important source of funds throughout the railway's construction. This domed, neo-classical building, modelled on the Pantheon in Rome, is particularly grand inside with its marble counters, massive columns and bronze trimmings everywhere.

● **Marché Bonsecours** Montrealers clearly delighted in these neo-classical, temple-style buildings. The old market hall at 350 rue Saint-Paul Est is a very striking example, with its doric columns and silver dome. The line of Georgian sash windows is something of a leap in period but the overall effect is lovely. Inside you'll find a collection of craft shops and small boutiques including the glass-blowing boutique, Gogo Glass.

● **Notre-Dame-de-Bonsecours Chapel** There's none of the grandeur here of the Notre-Dame Basilica but this pretty little church at 400 Saint-Paul Est is well worth a visit. It was a favourite of Montreal's sailors who would pray here for a safe voyage and then bring votive offerings on their return. Many of these are still there, such as the carved model ships hanging from the roof of the nave.

The church also houses the **Marguerite Bourgeoys Museum** (🖥 www. marguerite-bourgeoys.com), named after a French woman who came to Montreal in 1653 to open a school and teach the children of native people and settlers. It was thanks to her efforts that Montreal's first pilgrimage chapel was built in 1675, on the site of the current Notre-Dame-de-Bonsecours Chapel. Marguerite was canonised in 1982 by Pope John Paul II; the museum commemorates her life and work with a variety of religious artefacts. It's open Tuesday to Sunday 10am–5.30pm from May to October and 11am–3.30pm November to mid-January and mid-March to April; entrance costs $6.

● **Old Port** No longer used commercially, the old port has recently been landscaped and redeveloped with gardens, cycling paths, exhibition halls and an IMAX cinema. The views along the river are splendid and a lookout tower gives excellent views over the city. You can also see one of the old grain silos – a huge, grey block that apparently sent the visiting Le Corbusier into raptures.

Downtown
The pace of life shifts up a few gears as you move into the hustle and bustle of downtown Montreal. While many streets are dominated by skyscrapers, there are more than enough department stores, bars, museums, restaurants and even

churches to give Montreal a softer edge. The proliferation of young people here makes it as lively by night as it is by day.

● **Le Musée des Beaux Arts** Many of the paintings in this wonderful museum (🖳 www.mbam.qc.ca) were acquired from the private collections of Montreal's early 20th-century business magnates. The European collection, in particular, is excellent and includes works by El Greco, Canaletto, Renoir, Sisley, Monet, Giacometti, Dali and Picasso. The museum is at 1380 rue Sherbrooke Ouest and is open Tuesday 11am–5pm, Wednesday, Thursday and Friday 11am–9pm, Saturday and Sunday 10am–5pm. Entrance is a steep $15 (children under 12 go free), with half-price entry every Wednesday between 5pm and 9pm.

● **Centre Canadien d'Architecture (CCA)** Housed in a landmark, award-winning (if slightly brutal) building, skilfully adjoined to a grand 19th-century townhouse, the centre's vast galleries house a changing collection of drawings, models, photographs, prints and documents relating to a very diverse range of architectural themes. The adjoining house, known as the Shaughnessy mansion, was once the home of the great WC Van Horne, the man who saw the building of the Trans-Canada railway to completion; you can visit its beautiful reception rooms and conservatory. The centre occupies a whole block at 1920 rue Baile, on the corner with Atwater. From June to September opening hours are Wednesday to Sunday 10am–5pm and Thursday 10am–9pm. Entrance is $10, with free admission on Thursdays after 5.30pm; find out more at 🖳 www.cca.qc.ca.

● **McCord Museum of Canadian History** This enjoyable museum (🖳 www.mccord-museum.qc.ca) was founded in 1919 when David Ross McCord donated his collection of Canadiana to McGill University so that it might form the basis of a history museum. The exhibits, which include old photographs, native and immigrant clothing, paintings, china, toys and jewellery, are captivating and very well displayed, particularly in the First Nations gallery where textiles, beadwork, furs and carvings are shown to stunning effect. The museum is at 690 rue Sherbrooke Ouest and is open Tuesday to Friday 10am–6pm, and Saturday and Sunday 10am–5pm. Entrance is $12 for adults with free admission on the first Saturday of each month between 10am and noon.

● **McGill University** Just over the road from the McCord museum, this is one of Canada's most prestigious universities. The campus, with its limestone buildings and well-tended gardens, extends to the foot of the mountain and is a very pleasant place to stroll around.

● **Christ Church Cathedral** This Anglican cathedral, on the corner of Sainte-Catherine and University, quietly sums up some of the remarkable contrasts of Montreal: the graceful old building, containing some beautiful William Morris stained-glass windows, is set on top of a shopping mall. This connects it to a towering glass skyscraper next door, where the cathedral's offices are located!

● **Rue Ste-Catherine** This is the main shopping street in Montreal and offers some of the best shopping in Canada. It's always incredibly busy but has a vibrant rather than stressed atmosphere to it. Don't miss the Eaton department store at No 677, whose wonderful art deco dining room (9th floor) has remained unchanged since it opened in 1931.

● **Place-Ville-Marie** Designed by the architects who went on to create the pyramid in the Louvre, Paris, Place-Ville-Marie is a complex of towers built over the railway tracks. The most arresting one is the famous cruciform skyscraper, supposedly a symbol of the city's roots in Catholicism. It also provides a handy landmark. The tower houses hundreds of offices, including the headquarters of VIA Rail.

● **Sun Life Building** Right next door to Place-Ville-Marie is the former headquarters of the massive Sun Life Insurance company, who objected so strongly to Montreal's language laws that they moved their head offices to Toronto in the 1970s. This was the biggest building in the British Empire when it was erected in 1917 and, despite being dwarfed by surrounding skyscrapers today, it remains an impressive sight. It is also where the crown jewels were hidden during World War II.

● **Cathédrale Marie-Reine-du-Monde** Opposite the Sun Life Building is the green-roofed scale model of St Peter's in Rome; it's exactly one third of the original's size and is the third largest church in Quebec. It was built in the late 19th century in a flagrant attempt to overshadow the Notre-Dame Basilica in Old Montreal. Note the 13 copper statues above the entrance: these are of the patron saints of Montreal's parishes.

● **Windsor Station** When Van Horne decided that Montreal needed a new railway station to house the terminus of the transcontinental line, he got Bruce Price to draw up the plans. (Price was a leading American architect who went on to design the Château Frontenac and other CPR hotels.) The result was Windsor Station, a huge Romanesque building whose grandness reflected Montreal's importance as the railway centre of Canada. Although inter-city trains moved over to Central Station after World War II, it continues to be used by local commuter trains.

The station is open seven days a week to visitors and is located right next to the Molson Centre. A downstairs office at the station (Room G-1) houses the Canadian Pacific Archives, a massive collection of photographs and documents

---

Underground City

Each year more than 40 million tonnes of snow are ploughed up from Montreal's streets. Hardly surprising, then, that most Montrealers take to their incredible Underground City, also known as the Indoor City, during these winter months. This 18-mile system of shops, cinemas, restaurants, hotels and banks has even become something of a tourist attraction but be warned: it's notoriously difficult to find your way around, so be sure to equip yourself with a map (available at the tourist office and at most metro stations) before venturing down.

pertaining to CPR history. Members of the public aren't encouraged to come wandering in off the street but if you're interested you can always phone them at the station's Info-Tourism desk on ☎ 514-873-2015 and see if it's possible to visit.

Mont Royal

You can't come to Montreal without going up its little mountain which, at just 232m, is not a taxing climb. You will be rewarded with superb views over the city, a little like those over Paris from the Sacré Coeur. Besides the views, the expanse of parkland at the top of the hill is a fine place to wander about. You can also take in **St Joseph's Oratory**, a magnificent basilica built at the request of one Brother André, who is reputed to have performed miraculous healings. He was beatified by Pope John Paul II in 1982 and the site has since become an important pilgrimage destination for North Americans. The footpath up the hill starts at the northern end of rue Peel.

Maisonneuve

A few kilometres east of downtown is the Maisonneuve area, the site of three major attractions: the Olympic Stadium, the Biodôme and the Botanical Gardens. All three can be visited on a one-day 'Get an Eyeful' package which costs around $32 for adults and $16.50 for children under 17. The best way to get out there is by taking the métro to Pie IX; everything is well signposted from the métro exit.

● **Olympic Stadium** Mention the stadium to most Montrealers and you'll get a raising of the eyebrows and shrug of exasperation. The giant complex, with its 175-metre inclined tower supporting a supposedly retractable roof was built at colossal expense for the 1976 Olympic Games. Not only did it leave the city with an enormous debt but it didn't even work very well – the controversial roof was replaced in 1998 by a permanent roof costing a further $26 million. Still, the tower is an impressive construction and the shuttle ride up to the observation desk at the top is good fun even if it does set you back $14. Open daily 10am–6pm (until 9pm mid-June to 4 September), with regular tours in French and English costing $8. For more information contact ☎ 514-252-8687 or 🖥 www.rio.gouv.qc.ca

● **Botanical Gardens** Among the largest in the world, these thirty outdoor gardens include the beautiful replica of the old Ming Gardens of Shanghai, Montreal's twin city, designed by experts brought over from China.

The gardens also house the **Insectarium**, a fun museum devoted to creepie crawlies. The botanical gardens are open daily year-round, 9am–5pm (until 9pm from early September to late October). Entrance is $12.75 in summer and $9.75 in winter.

● **Biodôme** This amazing environment museum (🖥 www.biodome.qc.ca) contains four different ecosystems from the Americas under one roof: Tropical Forest, Laurentian Forest, St Lawrence Marine Ecosystem and (most interesting) Polar World. The habitats are home to thousands of plants and animals, living as though in their natural environment. Helpful staff, easily recognized by their safari-style hats, are on hand throughout the Biodome to answer any questions you might have or to point out animals hidden from view.

Opening times are 9am–5pm daily, year-round (until 6pm in summer); entrance is $12.75.

FESTIVALS

● **International Fireworks Competition**, around June and July. Spectacular displays in the beautiful setting of the Parc des Iles.
● **Montreal International Jazz Festival**, late June to early July (11 days). Outstanding, world-class cultural event attracting well over a million tourists annually. Two thousand international musicians (including lots of big names) and over three hundred shows, many of them free.
● **Just for Laughs Festival**, mid-July. The world's largest comedy festival, a fascinating insight into the contrasts of Anglo and Franco humour.
● **Montreal World Film Festival**, late August to early September. New films screened practically around the clock. At the end of the festival prizes are awarded, the top one being the Grand Prix des Amériques.

Montreal International Jazz Festival
PHOTO © MELISSA GRAHAM

MOVING ON

By rail

The service between Montreal and Toronto is the busiest in Canada. A good number of trains run daily between the two cities. Several trains a day also leave Montreal for Ottawa and for Quebec City, and there's a daily (except Tuesday) service to Halifax via Charny (close to Quebec City). For more information call VIA on ☎ 514-989-2626 (or ☎ 1-888-842-7245 when calling from outside Montreal).

Note that there is also an Amtrak rail service from Montreal to New York and Washington – the Amtrak toll-free information number is ☎ 1-800-872-7245.

By air

Montreal's international airport serves hundreds of internal and world-wide destinations. Autocar Connaisseur (☎ 514-934-1222) run a shuttle bus to the airport, picking up passengers at major hotels.

Other useful phone numbers include Montreal-Trudeau airport information: ☎ 514-394-7377; Air Canada: ☎ 514-422-5000; American Airlines: ☎ 514-397-9635; and British Airways: ☎ 514-287-9161.

Toronto

The country round this town, being very flat, is bare of scenic interest; but the town itself is full of life and motion, bustle, business and improvement.

Charles Dickens, *American Notes*

Toronto's had a considerable amount of bad press over the years and many people have agreed with Peter Ustinov's unflattering conclusion that it is 'a kind of New York run by the Swiss'. Yet the city is nowhere near as boring or sanitized as this characterization suggests. On the contrary you'll see beggars on the street and eccentrics on the underground, you'll hear lots of loud music pumping out of ghetto blasters and you'll see the funkiest people this side of London's Camden Town. Toronto, you'll quickly realize, is a crowded, noisy and very exciting place to be and fulfils European expectations of a big North American metropolis more than any other city in Canada.

One of the most refreshing things about Toronto is that it doesn't keep going on about its history – possibly because it has very little to go on about – but the welcome result is a moving, dynamic and forward-looking environment where new theatre, art and music flourish. It also boasts some outstanding museums, architecture and other attractions (notably the CN Tower). There really is plenty to do and see here, the only drawback being the vast amounts of money required to do it and see it.

HISTORY

Early settlement
The site was first occupied by the Huron Indians who named it Toronto, meaning 'Meeting place'. Lying on a sheltered harbour on the north shore of Lake Ontario, it was part of the connecting land route to Lake Huron.

In 1750 the French set up a fur-trading post here and built a stockade to protect their trading operations but the British ejected them in 1759 and destroyed the fort. They proceeded to ignore the place for several decades. However, when Loyalists to the British Crown started fleeing America after the War of Independence, many came and settled in the area.

Bought from the natives
In 1788 the Governor-in-Chief of Canada officially bought the site of Toronto from the Mississauga Indians. What was to become the nation's biggest city was a bargain at £1700, a few bales of cloth and some axes. The new purchase was renamed York and a few years later became the capital of Upper Canada. The first of the city's grid-patterned streets was laid out and the community slowly began to take shape.

America invades

When war broke out between England and America in 1812, York was invaded by 1700 US troops who pillaged the town and burnt down the Parliament Building. In revenge, British troops tried to burn down the building occupied by the US President in Washington. They didn't succeed but the damaged walls had to be white-washed, which is how it came to be known as the White House.

After the war ended in 1814, colonists began to come over in greater numbers: the city's population grew from 700 in 1816 to over 9000 in 1834. In this year the city was incorporated and given back its old name of Toronto.

Industrial and economic boom

With the arrival of the Grand Trunk and Great Western railways in the 1850s, Toronto entered a period of rapid economic expansion. It quickly emerged as an important agricultural, manufacturing and distribution centre and as its population and industrial clout boomed, expensive new buildings were erected at a similar pace. Following the difficult years of the 1930s' Depression, Toronto's economic strength was reaffirmed when the St Lawrence Seaway was opened in 1959, bringing with it a mass of trade and investment. The next few decades saw the construction of a multitude of gleaming skyscrapers and Toronto's business world was further enlarged by the arrival of many firms from Montreal, in flight from Quebec's language laws.

Toronto today

Toronto is Canada's biggest city with some 2.4 million inhabitants. Its population is astoundingly multicultural as a result of Toronto's policy of welcoming immigrants from around the globe and the city has been identified by the United Nations as the most ethnically diverse in the world. Racial relations are exemplary, giving weight to Toronto's claim that it is 'a city that works'. It is the financial, industrial and commercial capital of Canada and is also the most expensive city in the country in which to live.

ARRIVING IN TORONTO

By air

Most flights to Toronto arrive at the massive Lester B Pearson International Airport, 25km north-west of the city centre.

Pacific Western Airport Express buses (🖥 www.torontoairportexpress.com) will bring you into town for $16.50 one-way, stopping at a handful of major hotels from where free transfers are available to a further 32 hotels and hostels. Buses leave the airport every 20 minutes from 6am to 1am, and every 30 minutes in between these times; during rush-hour traffic, expect the journey to take from one hour thirty minutes to two hours. You can also, of course, take the quicker 40-minute option and use a taxi, which costs around $40.

Commuter flights from Ontario and Quebec arrive at the Toronto Island Airport, also known as Toronto City Centre Airport, from where a ferry and shuttle bus take travellers to the railway station.

By rail

Trains arrive at Union Station on Front St, near the CN Tower. It's right at the southern end of town but, if you need to go north, you can catch the subway here. This huge, imposing building was opened by the then Prince of Wales (the future King Edward VIII) in 1927 and is still the grandest railway station in Canada.

GETTING AROUND

Toronto's public transport system – a network of **buses**, **streetcars** and the **subway** – is arguably the best in Canada. It's operated by the Toronto Transit Commission (TTC); their telephone information line is ☎ 416-393-4636. Single tickets cost $2.75 or you can get a day pass for $8.50. Note that you need the exact fare, or a ticket or token (available at subway stations). The subway is open 6am–1.30am and when the subway is closed there are regular Blue Night Network buses running through the night along the main streets of Bloor-Danforth and Yonge.

Taxis are plentiful and can be flagged down on the street; or call Co-op Cabs (☎ 416-504-2667) or Diamond Taxicab (☎ 416-366-6868). **Cycles** and **rollerblades** can be rented at Wheel Excitement, 249 Queen's Quay W, south of Radisson Plaza (☎ 416-260-9000, 🖳 www.wheelexcitement.ca); or McBride Cycle, 2797 Dundas St W (bikes only; ☎ 416-763-5651, 🖳 www.mcbridecycle.com).

ORIENTATION

Toronto's downtown layout is very uncomplicated: it's contained within a rectangle formed by Front St in the south, Bloor St in the north, Jarvis St in the east and Spadina Ave in the west. A couple of blocks south of Front St is the harbour front. The biggest and busiest north–south street is Yonge St; the streets running across it at right angles are divided into East and West at this point. The distance between Bloor and Front is about 2^{1}/2km, while Jarvis to Spadina is just under 2km.

SERVICES

Tourist information

Tourism Toronto, whose head office is at 207 Queen's Quay Terminal, Suite 590, runs a seven-days-a-week information phone line on ☎ 416-203-2600, or ☎ 1-800-363-1990 from within North America.

You can visit them in person at their **Visitor Information Centre** (☎ 416-599-1548) inside the Metro Toronto Convention Centre at 255 Front St West, which provides maps and leaflets, including some surprisingly enlightened publications such as a guide for gay and lesbian travellers and a list of free activities in Toronto. They can also make hotel bookings; the centre is open daily 9am–5pm.

For information about the rest of Ontario, plus limited information on the city, head for **Ontario Tourism's Travel Centre** (☎ 416-314-5899) opposite the Eaton Centre at 595 Bay St and 20 Dundas St West, open Monday to Friday 10am–7pm, Saturday 10am–6pm and Sunday noon to 5pm.

Money

There is no shortage of **banks** in Toronto; whichever part of town you're in you'll find one nearby. In addition, Thomas Cook has numerous foreign exchange branches in the city including 100 Yonge St (15th Floor), 123 Queen St West and 9 Bloor St West.

Consulates

Australia (☎ 416-323-1155) 314-175 Bloor St East
Austria (☎ 416-863-0649) 1010-360 Bay St
Belgium (☎ 416-944-1422) 2006-2 Bloor St West
Britain (☎ 416-593-1290) 1910-777 Bay St
Denmark (☎ 416-962-5669) 310-151 Bloor St West
Finland (☎ 416-964-0066) 604-1200 Bay St
France (☎ 416-925-8041) 400-130 Bloor St West
Germany (☎ 416-925-2813) 77 Bloor St
Italy (☎ 416-977-1566) 136 Beverley St
Japan (☎ 416-363-7038) 77 King St West
Netherlands (☎ 416-598-2520) 2106-1 Dundas St West
Republic of Ireland (☎ 416-366-9300) 100 King St West
South Africa (☎ 416-364-0314) 2515-2 First Canadian Place
Spain (☎ 416-967-1661) 200 Front St West
Sweden (☎ 416-963-8768) 1504-2 Bloor St West
Switzerland (☎ 416-593-5371) 601-154 University Ave
USA (☎ 416-595-1700) 360 University Ave

Post, internet and laundry

Post office branches include those at 360 Bloor St West and 69 Yonge near the corner with King. **Internet access** is available at Cyberland Café at 257 Yonge St, opposite the Eaton Centre, and also the Internet Centre at 324 Yonge St, where terminals cost $3 per hour. Free internet can be found in post offices and, if you buy a coffee, at The Croissant Tree at 36 Toronto St, just off Adelaide East. Downtown **laundries** include Baldwin Laundromat, 23 Baldwin (two blocks north of Dundas West) and Speedy Automatic Coin Wash, 568 Church St (open 24 hours a day).

❏ **Toronto online**

🖥 **www.toronto.com** Information on Toronto's sights, accommodation, attractions and more, produced by Tourism Toronto.

🖥 **www.torontotourism.com** This site is strong on current events in Toronto and also some great online tools, such as maps of the city and a Fast Facts section known as Toronto 101.

🖥 **www.ontariotravel.net** Information about the whole province from Ontario Tourism.

WHERE TO STAY

Budget accommodation

Toronto has some excellent downtown hostels. At 76 Church St, the *HI Hostel* (☎ 416-971-4440, 🖥 www.hihostels.ca) is managed by an interior designer who's given the place a very stylish, funky look. Most dorms have three to four beds (from $27 for members, slightly more for non-members), and come with a private shower room and lockers. There are also a few private en-suite doubles, which cost $89 per room ($99 for non-members); it's extremely popular, so reserve well in advance.

Global Village Backpackers Hostel (☎ 416-703-8540, 🖥 www.globalbackp ackers.com) at 460 King St West is a large, brightly painted old house with dorm beds at $27 (six to ten beds per room) and $30 (four beds per room) as well as private doubles at $72.50. Global Village is the only hostel in Toronto with its own bar on the premises, and offers free wi-fi facilities to guests. Like the HI Hostel, the Global Village Backpackers Hostel has kitchen facilities and a patio area.

Just around the corner at 42 Widmer St is *Canadiana Backpackers* (☎ 416-598-9090, 🖥 www.canadianalodging.com), a renovated Victorian townhouse with dorm beds from $27 and double rooms from $75. There's lots on offer here, such as pancake breakfasts and weekly BBQs; the hostel even has its own TV room complete with reclining 'aeroplane style' seats and a selection of films, for those looking for a quiet night in. Close to the University is the small and friendly *Planet Travelers Hostel* (☎ 416-599-6789, 🖥 www.theplanetrave ler.com) at 175 Augusta Avenue, just off Dundas St West, which offers dorm beds with free lockers at $25 and private doubles at $60. The hostel is run by a lovely, helpful Scottish lady and thanks to its small size there's an intimate, relaxed feel to the place. Facilities include full kitchen, Saturday night BBQs and free breakfast, bed linen, towels and internet access.

From May to August, *Neil Wycik College* (☎ 416-977-2320, 🖥 www.neill-w ycik.com), at 96 Gerrard East, offers single rooms for $47.50 (or $38 for students, seniors and hostel members) and doubles and family rooms for $78 ($62.40 with discount). Rooms are private but they do share a kitchen/common room and washrooms with four or five other rooms. Some of the rooms are a bit spartan, as you might expect from university dorm rooms, but the location is fantastic, the staff are very friendly and there are fine views from the pleasant rooftop sun deck. Rates include continental breakfast and daily housekeeping.

Mid-range accommodation

Toronto has an ever-increasing number of **B&Bs**, many of them in handsomely renovated Victorian houses. A good one to try is stylishly decorated *The Mulberry Tree* (☎ 416-960-5249, 🖥 www.bbtoronto.com/mulberrytree) at 122 Isabella St, just south of Bloor at the corner of Jarvis, where friendly hosts Paul

---

❑ Accommodation prices quoted in this book are for **high season** (normally May or June to September). In low season many hotels offer substantial discounts.

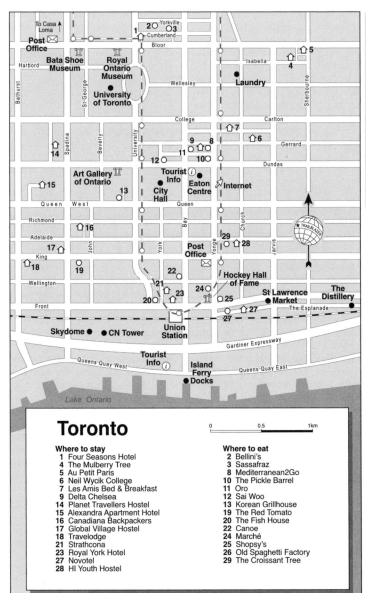

Toronto

0   0.5   1km

Where to stay
1 Four Seasons Hotel
4 The Mulberry Tree
5 Au Petit Paris
6 Neil Wycik College
7 Les Amis Bed & Breakfast
9 Delta Chelsea
14 Planet Travellers Hostel
15 Alexandra Apartment Hotel
16 Canadiana Backpackers
17 Global Village Hostel
18 Travelodge
21 Strathcona
23 Royal York Hotel
27 Novotel
28 HI Youth Hostel

Where to eat
2 Bellini's
3 Sassafraz
8 Mediterranean2Go
10 The Pickle Barrel
11 Oro
12 Sai Woo
13 Korean Grillhouse
19 The Red Tomato
20 The Fish House
22 Canoe
24 Marché
25 Shopsy's
26 Old Spaghetti Factory
29 The Croissant Tree

and Carol offer wonderful breakfasts and comfortable bedrooms full of character (doubles at \$125). A short walk away, at 3 Selby St, *Au Petit Paris* (☎ 416-928-1348, 🖥 www.bbtoronto.com/aupetitparis) offers four beautiful guest rooms (from \$125 a double) decorated with artwork and photographs shipped over from Paris. Vegetarian breakfast is served in a bright, cheerful breakfast room but the real gem is the rooftop terrace, which seems a world away from the busy streets of Toronto. The Parisian hosts own another B&B, too, at 31 Granby St: *Les Amis Bed & Breakfast* (☎ 416-591-0635, 🖥 www.bbtoronto. com) has attractive rooms (from \$105) with thick Japanese futon beds.

Another mid-priced option is the *Alexandra Apartment Hotel* (☎ 416-504-2121, 🖥 www.alexandrahotel.com) at 77 Ryerson Ave, a block of 60 small but spotless studios with kitchenette, cable TV, phone and private bathroom (with bath-tub and shower) from \$116 for doubles. One of the best-value 'proper' hotels is the well-located *Strathcona* (☎ 416-363-3321, 🖥 www.thestrathconahotel .com) at 60 York St, where the neat but small doubles go from \$135 in summer. Or try the recently refurbished *Travelodge Toronto Downtown West* (☎ 416-504-7441, 🖥 www.travelodgetorontodowntown.com), at 621 King St West; the clean, spacious rooms (\$149) are typical of the international chain and come with free continental breakfast, parking facilities and hi-speed internet access.

Upmarket hotels

If you want to do things in true style there's only one place to stay: the *Royal York Hotel* (☎ 416-368-2511, 🖥 www.fairmont.com) opposite the railway station. Built by Canadian Pacific Railways in 1929, the one-time tallest building in the British Empire is splendidly luxurious inside. Everything here is on a grand scale: it has 1365 rooms, boasts the largest hotel kitchens in Canada and no less than 72km of carpeting cover its vast halls and corridors. This is where the rich and famous stay when they're in town. Guests have included the Queen, Bob Hope, Ronald Reagan, Dolly Parton and the Dalai Lama. It has also been the location of a number of big movies, with the express lift recently starring alongside John Cusack in *Serendipity*. A night at the hotel is surprisingly affordable, with doubles starting from \$179 for a standard room; if you do book a room, ask to be on the lake side as there's no difference in price.

Other upmarket hotels include the swanky *Four Seasons Hotel* (☎ 416-964-0411, 🖥 www.fourseasons.com/toronto) whose beds are so comfortable that guests have asked to buy them, and whose restaurant is one of the best in Canada. It's located in the trendy Yorkville district at 21 Avenue Rd; standard doubles cost from \$340 during the week with discounts at weekends.

At 33 Gerrard West, the massive *Delta Chelsea* (☎ 416-595-1975 🖥 www. deltahotels.com) has lots of special facilities for children and doubles from \$175, while the *Novotel* (☎ 416-367-8900, 🖥 www.novoteltorontocentre.com), in an elegant landmark building at 45 The Esplanade, close to the train station, has smart doubles from around \$184. Many of the spacious, elegant rooms feature powerful 'rainforest showers' which are wonderfully invigorating – especially after a long day of sightseeing.

WHERE TO EAT

The highlight of Toronto's restaurant scene is its sheer diversity, owing to the multiculturalism of the city: from Korean to Greek, Italian to Chinese, there's something to suit all tastes and at very agreeable prices. Equally, at the top end of the market there are some fantastic places to go for a splurge, most of them sporting stylish décor, excellent food and a lively crowd.

Budget food

Some of the best-value places to eat are the numerous tiny restaurants in Chinatown; one of the oldest and most popular of these is *Sai Woo* at 130 Dundas West, which gets especially full late at night. Another long-standing Toronto favourite, dating from 1921, is *Shopsy's* at 33 Yonge St, with old wooden booths, a deli counter, a cigar stall and inexpensive snacks like chicken wings, potato skins, corned beef on rye and tasty burgers. A few blocks north at 312 Yonge St, the *Pickle Barrel* is best known for its jumbo sandwiches; it also serves cheap hot meals like pastas and noodles and has a pleasant patio area. Just around the corner at 3 Elm St, *Mediterranean2Go* takeaway offers tasty shawarmas for $2.99. A little more sophisticated and offering free internet is *The Croissant Tree* at 36 Toronto St, just off Adelaide East, where you can indulge in all sorts of toasted bagels.

The *Red Tomato*, in a dark basement at 321 King St West, may not be as smart as its neighbours but can't be beaten for value, serving delicious pizzas, pastas, stir-fries and salads, with all main courses around $10 to $12. There's plenty of choice nearby as well, as the whole block is taken up by pavement cafés and restaurants. Another good bet is the *Old Spaghetti Factory*, inside a former blacksmith's workshop at 54 The Esplanade; it offers excellent-value homemade pastas and good service.

For great food with a novel twist, head to the *Korean Grillhouse* at 214 Queen St West. Guests are seated at tables with their own barbecue placed in the centre and, in 'all-you-can-eat' fashion, you choose from a selection of meats, seafood and Korean specialities to be brought to your table, which you then cook yourself on the barbecue. The whole experience is highly enjoyable and the set prices of $13 for dinner and $9 for lunch are excellent value.

Mid-range and upmarket restaurants

Very popular with tourists, *Marché* (part of the Mövenpick chain) at 42 Yonge St, is a kind of mock market where you wander from stall to stall, pile your plate high with goodies like rösti potatoes and spit-roasted chicken, then pay for it all at the check-out (count on around $30 per head). For decently cooked fresh fish, *The Fish House*, near the CN Tower at 144 Front St, is a good place to go, offering a pleasing range of steamed, grilled, baked and fried fish, with most main courses around $30. One of Toronto's most enduringly popular eating spots is *Bellini's* at 101 Yorkville Ave (☎ 416-929-9111), a small, intimate and rather old-fashioned Italian restaurant whose clientele has included Elton John and Mick Jagger. The restaurant serves first-class pastas and risottos, with main courses ranging from $14 to $40, and a choice of three set dinner menus ($50, $60 or $78) in a refined setting, complete with crisp white tablecloths and attentive waiters. Nearby in a beautiful yellow building at 100 Cumberland St, *Sassafraz* (☎ 416-964-2222) is rather more chic, with its modern décor, wonderful glass ceiling and gurgling fountain; dinner for two with wine will cost from around $100 but the best time to come here is for Sunday brunch, which is accompanied by live jazz – reservations are recommended.

Another beautiful interior can be found at the excellent *Oro* (☎ 416-597-0155), 45 Elm St, where Italian, Portuguese and Oriental influences make up an adventurous menu featuring such items as 'pancetta-wrapped Canadian elk loin with sauce Rouennaise'; most main courses are around $20 to $40.

One of Toronto's most raved-about restaurants is *Truffles* at the Four Seasons Hotel, 21 Avenue Rd (☎ 416-964-0411; dinner only), a chic, elegant place serving elaborately prepared international dishes; a speciality is 'spaghettini with Perigord Black Gold truffle sauce'. Most mains are around $35–45 and there's also a five-course tasting menu ($85 or $135 with a selection of wines); note that the restaurant is closed on Sundays.

For a buzzing, glamorous atmosphere and sensational views, nowhere beats *Canoe* (☎ 416-364-0054) on the top (54th) floor of the Toronto Dominion building, 66 Wellington St. The food's excellent too, with some fine Canadian specialities like caribou and arctic char; a meal for two with wine can easily clock up to $150.

Another fine place for a splurge is the luxurious and intimate *Epic* at the Royal York Hotel, where French chef Jean-Charles Dupoire and sous-chef Brian Armstrong serve up mouthwatering treats like seared sea scallops and Quebec foie gras. The six-course tasting menu ($85 per person, or $140 with selected wines) is worth every penny and the service and attention to detail are second to none.

NIGHTLIFE AND ENTERTAINMENT

One of the liveliest stretches of town after dark is Queen West (see p120) between University and Spadina. Places to look out for are the *Black Bull* at No 298 (live bands); the *Horseshoe Tavern* at No 370 (more live bands); *Rivoli* at No 332 (lounge bar); the *Bamboo* at No 312 (African music) and the *Big Bop* at No 651 (nightclub). The city's trendy gay village runs down Church St.

Another popular nightlife centre is around Richmond and Adelaide streets, full of busy, studenty bars and pulsating nightclubs like *Limelight* at 250 Adelaide West and *Whiskey Saigon* at 250 Richmond St West (a huge, three-floor nightclub). More relaxed in tone is the Yorkville area, where a crowd of bars have rooftop patios, including *Remy's*, 115 Yorkville Ave, and *Hemmingways*, 142 Cumberland St (seven days a week) which is very popular with the young professional crowd and has a heated patio.

The best place to hear live jazz and blues in Toronto is *Grossman's*, a laid-back, unassuming venue at 379 Spadina, attracting excellent musicians. Perhaps the most memorable place to sip a cocktail is the glitzy bar at *Canoe* on the top floor of the Toronto Dominion building, 66 Wellington St, where the views out to the islands are magical. Another swanky bar with top-of-the-world views onto Toronto's skyline is *Atlantis*, 955 Lakeshore West at Ontario Place (take a taxi or bus No 121A or B from opposite the train station).

There's a thriving comedy scene in the city with one of the best comedy clubs, *Yuk Yuks* (☎ 416-967-6425) to be found at 224 Richmond St West. A number of big Hollywood names such as Jim Carrey started their careers here. Cover charges range from free to $10.

Toronto claims to be 'the third-largest **theatre** centre in the English-speaking world' after London and New York. There's certainly an enormous variety of shows being put on, from glitzy musicals (*Phantom* et al) to the best of contemporary theatre (particularly from the Canadian Stage Company; ☎ 416-368-3110). Check the local papers for listings. There's a half-price ticket outlet *T.O.Tix* (☎ 416-536-6468) at the Eaton Centre for same-day performances, Mews Level (open Tuesday to Saturday from noon to 7pm), or you can buy full-price tickets for most shows over the phone with Ticketmaster on ☎ 416-345-1839.

WHAT TO SEE

CN Tower

Never mind the five-mile queues, never mind the exorbitant entrance fee, the CN Tower is something that has to be done while in Toronto.

This long, spindly telecommunications tower that looks as if it might snap in two in a high wind is still the tallest free-standing structure in the world at 553m high. When your turn finally comes you ascend the first 442m to the **Observation Level** in a glass elevator on the outside of the tower. Once you're up you can enjoy the staggering views over the toy-town city from either an indoor or outdoor viewing deck. The particularly brave can also take a stroll across the gut-churning glass floor. Not being particularly brave myself, it

CN Tower
PHOTO © JIM MANTHORPE

took me half an hour to edge my way to the centre, at which point I nearly fainted when a 22-stone adolescent suddenly attempted a somersault, apparently to test the strength of the glass.

Serious height enthusiasts can go up an extra 100m to the **Skypod**, enclosed by a curved floor-to-ceiling glass wall, from where, on clear days, you can see as far as Niagara Falls, 137km away. The entrance to the CN Tower (🖳 www.cntower.ca) is on Front St, about five minutes' walk west of the railway station. It costs $21.49 (seniors $19.49) to get to the Observation Level and a further $4 to get to the Skypod; Hostelling International members receive a 10% discount. The Tower and Observation Deck are open daily, excluding 25 December, between 9am and 11pm.

Skydome

Right next door to the CN Tower is Toronto's answer to Montreal's Olympic Stadium: the Skydome (officially called the Rogers Centre), also with a fully retractable roof. The huge arena is home territory for the Toronto Blue Jays (baseball) and the Toronto Argonauts (football) and is the venue for numerous concerts and shows. It's certainly an impressive building but it's debatable whether it's worth parting with $13.50 for the behind-the-scenes hour-long 'Tour Experience' in the arena (daily, on the hour, 10am–6pm in the summer; ⌨ www.rogerscentre.com).

Hockey Hall of Fame

Continuing the sporting theme is this shrine to ice hockey – arguably Canada's national sport – on the corner of Front and Yonge. It's filled with a dazzling display of memorabilia (trophies, photos, movies, etc) which seems to send the Canadians and Americans wild. Opening hours during the summer are Monday to Saturday 9.30am–6pm, Sunday 10am–6pm, and during the winter Monday to Friday 10am–5pm, Saturday 10am–6pm, Sunday 10.30am–5pm. Entrance costs $12; for more information see ⌨ www.hhof.com.

City Hall

Unlike many daring edifices erected in the 1960s, this one continues to be raved about today. It comprises two tall, thin buildings curving towards each other with a short, dome-covered building in between them. City Hall is at Nathan Phillips Square (on Queen St West), which turns into a skating rink in winter. The old city hall still stands at the east side of the square (on the corner of Bay and Queen), its Romanesque grandeur somewhat diminished by its towering neighbours.

Queen West

Starting a few blocks west of the City Hall, Queen St West suddenly goes all young and trendy – a change in tone due mainly to the close proximity of Canada's biggest art school, the Ontario College of Art. Cafés, nightclubs, bookshops and restaurants are interspersed with art studios and fashion design workshops. This very lively and slightly downbeat area stretches between University and Spadina and is known simply as 'Queen West'.

Art Gallery of Ontario

This wonderful museum is a pleasure to visit. Good use of space and light makes it an airy and stress-free environment.

The first rooms you come to house the 19th- and early 20th-century collection, including works by Renoir, Degas, Sisley, Matisse, Monet and Picasso. Monet's gorgeous *Vétheuil in Summer* seems to light up in increasingly golden hues the further you stand back from it. Note also his *Charing Cross Bridge: Fog* which depicts a London fog the like of which I've never seen before – all pinks, greens and blues. In the same gallery look out for Otto Dix's startling *Portrait of Dr Heinrich Stadlemann*.

Up on Level 2 there's a very good collection of paintings by the Group of Seven (see box opposite). Their work powerfully evokes the vast wilderness of northern Ontario, which you pass through on the train journey between Toronto and Winnipeg. On the same level, a little further along from Andy Warhol's gun-slinging *Elvis*, is the Henry Moore Sculpture Centre which houses the world's largest public collection of Moore's work. The sculptor insisted on natural, overhead lighting and the effect is beautiful; his mammoth bronze women bathed in sunlight make an arresting sight.

The museum is at 317 Dundas St, on the edge of Chinatown, with an entrance on McCaul St, and is open as follows: Wednesdays, Thursdays, Fridays noon–9pm, Saturdays and Sundays 10am–5.30pm. Entry is $8 and free on Wednesdays from 6pm to 9pm. Due to renovation works that are scheduled to end early 2008, entry to some areas may be restricted; see 🖥 www.ago.net for more information.

Royal Ontario Museum

A few blocks north of Chinatown is the fabulous Royal Ontario Museum (ROM). The easiest way to get there is to take the subway and get off at Museum, then follow the signs to the entrance (Bloor at University). The enormous museum contains both arts- and science-based collections, including dinosaur skeletons (most of them from the Alberta Badlands), a display of luminous minerals that glow in the dark and exhibitions on the ancient civilizations of Greece, Rome and Egypt (including some amazing mummy cases). Best of all are the

The Group of Seven

If you plan to spend any length of time in Canadian art galleries you had better get to grips with the Group of Seven, still Canada's artistic pride and joy. The movement was initiated by the commercial artist, Tom Thomson, in 1912, following a trip to the Mississagi Forest Reserve in Northern Ontario. Thomson developed a bold new approach to painting Canada's wilderness, characterized by heavy colours, expressive patterns and a move away from similitude. His style was embraced by several of his friends who shared his frustration with the conservative nature of Canadian art, which had barely moved on from the 19th century. Together the artists began painting the wild and rugged terrain of Ontario's northern interior, where they honed their hallmark style of vibrant colours and stark, swirling landscapes.

In 1920, three years after Thomson's tragic death in a boating accident, his fellow artists – Frank Carmichael, Lawren Harris, AY Jackson, Franz Johnston, Arthur Lismer, JEH Macdonald and FH Varley – formed the Group of Seven and staged their first exhibition. They were wildly successful and their influence grew rapidly over the following years. Talent and innovation were helped by clever self-promotion and influential friends, which provoked resentment among Canada's established artists. The public, on the other hand, adored them, perhaps responding to their romantic evocation of the lonely, wild frontier.

The Group's work was to dominate Canadian art for the next thirty years. The irony of their success is that whilst they had set out to liberate Canadian art from the constraints of naturalism, their influence was so great that it stifled the development of alternative styles and became as restrictive as the artistic establishment they had replaced. Nonetheless, they engendered an important sense of national pride and showed that Canadian painters didn't have to look to Europe for the way forward.

Toronto's ethnic neighbourhoods

Officially deemed by the UN to be the most ethnically diverse city in the world, Toronto is made up of an exotic patchwork of cultural neighbourhoods. The largest ones are as follows:

● **Corso Italia**: Torontonians of Italian origin are outnumbered only by those of British extract. The Latin culture has been kept very much alive in 'Little Italy', centred along St Clair between Bathurst and Bloom.

● **Chinatown**: Toronto's Chinese population is the second biggest in North America, the biggest being in San Francisco. Starting with Sam Ching, a laundry shop owner who was Toronto's first Chinese immigrant at the turn of the 20th century, the community has grown to 350,000 people – equal to almost the entire population of Halifax. It's an exhilarating place to wander around, especially at the weekend when the street markets are in full swing and the shoppers are out in their thousands – walk along Spadina to Dundas and marvel at all the stalls filled with Chinese produce. All signs and prices are in Chinese and there's barely a Westerner in sight.

● **The Danforth**: East along Danforth Ave (between Pape and Woodbine) is the heart of 'Little Athens', where you'll find white-walled restaurants, little Greek bars and the National Bank of Greece.

● **The Jewish Community**: Centred mainly in the suburb of North York, Toronto's thriving Jewish community has no fewer than 60 synagogues and a fabulous supply of kosher delis.

● **Little Poland**: Along Roncesvalles Ave, west of downtown, the shops are stocked with Polish pastries and other delicacies. There is also a statue of the first Polish pope and a monument in honour of the 20,000 Poles who died in World War II.

● **West Indies in Toronto**: Spreading around the suburbs north of Highway 401 is the 300,000-strong Caribbean community. Over a million visitors a year come to see the community's Caribana carnival in July.

internationally famous Chinese galleries, whose highlights are the magnificent Ming tomb, and a series of 14 towering Buddhist sculptures dating from the 12th to 16th centuries. Other must-sees are the Dynamic Earth gallery, which explains phenomena such as earthquakes and volcanic eruptions with state-of-the-art displays, including a massive plastic volcano, and the Hands-on Biodiversity Gallery, looking at the interdependence of plants, animals and humans and featuring a real beehive, among other displays.

Note, however, that the museum is currently undergoing renovations which will increase the gallery space by over 40,000 square feet and should be completed by 2008. In the meantime not all exhibitions are open – you can find out more on 🖳 www.rom.on.ca. The museum is open 10am–6pm Monday to Saturday (with late closing on Friday at 9.30pm) and 11am–6pm on Sunday. High-season entrance is a costly $15 for adults and $12 for students and seniors (a few dollars less in winter) or $5 after 4.30pm on Fridays, and free for the last hour before closing between Saturday and Thursday.

Bata Shoe Museum

One block west of ROM, at 327 Bloor West, you'll find the Bata Shoe Museum, which houses a monumental and fascinating collection of footwear, taking in everything from Victorian wedding slippers and outrageous platform boots through to ancient Japanese sandals.

All the shoes are placed in their historical, functional and social context and are beautifully displayed. Among the highlights is a roomful of fine beaded moccasins produced by the Apaches of the American south-west, as well as a selection of shoes owned by the rich and famous, including Madonna, Marilyn Monroe and Elvis Presley.

The museum's opening hours are Tuesday to Saturday 10am–5pm (until 8pm on Thursday), and noon to 5pm on Sunday; entrance is $8.

Casa Loma

One of Toronto's quirkiest and most fascinating attractions is this grandiose mansion standing on a hillside. It was built in 1911 for Sir Henry Pellat, a self-made multimillionaire, and his wife, Lady Mary, who was the first Chief Commissioner of the Canadian Baden-Powell Girl Guide movement. Sir Henry lavished enormous quantities of his fortune on his 98-room castle in an effort to make it as ornate and opulent as it could possibly be. The palatial interior is fabulously over the top with a mixture of mediaeval-style banquet halls, secret passageways, marble bathrooms and fluffy boudoirs. Poor Sir Henry was able to enjoy these comforts for just ten years before bankruptcy forced him and his wife to move out and sell up.

These days the house is owned by the City of Toronto. It's a really fun place to visit and its beautiful grounds are a delight with their fountains, rhododendrons and 'secret garden'. Casa Loma (🖳 www.casaloma.org) is a short walk uphill from Dupont subway. It's open daily 9.30am– 5pm, with last admittance at 4pm; entrance is $19.

St Lawrence Market

Just outside the downtown core, on Front St between Church and Jarvis, the indoor St Lawrence Market (🖳 www.stlawrencemarket.com) is packed with a fabulous array of fresh fruits, vegetables, meats, cheeses, flowers and numerous craft stalls. It's made up of two historic market buildings: the Farmers' Market (also known as the North Market) and the South Market, which incorporates

---

🚂 Longest street in the world
The biggest and brashest thoroughfare in Toronto, **Yonge** (pronounced 'Young') **Street** is packed with skyscrapers, hotels, theatres, upmarket boutiques, scruffy discount stores, exclusive restaurants, greasy diners, thousands of people and much, much more. It's also the location (at Dundas) of the main entrance to the Eaton Centre, a veritable mega-mall that swallows up a million shoppers each week. Originally the street was built as a military pathway to link Lake Ontario to the Great Lakes in the north, which explains why it is so remarkably straight and long.

Not only is Yonge St one of Toronto's oldest and longest streets; it is also the world's longest street. Starting near Toronto's harbour front you could drive north along Yonge (petrol supplies permitting) all the way to Rainy River, Ontario – a distance of 1900km. If you were to drive that distance from London you'd end up in Morocco!

DAYTRIP TO NIAGARA FALLS

A visit to Toronto would be incomplete without making the two-hour journey south of the city to one of the world's most famous sights, Niagara Falls. No amount of hype can prepare you for the sound and view of the falls thundering down the wide, horseshoe cliff with almost unimaginable force. Some 790,000 gallons pour over the edge each second, partly obscured by a thick curtain of spray that frequently drenches onlookers when blown across by the wind. Inevitably the surrounding streets are overflowing with gift shops, themed restaurants and arcades filled with slot machines and cheesy rides – but not even this unbridled commercialism can spoil

things; indeed, some of the attractions are even rather fun.

The most rewarding are the **Journey Behind the Falls** ($11) along tunnels carved through the rock behind the waterfalls, with several viewing holes just a couple of metres from the water, and the famous *Maid of the Mist* boat ride (30 minutes; $13) towards the base of the falls.

It's also worth considering paying the $11 to go up the **Skylon Tower** which gives excellent views over the falls. Check online at 🖥 www.sky lon.com for a list of dates and times when the falls are lit up at night.

Getting here
Trains to Niagara Falls leave Toronto's Union Station daily at 8.30am, arrive around 10.30am and return to Toronto at 5.45pm, getting back into Union Station at 7.45pm. Tickets should ideally be bought at least a day in advance or earlier if you want to try and get discounted train tickets (a standard one-way ticket is around $33).

Toronto's original City Hall building. Selling everything from home-grown produce to Asian specialities, it's a food-lover's paradise and has a bustling, lively atmosphere. The Farmers' Market is open on Saturdays 5am–5pm, and the South Market is open Tuesdays and Thursdays 8am–6pm, Fridays 8am–7pm and Saturdays 5am–5pm. It's a short walk from downtown (three blocks east of the Hockey Hall of Fame), or you can take a streetcar east along King St (get off at the St Lawrence Hall stop, a couple of minutes' walk from the market buildings).

The Distillery

Some five blocks further east of the St Lawrence Market, the Distillery district (referred to by locals as simply the Distillery) is one of Toronto's up and coming areas. It's centred around a block of recently renovated 19th-century warehouses on Mill St at the intersection with Parliament St, which were originally part of the Gooderham and Worts Distillery – at one time the biggest whisky

The Niagara Falls train station is about 4km from the falls themselves, which can be reached either by taxi (about $10) or on the 'People Mover' shuttle bus (all-day ticket $6, or $3 for a one-way ticket) plying up and down Niagara Parkway, alongside the river. For the 'People Mover', from the train station cross over the road to the small bus station directly opposite, where you can buy your day pass and catch the bus.

Alternatively, you could try one of the many **organized bus trips** from Toronto. One of the best outfits is the small and informal JoJo Tours (☎ 416-201-6465, ⌨ www. home.interlog.com/~jojotour/) with day trips to the falls for $50 in summer, giving you three to four hours' free time at Niagara along with some wine-tasting at a few of Canada's most famous vineyards on the return journey.

Niagara-on-the-Lake and the wineries

A short drive from the falls through an idyllic stretch of vineyards is **Niagara-on-the-Lake**, a quaint little town full of pretty clapboard buildings and neat gardens. It's a lovely place for a wander and has the added attraction of being close to an abundance of fantastic **wineries** scattered around this part of southern Ontario, which thrive on the region's climate, soil conditions and latitudinal position. A good one to aim for, within walking distance of town, is the family-owned Peller Estates (☎ 905-468 4678, ⌨ www.peller.com), which boasts a beautiful setting with gorgeous views of the Niagara Escarpment. Once there, you can take a tour (from $10) around the winery and taste a variety of wines, including a local speciality, ice wine, a very sweet dessert wine made from frozen grapes. Other samples at the Tasting Bar range from $1 to $5, depending on the wine.

The easiest way to get to Niagara-on-the-Lake from Niagara Falls is on the Niagara Shuttle bus (☎ 905-358-3232; May–Oct, three daily, rest of year one daily), leaving from the bus station opposite the train station, with other pick-up points around town. Alternatively, a taxi will cost you around $30 each way. A fun way to explore the vineyards near Niagara-on-the-Lake is by **bicycle**, which can be hired from Zoom, 280 Hunter Rd (☎ 905-468-4691).

distillery in the British Empire. Today, the cobbled streets are lined with a variety of stores, restaurants, cafés and charming boutiques, popular with tourists and locals alike. Chocoholics should head straight to the Soma Chocolatemaker, where the shelves and cabinets are laden with chocolate delights: a mug of Mayan hot chocolate here is highly recommended. Other places worth visiting include the Sandra Ainsley Gallery (located in building 32-101), selling exquisite (and expensive) pieces of glasswork, and Mill Street Brewery which produces local ales and offers tours around the brewery for a mere $3 (or $8 if you'd like to take home a Mill Street pint glass). To get to the Distillery from downtown, either take bus No 172 eastbound from Front St or Bay St, or take the streetcar east along King St and get off at King and Parliament. For more information on the Distillery check out ⌨ www.thedis tillerydistrict.com, which includes a map showing the location and opening hours of all of the stores.

The Islands

Having expended vast amounts of energy and money cramming in Toronto's many attractions, most visitors find a trip to the islands a well-deserved break. For just $6 for a return ticket, you can take a 15-minute ferry ride to one of three interconnecting islands – Ward's Island, Centre Island, or Hanlan's Point – where you can wander around the parkland, take a picnic, stroll along the beach and generally relax. It's worth it for the view alone: Toronto's downtown skyline is breathtaking from the ferry.

The Island Ferry Docks are right at the bottom of Bay St on the lakeshore; you can walk from Union subway or go one stop from there on the connecting Harbourfront LRT line; note that the ferry goes only to Ward's Island in winter.

FESTIVALS

● **du Maurier Ltd Downtown Jazz Festival**, late June to early July. Canadian and international jazz musicians.

● **International Dragon Boat Race Festival**, late June. Boat races and lots of hoopla on Centre Island.

● **Caribana**, late July to early August. Massive Caribbean festival of music and dance, with a fabulous parade.

● **Toronto International Film Festival**, mid-September. Highly regarded festival showing new films from around the world.

MOVING ON

By rail

The *Canadian* leaves Toronto for Vancouver on Tuesdays, Thursdays and Saturdays. The journey takes three days and three nights. There are frequent daily services to Montreal (four hours on the express) and Ottawa (just over four hours). In addition, Amtrak connections provide a service to New York and Chicago.

The VIA information number is ☎ 416-366-8411 (or ☎ 1-888-842-7245 when calling from outside Toronto). The Amtrak number is ☎ 1-800-872-7245.

By air

To get to Pearson International Airport take the Airport Express bus (☎ 905-564-3232). It picks up passengers from several major hotels, including the Royal York, opposite the train station. To arrange a free transfer from your hotel to the bus pick-up point, call ☎ 861-1234.

Useful airline numbers include Air Canada (☎ 416-925-2311) and American Airlines (☎ 1-800-433-7300).

Winnipeg

The manners of Winnipeg, of the West, impress the stranger as better than those of the East, more friendly, more hearty, more certain to achieve graciousness, if not grace.
    Rupert Brooke, in a letter from 1913, as published in *Letters from America* (1916)

Winnipeg is a convenient place to take a break, being right in the middle of the country: it lies midway between the Atlantic and the Pacific, just 20km from the longitudinal centre of Canada. Its short but hot summers coax the crowds out of the malls and onto the streets and Winnipeg in July is a lively city. Out of season, however, it's a drab and chilly place. Winters are long and bitterly cold and the intersection of Winnipeg's two main streets has the unenviable reputation of being the windiest spot in the world.

The city is described in Carol Shields' *The Republic of Love* as 'a place with a short tough history and a pug-faced name' and receives less than flattering treatment at the hands of the English writer, Mark Lawson, in *The Battle for Room Service*: 'it was somehow just one of those places that sounded as if it might be Indian for shit-hole.' The people of Winnipeg, however, are known for their warmth and friendliness. Perhaps this is the result of a conscious effort on the part of the locals to live up to the provincial slogan, 'Friendly Manitoba', yet each time I've visited Winnipeg I've had some wonderful strangers take me under their wing. I'm inclined, in the end, to agree with one of Shields' characters who declares: 'I love Winnipeg because the people here are the salt of the earth. You walk down Portage and you get smiles from everyone, even the cops.'

HISTORY

The fur trade
Winnipeg is situated where the Red and Assiniboine rivers meet. This junction, known as The Forks, was an important centre of the fur trade: in 1738 Sieur de la Vérendrye erected a post here, which was later taken over by the French-owned North West Company (known as 'the Nor'westers'). It soon became a playing field for the bitter antagonism between the Nor'westers and their rivals, the Hudson's Bay Company (or 'the HBC').

The Red River Colony
In 1812 the Earl of Selkirk of the HBC set about creating a settlement near The Forks, which he named the Red River Colony. The life of the new settlers, most of whom had come from Scotland, was not an easy one. The Nor'Westers felt threatened by their presence and systematically attempted to destroy the colony. The aggression reached a head in 1816 when the Seven Oaks Massacre left 21 of the settlers dead. The problems were in a large part resolved when the North West Company and the Hudson's Bay Company amalgamated in 1821 (keeping

the HBC name). The Red River Colony began to grow in size, this time populated mainly by local Métis (of French and Indian extraction).

The Riel rebellions

After Canada became a dominion in 1867, the new government purchased the land occupied by the Red River Colony from the Hudson's Bay Company. They somewhat insensitively began to reorganize the settlement without consulting its inhabitants. The Métis staged a rebellion (see p35) organized by Louis Riel which resulted in the creation of the province of Manitoba but also in the exile of Riel.

When a second Métis rebellion broke out 15 years later, Riel was summoned back to lead his people once more. This time the results were less successful and Riel was hanged for high treason.

The boom years

When it became clear that Winnipeg was going to be an important stop on the new transcontinental railway, it became in 1881 the site of a feverish and undisciplined land boom. Thousands of speculators rushed in to buy and sell lots and as the value of land rocketed, vast fortunes were made overnight.

Over the following years a steady flow of immigrants arrived to settle and farm the land, the influx reaching an all-time high between 1901 and 1914. In just a few decades it had grown from a small settlement of 241 people in 1871 to Canada's third-largest city in 1911, with a population of 136,000. The Winnipeg Grain Exchange was exporting grain all around the world and the city was the transportation, distribution and financial centre of western Canada.

Winnipeg today

By 1915 the boom was over and Winnipeg entered a period of recession. Poor working conditions and a burgeoning trade union movement resulted in the abortive Winnipeg General Strike in 1919, Canada's most famous strike to date. The situation didn't improve as Canada entered the 1920s in the grip of the world-wide Great Depression.

The economy picked up after the Second World War and Winnipeg once more established itself as the transportation hub of the west. Its prosperity has been undermined, however, by the westward shift of economic development into cities like Saskatoon and Regina. Today Winnipeg has a population of 650,000 and is the seventh-biggest city in Canada.

GETTING AROUND

The local **bus** service is operated by Winnipeg Transit (☎ 204-986-5700). The Downtown Spirit, which does a loop taking in Main, Portage, Vaughan and Broadway (calling at The Forks market), is free; otherwise, regular bus routes cost $2 per ticket. From May to October there's also a **water-bus service** connecting Exchange Dock with The Forks and other points along the Assiniboine River. Single tickets are $2.50 or a day pass is $15. **Taxi** companies include Unicity Taxi (☎ 204-925-3131) and Duffy's Taxis (☎ 204-925-0101).

❑ **Winnipeg online**
🖥 **www.destinationwinnipeg.ca** Tourism Winnipeg's official website, with lots of practical information on the city.

🖥 **www.travelmanitoba.com** Well put-together site with lots of travel information on the whole province, and a section with suggestions on what to do in Manitoba.

If you'd rather get around by **bike**, you can rent mountain bikes at Gord's Bike Centre (☎ 204-284-2952) at 7 Donald St and Olympia Cycle & Ski (☎ 204-888-4586), at 1813 Portage Ave. Both places charge around $20 for a day's rental. Stop off at the Tourist Information Centre and pick up the *Cyclist's Map of Winnipeg* for $3, which has lots of great routes and tracks, regardless of the season or how good your cycling skills are.

ORIENTATION

The train station is very central, on Main St, and is no more than 15 minutes' walk from most hotels.

The lay-out of the city has developed around the Red and Assiniboine rivers – the downtown area slots into the corner where the two rivers meet. The two busiest thoroughfares are Main St (north–south, parallel to the Red River) and Portage Ave (east–west, parallel to the Assiniboine).

SERVICES

Tourist information

The staff at the **Tourism Winnipeg** office (☎ 204-943-1970, or ☎ 1-800-665-0204 toll-free from anywhere in North America), at 259 Portage Ave, are very helpful; they are open Monday to Friday 8.30am–4.30pm.

There's also a **Travel Manitoba Information Centre** (☎ 204-945-3777 or ☎ 1-800-665-0040) at The Forks, opposite the Johnston Terminal; it incorporates a very interesting if small museum known as the Theme Pavilion which depicts the history of Manitoba and includes a life-size polar bear and other amusing displays. It also has a free internet terminal. The centre is open daily 10am–6pm, until 8pm on Friday and Saturday in summer.

Money

There are plenty of banks about, including the Custom House Currency Exchange at 231 Portage Ave. The Toronto Dominion Bank is at Portage and Main and the Assiniboine Credit Union can be found at York and Main.

❑ Accommodation prices quoted in this book are for **high season** (normally May or June to September). In low season many hotels offer substantial discounts.

Consulates

Belgium (☎ 204-261-1415) 15 Acadia Bay
Denmark (☎ 204-233-8541) 239 Aubert St, St-Boniface
Germany (☎ 204-475-3088) Suite 101, 1200 Pembina, Fort Garry
Italy (☎ 204-488-8745) 1044 Wilkes
Netherlands (☎ 204-487-1211) 69 Shorecrest Dr
Norway (☎ 204-489-1626) 336 Lindenwood Dr East
Sweden (☎ 204-233-3373) 1035 Mission St

Post, internet and laundry

Winnipeg's main **post office** is at 266 Graham Ave, at the corner with Smith.
Internet access is available at the post office, as well as at the public library at
251 Donald (on the corner with Graham) and at Tourism Manitoba at The Forks.
There's also Osborne Cyber Café at 118A Osborne St (Monday to Friday
10am–midnight). The closest **laundry** to the downtown core is Sit and Spin at
213 Osborne.

WHERE TO STAY

Winnipeg has a good spread of accommodation, particularly in the mid-range
bracket. If you've just arrived from Montreal or Toronto you'll notice that you
get a lot more for your money here, even at the upper end of the scale.

Budget accommodation

HI Ivey House International Hostel (☎ 204-772-3022, 🖳 www.hihostels.ca) is
at 210 Maryland, about a 15-minute walk west of downtown. It's a small but
clean and friendly hostel in an old house with big sunny rooms. Standard dorm
rates are $20 for members and $24 for non-members; if you'd prefer a private
room, a double costs $48 or $58 for non-members. The hostel has the usual
facilities, such as kitchen, internet access, etc and offers bike and walking tours.
To get there from the train station, take bus No 29 to Broadway and Sherbrooke,
which is one block east of the hostel.

A few doors down at No 168, on the corner of Alloway, is the *Backpackers'
Guest House International* (☎ 204-772-1272, 🖳 www.backpackerswinnipeg.
com) – it has dorm beds and private rooms, cable TV, a games room in the basement, laundry facilities and bike rental. Dorm room rates are $22 for youth hos-
tel members and $25 for non-members; private rooms are $45 for one person
(with an additional $7 added for each extra person staying in the room). It some-
times closes from November to March, so it's best to phone in advance if you're
travelling during those months.

Mid-range hotels

The *St Regis Hotel* (☎ 204-942-0171, 🖳 www.stregishotel.net) at 285 Smith,
just south of Portage Ave, was built in 1911 at the height of the immigration
boom. The rooms aren't exactly flash but they're spacious, clean, come with a
TV and private bathroom and are very cheap for what you get, starting at $68 for
a double. Cheaper still, at $60 a double, is the *Downtowner Motor Hotel*

To HI Ivey House International Hostel,
Backpackers Guest House International
& Assiniboine Park

Colony

Osborne

Art
Gallery

Colony

To laundry,
Osborne Village
& Corrydon

Memorial

Vaughan

**Legislative
Building**

Kennedy

Webb

Kennedy

Edmonton

Ellice

Qu'Appelle

Carlton

Cumberland

Notre Dame

Hargrave

Donald

Internet

St Mary

Graham

Portage

**Tourism
Winnipeg**

Princess

Smith

**Post
Office**

King

River

Assiniboine

Broadway

York

Garry

McDermot

Assiniboine River

Bannatyne

Fort

E X C H A N G E
D I S T R I C T

Albert

Main

**Manitoba
Museum**

**Railway
Station**

Waterfront

Water

Pioneer

*THE
FORKS*

**Tourist
Info**

Red River

To St Boniface

1	Holiday Inn
2	Downtowner Motor Hotel
3	Carlton Inn
4	East India Company
5	Delta Winnipeg
6	Pasta La Vista
7	St Regis Hotel
8	Hotel Fort Garry
9	VJ's Drive Inn
10	The Ivory
11	Earl's
12	Mondetta World Café
13	The Old Spaghetti Factory
14	Inn at the Forks

Winnipeg

0   100   200m

(☎ 204-943-5581, 🖳 www.downtowner.ca), at 330 Kennedy St, right behind the Portage Place shopping mall. The area is a little run-down but the recently refurbished rooms are good value. Nudging up the scale in comfort, the *Carlton Inn* (☎ 204-942-0881, 🖳 www.carltoninn.mb.ca) at 220 Carlton St, offers neat, well-maintained rooms plus a small pool, sauna and gym, with rates going from $81 a double. Adjoined to the hotel is the smart Paragon restaurant which serves up great Greek food and has live jazz sets every Friday at 5pm.

The smartest mid-range choice is the *Holiday Inn* (☎ 204-783-9490, 🖳 www.holiday-inn.com/winnipegdtwn), at 360 Colony St, which comes with a pool and a small gym; doubles here cost $119 during the week and $109 at weekends. Finally, if you don't mind staying out of the city centre you could always try one of the B&Bs in the leafy residential neighbourhoods: **Heritage Bed and Breakfast Homes of Winnipeg** (🖳 www.bbcanada.com/associations/Winnipeg) offers five large and characterful B&Bs with rates from $50.

Upmarket hotels

Close to the railway station at 222 Broadway, the *Hotel Fort Garry* (☎ 204-942-8251, 🖳 www.fortgarryhotel.com) is without doubt Winnipeg's most distinctive and atmospheric hotel. Built in 1913 by the Grand Trunk Pacific Railway, it's wonderfully grand inside, featuring a beautiful domed lounge and a gorgeous lobby. Residents have free use of the adjacent pool and fitness centre. Doubles (including a fine breakfast) start at around $139, going up to $209 for an executive suite. Keep your wits about you if you happen to be on the eighth floor – it is said to be haunted.

The newly renovated *Delta Winnipeg* (☎ 204-942-0551, 🖳 www.deltawinnipeg.com) at 350 St Mary Ave is the largest hotel in Canada. It's smart and modern with excellent facilities, including an indoor and outdoor pool and large gym. Another nice touch is the heated bathroom floors and hi-speed internet access in all the rooms; standard doubles start from $139. Another stylish hotel is the *Inn at the Forks* (☎ 204-942-6555, 🖳 www.innforks.com) which boasts a great location right next to the The Forks market, a short distance from the VIA station. Rooms here are spacious and immaculate, as you might expect from a hotel of this standard, and if you feel in need of some serious pampering the Riverstone Spa, located within the hotel, will do the trick. Rates start at $129.

WHERE TO EAT

The first thing you'll notice about Winnipeg's restaurants is that so many of them are Italian, reflecting the city's immigration history in the early 20th century. Most of them are also very good and reasonably priced to boot.

Budget food

For a really cheap meal you could do worse than try *VJ's Drive Inn*, a shack opposite the train station serving homemade burgers, hot dogs and fries, and apparently famous throughout the prairies. There are also plenty of bargain food stalls at **The Forks market**, ranging from bagels to stir-fries, accompanied by a lively atmosphere.

One of the most popular eating places in town is *Earl's* at 191 Main St, where you can eat burgers, pastas, pizzas, fried chicken and the like in a large, bright and invariably packed-out dining room. If the weather is cooperative, you can make the most of the spacious outdoor patio, overlooking Main St.

For something a bit different, try the **East India Company**'s $10.95 lunch buffet or $16.95 dinner buffet (Monday to Friday) at 349 York St, surrounded by sumptuous Indian decorative art. Alternatively, *The Old Spaghetti Factory* is housed in the Old Johnson Railway Storage Building at The Forks. Part of a chain, it offers cheap but dependable food (typically $10 to $15) and friendly, efficient service.

Mid-range and upmarket restaurants

Some of the best places to eat are out of downtown in the surrounding neighbourhoods, where Winnipeg's ethnic communities are concentrated. One of these is **Corrydon Avenue** which is lined with Italian cafés and restaurants (to get there take the No 18 bus from Main St). *Civita*, at No 691, has an Italian-meets-Californian feel to it – the food is superb and moderately priced at $10 to $20 for mains and the atmosphere and service are very friendly. Another highly recommended restaurant is *Sette Bello* (☎ 204-477 9105) at No 788. It serves traditional Italian food and does a roaring trade – booking is advised on a Saturday night.

Closer to the city centre, on the south side of the Assiniboine River is **Osborne Village** which has a lot of good-value, interesting eating places. One of the best is the *Tap & Grill* (137 Osborne St) whose unpromising name and exterior conceal a beautiful, tropical-plant filled room where delicious Mediterranean grills are served. The Village is about a 10-minute walk from the Legislative Building, or you can take the No 16 bus from Graham at Vaughan.

Downtown, one of the best Italians is the relaxed, casual *Pasta La Vista* on the corner of Hargrave and St Mary, which serves wood-fired pizzas and a wide range of pastas for around $15 to $20 a main course.

If you're fed up with Italian, try *Mondetta World Café* at 25 Forks Market Rd for an astonishingly wide range of international dishes, from East African eggplant with garam masala to Japanese pork dumplings. The interior is super-stylish but the music can be a bit loud and the place functions more as a bar late at night.

There's also a very smart Indian restaurant, *The Ivory*, at 200 Main St (not far from the train station) with a funky interior and a reputation for great dishes.

Finally, mention must be made of the fabulous Sunday brunch served at the *Hotel Fort Garry* (☎ 204-942-8251), where a breathtaking range of fruits, salads, hams, cold fish, pastries and cakes (as well as traditional hot breakfasts) are spread out in the grand lobby and eaten in the domed lounge (if they try to seat you in the other dining room, insist on waiting for a free lounge table); the buffet costs around $21 per person and reservations are essential, even for hotel guests.

NIGHTLIFE

Thanks to its large student population, Winnipeg has a lively nightlife scene. Curiously, the city has a number of very popular pseudo-British pubs, including the *Elephant & Castle*, next door to the Delta Winnipeg at 350 St Mary, and the *Toad in the Hole* in Osborne Village at 112 Osborne.

For more authentic stuff you should try out one of the local country and western bars frequented by burly men wearing stetsons and cowboy boots; one of the best, especially for live music and country dancing, is *Palomino Club* at 1133 Portage Ave (a short cab ride from the centre), which is open until 2am.

There's a concentration of nightclubs around the Exchange District, including *Kaito* at 441 Main St, in a funky converted bank building, and *The Gallery* at 165 McDermot Ave.

One of the best places to listen to jazz in Winnipeg is *The Blue Note Café*, an intimate, relaxed place at 875 Portage. More sedate, and very refined, is the bar at the *Hotel Fort Garry*, which has live piano music most evenings.

A good place for live blues is the *Times Change High and Lonesome Club* on Main with St Mary (Wednesday to Sunday until 2am). Another, even better one is the *Windsor Hotel Bar* at 187 Garry St. Known to locals as the House of Blues, it's famous for attracting internationally renowned blues artists. It's also famous for putting up Charlie Chaplin who is said to have penned a letter to a friend on the hotel's headed paper declaring his intention to move to Hollywood to pursue a career in acting. A huge Chaplin mural decorates the outside back wall of the hotel.

Charlie Chaplin was here: mural at the Windsor Hotel
PHOTO © JIM MANTHORPE

WHAT TO SEE

The Forks

Right behind Union Station is The Forks, where the Red and Assiniboine rivers meet. It used to be a railway service and repair site but has been converted to a market. The buildings are full of food, crafts, jewellery, clothes, restaurants, cafés and the like, bearing more than a passing resemblance to London (England)'s Covent Garden, and there are plenty of street entertainers outside. It's very lively and has a buzzing atmosphere, especially in the summer, and if the hustle and bustle become too much there are some lovely pathways leading down to the river and beyond.

Union Station and Winnipeg Railway Museum

Close to the Forks, Winnipeg's railway station, which was designed by the same architects as New York's Grand Central Station, is one of the most impressive in Canada, featuring a beautiful domed ceiling above the main hall.

Upstairs on Tracks 1 and 2, the Winnipeg Railway Museum (☎ 204-942-4632) houses several gems including the grand old *Countess of Dufferin*, built in 1872, and the first locomotive in the Canadian West. Other exhibits include a Baldwin locomotive that was used to build part of the Canadian Pacific Railway, a CNR Caboose that (if you ask nicely) you can climb aboard, and a 1920s' railbus. There's also a well-stocked gift shop selling everything from fridge magnets to clocks.

The museum, run on a voluntary basis by the Midwestern Rail Association, is open from late June to early September from Friday to Sunday between the hours of noon and 5pm, and in winter it's open weekends only, from noon to 4pm. They often try to be open when *The Canadian* is passing through, too, when it makes an excellent place to stretch your legs during the one-hour stop. A modest entrance price is charged.

Manitoba Museum

This is Winnipeg's best museum by a long shot. With an emphasis on the province's natural and human history, highlights include a representation of the Arctic tundra with an impressive polar bear display, a Grasslands gallery with a big tepee and other items typical of life on the plains and, best of all, a full-size replica of the ketch that brought the founders of the Hudson's Bay Company to Canada (you can climb on board and wander around), as well as a life-size reconstruction of Winnipeg during the 1920s in which you can also stroll around.

The museum (🖵 www.manitobamuseum.ca) is at the Centennial Centre on Main St, opposite the City Hall. From June to August it's open daily 10am–6pm and until 9pm on Thursday, and during the rest of the year Tuesday to Friday 10am–4pm, weekends 11am–4pm. Admission is $8, or $18 for a Value Pass which also gets you into the attached **Planetarium** (excellent multimedia shows which recreate the sky at night, suitable for all ages) and **The Science Centre** (a hands-on science gallery, geared towards kids).

Exchange District

In the boom years of 1880–1915 large numbers of banks, warehouses and other commercial buildings sprang up in Winnipeg. The centre of this expansion was the Exchange District, close to the Manitoba Museum, where the old buildings with their elaborate advertisements painted on the walls have recently been renovated and gentrified. They now house offices, shops, restaurants and pubs. It's an interesting place to wander around and certainly contains the best examples of Winnipeg's otherwise uninspiring architecture. Guided historic walking tours ($6) are available during summer months; see (🖵 www.exchangedistrict.org).

Winnipeg Art Gallery

At the northern end of downtown, the Winnipeg Art Gallery (🖵 www.wag.mb.ca) houses mainly temporary exhibitions of modern Canadian art which change every six to eight weeks. One of the rooms is used exclusively for Inuit collections and the museum has a reputation for showing the most comprehensive range of Inuit art in the country.

The museum is located at 300 Memorial Blvd and is open Tuesday to Sunday 11am–5pm (and until 9pm on Thursdays); entrance is $6.

CITY GUIDES & PLANS

Legislative Building

Dating from 1919, Manitoba's seat of government – a few blocks west of the Art Gallery at 450 Broadway – is an imposing building. Its large dome is topped by Winnipeg's most famous symbol: the Golden Boy, a four-metre-tall gilded statue of a messenger carrying a sheaf of grain in one arm and a torch in the other (and supposedly embodying the spirit of youth and enterprise). During the summer months there are free guided tours around the building.

Winnie-the-Bear
PHOTO © JIM MANTHORPE

Assiniboine Park

About 8km west of downtown is this 376-acre park, containing a zoo (admission $4.25 in summer, $3.75 in winter) with over one thousand animals.

Look out for the statue of Winnie-the-Bear near the main entrance, one-time resident of the zoo, named after the city and donated to London Zoo as a cub. It happened that young Christopher Robin named his own teddy bear after the animal, giving rise to the Winnie-the-Pooh stories that his father A A Milne wrote.

The park is also home to a conservatory (excellent tropical plants) and the Leo Mol Sculpture Garden, with its religious and wildlife sculptures. To get to the park take the No 18 bus from Main at Pioneer; the park entrance is at 2355 Corydon Ave.

Winnipeg's Book Walk

Any bookworms visiting the city might be interested to know that Winnipeg offers a self-guided tour of its Book and Collectible District. The leaflet, which can be picked up at tourist offices, takes you on a leisurely stroll through a variety of thrift stores, second-hand bookstores and quirky antique shops. If you've a long train ride ahead, this is a good opportunity to stock up on books – and if not, it's still a chance to get to know a different side of Winnipeg. For more information, contact Kelly Hughes on ☎ 204-943-7555 or 🖳 aquabooks@gmail.com.

Old Saint-Boniface

Cross over the river from the VIA station and the Forks and you'll find yourself in Old Saint-Boniface, the heart of Winnipeg's Franco-Manitoban community, which prides itself on its history and ambiance. Home to the largest francophone community west of the Great Lakes, the area is steeped in French and Métis culture – eloquently celebrated at the impressive St-Boniface Museum (housed in the oldest building in Winnipeg and the oldest log structure in North America). St-Boniface is also the site of the striking remains of a burned-down cathedral, some modern galleries and shops featuring the works of local artists and craftsmen, and plenty of inviting cafés and restaurants. Guided walking tours of Saint-Boniface, led by knowledgeable staff in period costume, are offered by Tourismeriel: for more details contact ☎ 204-233-8343 or visit ⌨ www.tourismeriel.com.

Prairie Dog Central Railway

This beautiful early 20th-century train makes the 36-mile round trip (two and a half hours) every Saturday and Sunday between June and September. The *Prairie Dog Central*'s steam engine was built in Scotland in 1882, and for 36 years pulled CPR passenger trains between Fort William and Kenora. These days it runs north from Inkster Junction Station (a 20-minute drive from central Winnipeg) to Grosse Isle, and while it can hardly claim to be the most scenic rail ride in the country it's certainly one of the most stylish; the polished oak and mahogany inside the old coaches are magnificent. The train stops off at Warren before reaching Grosse Isle and local residents set up stalls on the platform selling cakes, hot drinks and local crafts. The staff are all in costume and it really is a great family day out.

Trains depart at 10.30am; the regular fare is $18, though check in advance as some special events can mean that the fare is either increased or discounted. It's possible to make advance reservations online or by phone and for those without their own transport, the *Prairie Dog Central* provides its own courtesy shuttle bus to Inkster station, with pick-up points at the Inn at the Forks and the Clarion Hotel, 1445 Portage Ave (☎ 204-774-5110). For more information on the *Prairie Dog Central*, call ☎ 204-832-5259 or visit ⌨ www.pdcrailway.com.

FESTIVALS

● **Winnipeg Jazz Festival**, mid to end of June. Week-long programme of indoor and outdoor jazz concerts.
● **Red River Exhibition**, last week in June. Manitoba's largest fair: music, parades, shows and games.
● **Folk Festival**, mid-July. Huge gathering of Canadian and international folk musicians.
● **Folklorama**, early to mid August. A multicultural celebration of the peoples of the world – over 40 pavilions throughout the city, with singing, dancing, arts and crafts, ethnic foods and more.

MOVING ON

The *Canadian* leaves for Vancouver (about 40 hours from Winnipeg) on Wednesdays, Fridays and Sundays, and for Toronto (about 30 hours) on Tuesdays, Thursdays and Sundays.

The *Hudson Bay* leaves Winnipeg for Churchill on Tuesdays, Thursdays and Sundays – the journey takes around 35 hours. The VIA information line is ☎ 1-888-842-7245.

Edmonton

Edmonton, the headquarters of the Hudson Bay Company's Saskatchewan trade... is a large, five-sided fort with the usual flanking bastions and high stockades. It has within these stockades many commodious and well-built wooden houses, and differs in the cleanliness and order of its arrangements from the general run of trading forts in the Indian country.
Butler, *The Great Lone Land*, 1872

Situated on the northern edge of the prairies, Alberta's provincial capital is a city grown rich from wheat and oil. Despite its affluence, however, of all the cities along the line it has the least to recommend itself to the rail traveller. It's not that there's nothing to do or see here; on the contrary there are some great attractions but, unfortunately, most of them are far from the city centre and reaching them by public transport can be tedious.

The downtown area is a little lifeless owing to the collapse of a large number of shopping outlets since the opening of the giant West Edmonton Mall. This shopping complex, the largest in the world, ranks as Edmonton's number one tourist attraction – a fact that may well start the warning bells ringing... Finally, Edmonton is so close to Jasper that there seems little point, for westbound travellers anyway, in delaying the spectacular ride through the Rockies.

HISTORY

Fur-trading outpost
Edmonton began life in 1795 when the Hudson's Bay Company (HBC) erected Edmonton House as a fur-trading base. This was established to compete with the nearby Fort Augustus, founded a few months earlier by the HBC's great rival, the North West Company. The two companies traded with the local Cree and Blackfoot Indians for beaver pelts, otter and muskrat furs and Edmonton quickly became the headquarters of the fur trade in the western prairies. It was also a major stopping-off point for travellers to the North or to the Pacific.

Sold to the Dominion
It wasn't until the Hudson's Bay Company sold the best part of its land to the Dominion of Canada in 1870 that settlers began to set up home outside the HBC stockade. Businesses sprang up and by the 1890s the new town was operating coal mines, saw mills and a boatbuilding factory. In 1897 the Yukon gold rush brought thousands of fortune-seekers en route for the gold fields. Many stayed and by the turn of the 20th century Edmonton's population had grown to 4000.

Booming provincial capital
Following its incorporation as a city in 1904, Edmonton became Alberta's capital when the province was created in 1905. By then the population was 9000, a number that grew rapidly in the next few decades. Although it had been

ignored in favour of Calgary by the Canadian Pacific Railway, it was a major stop on two new lines by 1915. It also became an important transportation and supply centre with the construction of the Alaska Highway in 1942.

Shortly after this, Edmonton's success was assured when oil was discovered at Leduc Number One Well in 1947. Over the following years, oil was struck in thousands of wells within a 160km radius of the city and Edmonton became known as the 'Oil Capital of Canada'.

Edmonton today

Today around one million people live in Greater Edmonton, making it Canada's sixth-largest city. The wealth bestowed on it by the oil industry has transformed the downtown district into a jumble of glass-plated skyscrapers.

As the impact of oil on Edmonton's economy begins to scale down, businesses such as forestry, pharmaceuticals and electronics are starting to play a more important role.

GETTING AROUND

If you stick to the downtown core you'll be able to get around on foot, but for visits to attractions such as the famous Mall you'll need to use Edmonton Transit (☎ 780-496-1611), a mixture of **bus** and **light-rail** transit (LRT) networks. Fares are $2.25. Ask for a transfer when you board the bus as this allows you to change buses during the following 90 minutes. **Taxi companies** include Alberta Co-Op (☎ 780-425-2525) and Yellow Cab (☎ 780-462-3456).

ORIENTATION

The railway station is at 12360–121 St, 6km north-west of downtown; the only way into the centre is to take a cab, which usually works out at about $10.

Downtown Edmonton, which is surprisingly compact, sits on the northern bank of the North Saskatchewan River. The city's biggest and busiest thoroughfare is Jasper Ave. The other avenues and streets are numbered, not named: avenues run from east to west, their numbers increasing as you go north; streets run from north to south with their numbers increasing as you move east.

SERVICES

Tourist information

The main **tourist office** (☎ 780-496-8400 or ☎ 1-800-463-4667) is in the World Trade Centre at 9990 Jasper Ave. It's open 6am–9pm from Monday to Friday, and 9am–5pm at weekends during the summer; it stocks a comprehensive range of maps, brochures and other material.

Money

All the major banks can be found along Jasper Ave. There's also an American Express office at 10180–101 St, and a Thomas Cook Foreign Exchange in the West Edmonton Mall.

CITY GUIDES & PLANS

❏ **Edmonton online**

💻 **www.discoveredmonton.com** General round-up of the city's attractions, accommodation and restaurants, plus ideas for touring the Rockies from Edmonton.

💻 **www.travelalberta.com** Heaps of information on the whole province, including a good section on Edmonton.

💻 **www.edmonton.com** Provides general information on the Greater Edmonton area.

Consulates

Belgium (☎ 780-496-9565) Suite 107, 4990–92nd Ave
Denmark (☎ 780-426-1457) Suite 1112, 10235–101st St
Finland (☎ 780-426-7865) 1400–10303 Jasper Ave
France (☎ 780-428-0232) 6th floor, 9707–110th St
Germany (☎ 780-422-6175) Suite 201, 8003–102nd St
Italy (☎ 780-423-5153) Suite 1900, Merrill Lynch Tower
Netherlands (☎ 780-428-7513) 10214–112th St
Norway (☎ 780-440-2292) 2310–80th Ave
Sweden (☎ 780-421-2482) Suite 2500, 10104–103rd Ave
Switzerland (☎ 780-426-9221) 4926–89th St

Post, internet and laundry

The main downtown **post office** is at 9808–103A Ave. **Internet access** is available at Bytes Internet Café, 1668 West Edmonton Mall and Planet Inc. Cyber Café, 201, 10442–82nd Ave NW (in Old Strathcona).

The most conveniently located **laundries** are Easy Self Serve Laundry at 10992–124th St (west of downtown) and Soap Time Laundry, 7626–104th St, near Old Strathcona.

WHERE TO STAY

Budget accommodation

The *HI Hostel* (☎ 780-988-6836, 💻 www.hihostels.ca) is at 10647–81st Ave in Old Strathcona, the lively shopping and restaurant district across the river from downtown. Beds start from $24 for members and $28 for non-members; there are also a few private doubles at $56 and $64 respectively. The hostel is directly behind Whyte Avenue, otherwise known as 'Party Street', so if it's nightlife you're after, this is the place to head.

The friendly, centrally located *YMCA* (☎ 780-421-9622, 💻 www.edmonton. ymca.ca) at 10030–102A Ave has comfortable singles (with a women-only floor) from $38 and dorm beds for men starting at $25, as well as a number of double rooms for $51.

Mid-range hotels

The cheapest downtown hotel is the *Grand Hotel* (☎ 780-422-6365, 💻 resgrand @telusplanet.net) at 10266–103rd St, which has adequate en-suite doubles

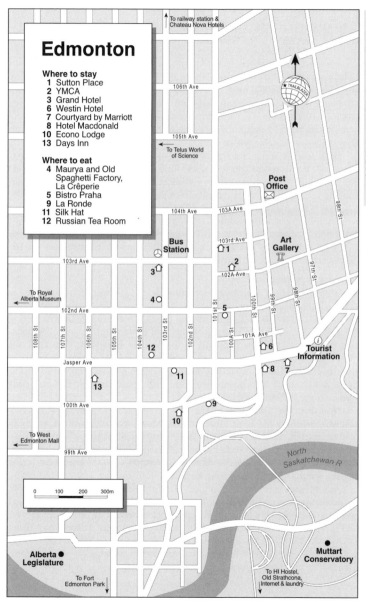

Edmonton

Where to stay
1 Sutton Place
2 YMCA
3 Grand Hotel
6 Westin Hotel
7 Courtyard by Marriott
8 Hotel Macdonald
10 Econo Lodge
13 Days Inn

Where to eat
4 Maurya and Old Spaghetti Factory, La Crêperie
5 Bistro Praha
9 La Ronde
11 Silk Hat
12 Russian Tea Room

To railway station & Chateau Nova Hotels

106th Ave

105th Ave

To Telus World of Science

104th Ave

103A Ave

Post Office

Art Gallery

Bus Station

103rd Ave

102A Ave

To Royal Alberta Museum

102nd Ave

108th St
107th St
106th St
105th St
104th St
103rd St
102nd St
101st St
100A St
100th St
99th St
98th St
97th St

Jasper Ave

101A Ave

Tourist Information

100th Ave

To West Edmonton Mall

99th Ave

North Saskatchewan R

0   100   200   300m

Alberta Legislature

Muttart Conservatory

To Fort Edmonton Park

To HI Hostel, Old Strathcona, Internet & laundry

❑ Accommodation prices quoted in this book are for **high season** (normally May or June to September). In low season many hotels offer substantial discounts.

(with rather lurid 1970s' carpets and small beds) for $58 and rooms with a shared bathroom for $38; both types come with full breakfast included. Another affordable choice is the ***Econo Lodge*** (☎ 780-428-6442, 🖳 www.econolodge. com) at 10209–100th Ave, which has anonymous but well-maintained motel-style rooms for $69 and a curiously named Chinese/Western restaurant, The Ginger Ginger, which opens at 7am.

Days Inn (☎ 780-423-1925), at 10041–106th St, looks a bit spartan from the outside but its rooms (starting at $80 for a standard bedroom) are neat, modern and good value; breakfast is served at the friendly Albert's restaurant. Moving up a notch, a short cab-ride from the train station at 159 Airport Rd, ***Chateau Nova Hotel and Suites*** (☎ 780-424-6682, 🖳 www.novahotels.ca) is a new establishment with beautiful, spacious rooms and a business centre with free internet access for all guests. The location is perfect if you just want an overnight stop before getting back on the train, but isn't convenient for the downtown area (about a $7 cab ride away).

Upmarket hotels

The ***Fairmont Hotel Macdonald*** (☎ 780-424-5181, 🖳 www.fairmont.com) at 10065–100th St was built in 1915 by the Grand Trunk Railway and was revamped with a $30 million renovation package before reopening in 1991 – exquisitely refurbished, all ivories, whites and Edwardian elegance. The location is unbeatable, as the hotel sits in the heart of downtown Edmonton yet offers spectacular views over the river valley. Guests can admire the views as they sip cocktails in the beautiful Confederation Lounge or perhaps take a stroll in the immaculate hotel gardens, complete with ornate fountain. Standard doubles go from $329 to $459.

Next door, the ***Courtyard by Marriott*** (☎ 780-423-9999, 🖳 www.marriott. com/yegcy) offers the same great riverside views from many of its rooms as well as from its outdoor deck area. This recently renovated hotel has a variety of very spacious, pristine suites, some with Jacuzzi baths, and offers free laundry facilities to all guests. Weekend rates start at $99, with standard room prices ranging from $129 to $149 during weekdays.

Across the road, well-appointed ***Westin Edmonton*** (☎ 780-426-3636, 🖳 www.westin.com/Edmonton) is another good choice with its spacious rooms, contemporary décor and trademark 'Heavenly Beds'. Rates are around $85 to $180 according to demand. The recently refurbished ***Sutton Place Hotel*** (☎ 780-428-7111, 🖳 www.edmonton.suttonplace.com) at 10235–101st St boasts a fantastic rooftop indoor pool and hot tub and an impressive, elegant lobby. Standard rooms range between $284 and $304 during high season.

WHERE TO EAT

Downtown Edmonton has a reasonable selection of restaurants and cafés but if you want a more vibrant atmosphere at night head over to the livelier district of Old Strathcona, just across the river (take bus No 6 on 100th St at Jasper Ave, opposite Fairmont Hotel Macdonald).

Budget food

The *Silk Hat* at 10251 Jasper Ave, with its gleaming counter and worn, diner-style booths complete with mini-juke boxes on each table, looks like something out of a 1950s' American movie. As it's just been taken over by new management, it is to be hoped that the charming interior isn't altered too much. It's very popular with locals for a quiet coffee or a quick lunch.

Another inexpensive choice is the *Russian Tea Room* at 10312 Jasper Ave. It lacks the quirky style of the Silk Hat but does tasty lunchtime specials as well as plenty of snacks, chicken and beef dishes and large cakes. It also offers psychic readings at the back of the restaurant (from around $20)!

Creeping out of the budget range but still excellent value is *Bistro Praha* on the small, pedestrianized section of 100A St; its Wiener schnitzel is the best in town and has a charming outdoor terrace.

In Old Strathcona, most places to eat are on Whyte Ave, including *Boston Pizza* at No 10854, *Da-De-O New Orleans Diner and Bar* at No 10548A (known for its Cajun chicken), the chilled-out *Bagel Tree Café* at No 10355, *Tasty Toms on Whyte* on the corner of 100 St, plus lots of fast-food outlets.

Mid-range and upmarket restaurants

Downtown, there's a cluster of affordable mid-priced restaurants at the Boardwalk Market on 103rd St at 102nd Ave, including the always-reliable *Old Spaghetti Factory*, *Maurya Indian Restaurant* and *The Crêperie*, an intimate, attractive restaurant offering a huge choice of crêpes and some imaginative, well-prepared meat dishes.

One of the nicest places to eat in town is The Fairmont Hotel Macdonald's *Harvest Room*, which has beautiful views over the river and an outdoor terrace. Most main dishes are around $20–30 but sandwiches and light snacks are also available.

Another good place for a splurge is *La Ronde*, Edmonton's revolving restaurant on top of the Crowne Plaza-Chateau Lacombe at 10111 Bellamy Hill (☎ 780-428-6611), where you can admire the views of downtown Edmonton and the river valley and eat from around $20.

Back over on Whyte Ave in Old Strathcona, at No 9602 *Unheardof Restaurant* is popular for both its signature seafood dishes and selection of creative specialities which change on a twice-weekly basis, such as pistachio halibut fillet and cacao balsamic pork tenderloin. Recently named one of Canada's top 100 restaurants in the *EnRoute Magazine*, reservations are advised as it can get pretty busy (☎ 780-432-0480 from 5.30pm onwards, closed on Mondays).

NIGHTLIFE

Edmonton's nightlife scene is concentrated in Old Strathcona, which boasts numerous bars and pubs, most of them affecting a British or Irish style. Most are on Whyte Ave, including *Mickey Finn's Tap House* at No 10511, *O'Byrnes* at No 10620, *The Pig and Whistle* at No 9912 and the *Sherlock Holmes* at No 10341; one of the most popular is the *Elephant and Castle* at No 10314, serving generous portions of typical bar food (such as nachos and wings), but it can get packed out during ice hockey season when fans flock there to watch the Oilers play, so get there early to grab a good seat.

The best blues can be found at *Blues on Whyte* in the spacious bar of the Commercial Hotel, 10329 Whyte Ave. This Edmonton institution opens every evening and has excellent live blues most nights (expect a small cover charge).

Popular with tourists are the weekend night cruises on the *Edmonton Queen Riverboat*, moored at Rafter's Landing on the south bank of the river, close to the Muttart Conservatory. Drinks are served on the upper deck and you get excellent views onto Edmonton's illuminated skyline as you drift past, sipping cocktails. Another fine venue for a drink is the elegant bar at *Hotel Macdonald*, where the 1915 décor and soft jazz music lend an air of style and romance.

WHAT TO SEE

In town

● **Art Gallery of Alberta** (🖥 www.artgalleryalberta.com) houses temporary exhibitions focusing on contemporary Canadian painting, and a permanent collection ('From Sea to Sea') taking in Canadian painting from the late 19th century to today, including works by the Group of Seven (see p121) and Emily Carr. Centrally located at 2 Sir Winston Churchill Square, the gallery is currently undergoing an extensive renovation project with Los Angeles architect Randall Stout at the helm. The work should be completed by 2009 but until then the collection will be moving to temporary premises – check with the Tourist Information Centre in advance or call ☎ 780-422-6223 for further information. Admission is $10 for adults and opening hours are 10.30am–5pm Tuesday, Wednesday and Friday (till 8pm Thursday) and 11am–5pm at the weekend.

● **Alberta Legislature** This beautiful neo-classical building (🖥 www.assem bly.ab.ca) is worth a visit if only for the tranquillity of its gardens and fountains. It was built in 1912 on the site of Fort Edmonton (the stockade belonging to the Hudson's Bay Company) at 97th Ave and 107 St. The entrance is minutes from the streetcar platform and there are free guided tours inside, lasting roughly 30–45 minutes, throughout the day – for details call ☎ 780-427-7362. Summer hours are Monday to Friday 8.30am to 5pm, weekends 9am to 5pm, with tours running on the hour from 9am and then on the half hour from midday onwards.

● **Royal Alberta Museum** Upgraded from 'Provincial' to 'Royal' by Queen Elizabeth II during her 2005 trip, the museum (🖥 www.royalalbertamuseum.ca) has some interesting displays falling into three broad categories: natural history, habitat groups and human history. Highlights include some fossils of extinct animals from Alberta and hundreds of examples of Canadian taxidermy at its best. The Syncrude Gallery of Aboriginal Culture looks back at over 11,000 years of aboriginal history and the grounds feature an impressive sculpture park. The museum is open daily 9am–5pm; entrance is $10, or half-price at weekends between 9am and 11am. It's at 12845–102nd Ave; to get there take the No 1 or 20 bus west along Jasper Ave.

● **West Edmonton Mall** This mother of all malls is listed in the *Guinness Book of Records* as being the 'largest shopping mall in the world' and having the 'world's largest car park.' It's certainly big, covering an area of 48 city blocks. Inside, not only can you shop 'til you drop, you can also do a spot of bungee-jumping, take a submarine ride, watch three performing sea lions, take a whirl on the enormous ice rink, lose your money at the casino and wrap it all up with a penitential visit to the chapel. It's quite a fun place to visit and is very well designed with lots of natural lighting to stop you from feeling claustrophobic. Of course, a shopping mall's really just a shopping mall no matter how much you jazz it up but that doesn't stop 37,000 tourists a day from visiting this one. To join the crowds take bus No 100 west along Jasper Ave; while to find out more about what's waiting for you, check 🖳 www.westedmontonmall.com.

● **Muttart Conservatory** Highly recommended as a post-mall relaxation exercise, the conservatory, which consists of four pyramid-shaped greenhouses, lies on the southern bank of the river, not too far from downtown. The plants inside represent three climatic zones: arid, temperate and tropical, while the fourth pyramid houses a changing display. It's a lovely, peaceful place to stroll around and the plants are glorious, especially in the tropical pyramid; one local told me she goes there to cheer herself up in the middle of Edmonton's cold winters. Admission to the conservatory costs $7.75. It's at 9626–96A St and is open year round: Monday to Friday 9am–5.30pm, weekends and holidays 11am–5.30pm. To get there take the No 85 or 86 bus on 100 St opposite the Fairmont Hotel Macdonald or, if you fancy the short walk, head down the steps behind the Shaw Conference Centre and cross the bridge.

● **Old Strathcona** Also on the south bank of the river, Old Strathcona is in many respects the most enjoyable part of Edmonton to stroll around – it boasts many well-preserved old buildings and lots of pavement cafés, restaurants and small boutiques. While you're here, you could pay a visit to the **C&E Railway Museum** at 10447–86th Ave which displays a modest collection of railway memorabilia and old photographs. The museum (admission by donation) is open Tuesday to Saturday from 10am to 4pm during the summer months; if you're not here in the summer, phone ☎ 780-433-9739. Another attraction in Old Strathcona is the lively **farmers' market**, where you'll find numerous colourful fresh produce stalls and craft shops. The market's open year-round on Saturdays 8am–3pm.

To get to Old Strathcona from downtown, take bus No 6 from 100 St at Jasper Ave, opposite The Fairmont Hotel Macdonald. Alternatively, if you'd prefer to get there in style you could hop aboard the High Level Bridge Streetcar, 'the world's highest streetcar river crossing' from Jasper Ave, over the North Saskatchewan River to 103rd St, behind the farmers' market (🖳 www.edmonton-radial-rail way.ab.ca). The views over the river are quite amazing and the three-kilometre trip is a very pleasant way to see the city from above. The streetcar operates at 20- to 40-minute intervals between 9am and 9.40pm, daily from mid-May to early September, and Friday to Sunday during the rest of the year. Tickets cost $4.

Out of town

● **Fort Edmonton Park** This 'living museum' (🖳 www.fortedmontonpark. com) represents four periods of Edmonton's past with reconstructions of the old Hudson's Bay Company fur-trading fort and three streets (1885 St, 1905 St and 1920 St). It makes an excellent day out is and well worth the visit, providing a clear picture of how life and trade were organized in these early outposts. Staff dress in period costume and take on various roles relating to the different areas of the park – you may find yourself drinking tea with a group of friendly cowboys on 1885 St or being waited on at lunch by attentive staff kitted out in immaculate twenties attire in the fantastic Hotel Selkirk on 1920 St. The site is extensive but if you tire of walking around on foot, transport is provided by way of an old steam locomotive, a tram and even a horse and carriage.

It's located quite a distance from downtown but you can get there by public transport. First off all take a southbound train to the University LRT station, and from there pick up a shuttle bus from stop 2002, right next to the station (May–Oct, hourly from 11.06am to 5.06pm, with the last bus leaving the Park at 5.46pm). If you miss the shuttle bus, take the No 4, 30, 32 or 106 bus from the same stop. The Park's opening hours are: spring (mid-May to late June) Monday to Friday 10am–4pm, weekends 10am–6pm; summer (late June to early September) daily 10am–6pm; autumn (September) guided wagon tours Monday to Saturday between 11am and 3pm, Sunday 10am–6pm. Entrance costs $9.75 for adults, with family passes for $29.50.

● **Telus World of Science** This excellent complex includes Canada's biggest planetarium and a huge IMAX theatre. Shows are screened on various scientific topics with the help of state-of-the-art audiovisual effects. Visitors can walk through five interactive galleries and there's also an observatory, a centre for live demonstrations and facilities for going on simulated trips in space. Brilliant stuff. For information on schedules call ☎ 780-451-3344 or check 🖳 www.odyssium. com. From late June to early September the centre is open daily 10am– 9pm, and for the rest of the year Friday and Saturday 10am–9pm, and Sunday to Thursday 10am–5pm. Admission is $10.95, or $15.95 including an IMAX ticket. To get there take the No 5 or 135 bus west along Jasper Ave.

FESTIVALS

● **Jazz City International**, late June to early July. Good selection of jazz artists, Canadian and international.

● **Klondike Days**, for one week mid to late July. Big and brash celebration of the good old gold-rush days.

● **Folk Music Festival**, early August. Internationally renowned event attracting huge crowds. A wide range of styles represented.

● **Fringe Theatre Event**, mid-August. More than 800 performances are spread over nine days. The quality is highly variable, as with any fringe festival, but on the whole it's worth visiting.

MOVING ON

The *Canadian* leaves for Vancouver on Mondays, Thursdays and Saturdays, and for Toronto on Mondays, Wednesdays and Saturdays. For more details call VIA on ☎ 1-888-842-7245.

Jasper

A ride of two miles took us to Jasper's, where we arrived exactly fifteen days after leaving Edmonton... This station is now all but abandoned by the Hudson's Bay Cy. It was former- ly of considerable importance, not only from the number of fur-bearing animals around, but because it was the centre of a regular line of communication between Norway House and Edmonton on the one side, and the Columbia District and Fort Vancouver on the other. An agent and three or four men were then stationed at it all the year round...Now, the houses are untenanted, locked and shuttered. Twice a year an agent comes up from Edmonton to trade with the Indians of the surrounding country and carry back the furs.

Rev Grant, *Ocean to Ocean* (1873)

Jasper is a quieter, calmer alternative to busy Banff. Nestled deep in the Canadian Rockies, the town sits in the largest national park in the Rocky Mountains – Jasper National Park – which covers an incredible 10,878 kilome- tres and is home to not only stunning scenery but a variety of wildlife, includ- ing 277 species of birds and just under 70 species of mammals.

Archaeologists believe that people were present in the region over 9000 years ago, joining the existing inhabitants of the area such as the mountain goats, moose, bison and elk to name but a few. However, it wasn't until 1907 that the Jasper National Park was founded.

Unlike the more popular tourist resorts of Banff and Whistler, Jasper is sur- prisingly uncommercial and retains a definite charm, even though thousands of tourists flock here each year to admire and explore the surrounding wilderness. The backdrop of the Rocky Mountains, the sparkling turquoise waters of the winding Athabasca River, the animals grazing nonchalantly by the side of the road – Jasper is a photographer's heaven and yet, despite endless rolls of film, it is almost impossible to capture the beauty and sheer grandeur of the scenery around you.

ARRIVING IN JASPER

By train

If you are taking *The Canadian* from Toronto to Vancouver, or vice versa, then you will most likely arrive in Jasper on either Monday, Thursday or Saturday, with train times scheduled so that you pass through the Rockies during daylight. *The Rocky Mountaineer* arrives in Jasper every Wednesday, Friday and Sunday from Whistler and every Monday, Wednesday and Friday from Kamloops. The train station is right in the centre of the downtown core on Connaught Drive and there are always a number of taxis nearby to take you the short distance to your lodgings.

By bus

Greyhound (🖳 www.greyhound.ca) provides a daily service to Jasper from Edmonton which takes roughly 5 hours and costs $59.30 for a single ticket. Travelling up from Banff, Lake Louise or Calgary, your best option is the Brewster Bus, a pleasant, air-conditioned coach making regular trips between Calgary and Jasper. A one-way ticket from Banff to Jasper is $66; from Calgary it's $113. Brewster also offers great sightseeing tours of the local area, including the Columbia Icefields; call ahead to check what is available on ☎ 1-800-760-6934 or visit 🖳 www.sightseeingtourscanada.ca.

ORIENTATION AND GETTING AROUND

Jasper town is so compact that you will be able to take it all in on foot. The two main streets where the majority of shops, restaurants and bars are situated are Connaught Drive, on which the rail station is located and, running parallel behind it, Patricia St. If you need a taxi, Mountain Express (☎ 780-852-4555) are reliable. Alternatively, if you're staying in the HI hostel or venturing up to the Jasper Tramway, the town offers a great **shuttle service** which runs frequently throughout the day from 9am to 8pm (summer months); a single ticket costs $3. The shuttle stops at the totem pole on Connaught Drive and heads up to the Tramway, with plenty of rooftop space for luggage.

SERVICES

Tourist information

The friendly **Jasper Park Information Centre** (☎ 780-852-6176, 🖳 www.jaspercanadianrockies.com) is housed in a beautiful, historic building at 500

❑ **Jasper online**

🖳 **www.visit-jasper.com/home1.html** Independent but useful site on Jasper.

🖳 **www.canadianrockies.net/jasper/** Site on Jasper National Park

🖳 **www.jaspercanadianrockies.com/** Official website of Jasper Tourism and Commerce

Connaught Drive. The centre is open year round, from 8.30am to 7pm in high season, 9am until 4pm in winter.

Money

There are several banks in the centre of the town, including a TD Waterhouse bank at 606 Patricia St and a CIBC bank at 416 Connaught Drive.

Post, internet and laundry

The **post office** lies on Patricia St, or you can head to More Than Mail on Connaught Drive which offers facilities such as **faxing**.

The fantastic Coin Clean **Laundry** on Patricia St has huge washing machines and dryers and a little counter selling coffee and muffins to help pass the time away. Directly above is one of the town's many **internet cafés**, promising competitive prices.

WHERE TO STAY

There is no shortage of accommodation in Jasper, ranging from campsites and rustic cabins to luxurious hotels and resorts. It can, however, easily become booked up in high season so book ahead; that said, some hotels do offer last-minute deals so if you're willing to take a risk outside the high season, you can sometimes get a great deal.

Budget accommodation

Jasper National Park has five HI hostels within its boundaries. The nearest one to the town site (and the least primitive!) is the *HI Jasper Hostel* (☎ 780-852-3215; 🖥 www.hihostels.ca), which lies a short distance out of the town centre on Whistler's Mountain. The building is rather like a large wooden cabin but has a large, fully fitted kitchen, indoor showers and a cosy lounge area. Private rooms are available (from $50) as well as large dorm rooms ($20 per bed), one specifically for females, the other mixed. The Jasper Shuttle runs between the town centre and the hostel several times a day ($3) or you can walk (45 minutes-plus), though watch out for the wildlife!

Mid- and upper-range hotels

For home comforts in a rustic setting, you'll enjoy spending time at the *Pine Bungalows* (☎ 780-852-3491; 🖥 www.pinebungalows.com), a 30-minute walk (or $10 taxi ride) from the centre. This family-owned business understands that a vacation in Jasper is all about enjoying the natural surroundings, which is why you won't find televisions or telephones in your room. The cabins offer comfortable beds and sparkling clean bathrooms and some even have kitchen facilities. Rates start at $150.

A few minutes' walk from the centre of the town, the very welcoming *105 Patricia Street* (☎ 780-852-4346; 🖥 www3.telus.net/105patriciastreet) is a charming place with two immaculate suites, each with fridge, microwave and kettle, though note that breakfast is not included. Rates are based on double occupancy and are set at $100.

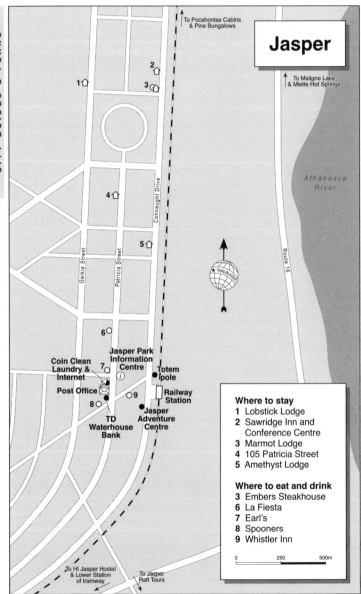

To Pocahontas Cabins
& Pine Bungalows

Jasper

1 ⌂

2 ⌂

3 ⌂

To Maligne Lake
& Miette Hot Springs

Athabasca
River

Connaught Drive

Route 16

4 ⌂

5 ⌂

★ TRAILBLAZER

Geikie Street

Patricia Street

6 ○

Jasper Park
Information
Centre

Coin Clean
Laundry &
Internet

7 ○

(i)

Totem
pole

Post Office ⊠

9 ○

Railway
Station

8 ○

TD
Waterhouse
Bank

Jasper
Adventure
Centre

Where to stay
1 Lobstick Lodge
2 Sawridge Inn and
  Conference Centre
3 Marmot Lodge
4 105 Patricia Street
5 Amethyst Lodge

Where to eat and drink
3 Embers Steakhouse
6 La Fiesta
7 Earl's
8 Spooners
9 Whistler Inn

0   250   500m

To HI Jasper Hostel
& Lower Station
of tramway

To Jasper
Raft Tours

❑ Accommodation prices quoted in this book are for **high season** (normally May or June to September). In low season many hotels offer substantial discounts.

Opened in 1983, the warm and hospitable *Sawridge Inn and Conference Centre* (☎ 780-852-6590; 🖳 www.sawridgejasper.com), in a great location on Connaught Drive, is naturally lit with an abundance of skylights and boasts 153 bedrooms and suites, its own spa – complete with two hot tubs, a sauna and pool – as well as cosy Champs bar, with its leather couches, a pool table and flatscreen TV. Rates range between $175 and $300.

Mountain Park Lodges is another prominent organization on the Jasper accommodation scene, with four properties. The recently renovated *Lobstick Lodge* (☎ 780-852-4431) at 94 Geikie St takes its name from how native people in the Rockies marked territory. The branches of a tree were lopped off, with the exception of those near the top, and what remained was known as a lobstick. Situated a short distance from downtown, this hotel offers 139 comfortable rooms, some with full kitchen facilities, and rooms start from just $89, though a standard room in high season is around $225.

More centrally located at 200 Connaught Drive, *Amethyst Lodge* (☎ 780-852-3394) has some great facilities including two outdoor hot tubs; rates range from $79/$219 in low/high season.

Nearby, *Marmot Lodge* (☎ 780-852-4471) at 86 Connaught Drive looks like a motel but head indoors and you will be greatly impressed with the high standards. The spacious rooms boast full kitchen facilities, while in the Lodge grounds there's a BBQ area, stand-alone hot tub and an indoor pool. Standard rooms start at $85/$215 in low/high season.

Finally, for something different try the *Pocahontas Cabins* (☎ 780-866-3732; 🖳 www.mpljasper.com) on Highway 16 East. This peaceful resort consists of a range of cabins, from the basic Settler's Cabin to the ultra-luxurious Executive Cabins that come complete with second-floor Queen bedrooms and spectacular mountain views. The only downside is that they're a 25-minute drive out of town but if you're looking for a tranquil retreat, this accommodation will certainly appeal. Cabins range from $129 to $249 in high season, $89 to $199 during the rest of the year.

WHERE TO EAT

There is no shortage of places to eat out in Jasper, from friendly breakfast cafés like *Spooners* on Patricia St, where you can tuck into their tasty breakfast burritos on the balcony surrounded by flower baskets and fantastic views of the Rockies, to cosy Mexican restaurants like *La Fiesta*, 504 Patricia St, which offers Spanish fusion cuisine such as tapas dishes, fajitas and enchiladas. A staple favourite is the chain restaurant *Earl's*, on the 2nd floor at 600 Patricia St, which has great steaks and salads and appealing drinks offers practically every night of the week (the martinis are great!). Many of the hotels also feature impressive restaurants, such as *Embers Steakhouse*, part of the Mountain Park Lodges chain, which serves breakfast and dinner and has events throughout the year, including the ever-popular Scotch tasting in January!

NIGHTLIFE

The Whistler's Inn, located between Patricia and Connaught opposite the Tourist Information office, is a snug pub with worn-in couches and a friendly atmosphere that's proving very popular with the locals. For those who prefer to dance the night away, the two main hotspots are *Pete's Club*, upstairs at 614 Patricia St, which fills up every weekend with a young and lively bunch, and the *Atha-B* nightclub, 510 Patricia St, which rivals Pete's with its packed-out dancefloors and equally fun clientele.

THINGS TO DO

The breathtaking scenery of Jasper means that there is always something to observe or discover in this quaint town and its surroundings and although many activities come at a price due to the high number of tourists who flock here each year, they are definitely worth it!

Maligne Lake

If you have time to make only one day-trip during your stay, then spend it exploring the largest lake in the Canadian Rockies. Maligne (⌨ www.malignelake.com) is located an hour's drive from Jasper; you can get there in comfort by booking a seat on the **Maligne Lake Shuttle** which runs from outside its office at 616 Patricia St three to four times a day. On the way, keep your eyes peeled for wildlife – the last time we did this trip we were lucky enough to see a mother black bear and her cubs idling up the side of the road! At the lake you can sit back and enjoy the views or take the Spirit Island Scenic Cruise (☎ 780-852-3370) out onto the beautiful turquoise glacial waters, which calls in at a wonderfully picturesque stretch of shore on the way. A return ticket on the shuttle costs $32.10; the boat cruise is $41 and departs on the hour between 10am and 5pm in high season.

Jasper Tramway

For those with a head for heights, a cable car ride known as the Tramway (⌨ www.jaspertramway.com) provides breathtaking views of the national park. Climbing to 2277 metres at the top of Whistler's Mountain, the Tramway begins its journey 10 minutes out of town at the lower station (1304 metres), situated at the top of Whistler's Mountain Road. The Tramway journey takes roughly 10 minutes. At the end you can admire the views over a drink from the fully licensed Treeline Restaurant or, if you're feeling particularly adventurous, venture out on the summit hiking trail which leads to even more spectacular views (appropriate footwear essential).

The Tramway runs 9am—8pm from late June to late August ($24 per adult, discounts for children and seniors). To reach the lower station from downtown you can take the shuttle bus from the Totem Pole on Connaught Drive; a return journey, including admission to the tramway, costs $29 and can be bought from the driver.

Miette Hot Springs
Perfect after a strenuous day of sightseeing, the Miette Hot Springs are located a short drive from the town centre. With views of the mountains to savour, the mineral-rich waters come straight from within the Rockies at 54°C before being cooled to a bearable 40°C in two pools, with a third 'cool pool' nearby. Thousands of people flock here to soak up the scenery and enjoy the incredible wildlife, with bighorn sheep and deer grazing in the nearby parking area. The springs are open from May to early October, with opening hours 10.30am–9pm in May and September, 8.30am–10.30pm in summer. Admission costs $7. Unless you have access to a vehicle, you will need to take a shuttle to the springs. **Jasper Adventure Centre** (☎ 780-852-5595; 🖳 www.jasperadventurecentre.com) offers regular tours to the springs; the journey itself takes roughly an hour.

Rafting
Whitewater rafting is a highly popular activity in the Jasper National Park with the Athabasca and Sunwapta rivers providing opportunities for people of all levels. **Jasper Raft Tours** (☎ 780-852-2665; 🖳 www.jasperrafttours.com) provide a great way to enjoy the river in a relaxing way, with round trips down the Athabasca on a raft that can seat between 12 to 20 people, led by an experienced guide who steers you through gentle rapids graded at a pleasant level 1-2. Raft tours run between mid-May to late September and cost $47 for adults and $15 for children under 15.

MOVING ON

By rail
The *Canadian* leaves for Vancouver (17 hours 30 mins) on Mondays, Thursdays and Saturdays and for Toronto (54 hours) on Mondays, Wednesdays and Saturdays. For more information visit 🖳 www.viarail.ca. The *Rocky Mountaineer Yellowhead Route* leaves for Vancouver via Kamloops (two days and one night) on Tuesdays, Thursdays and Sundays. The *Rocky Mountaineer Fraser Discovery Route* leaves for Whistler via Quesnel (two days and one night) on Tuesdays, Thursdays and Saturdays. Both Rocky Mountaineer routes are seasonal (April/May to late October) so check in advance for alternative transportation if you are visiting during the winter months. For more information, visit 🖳 www.rockymountaineer.com.

By bus
There are frequent daily departures from Jasper to Edmonton and limited indirect services between Banff, Calgary and Jasper on the **Greyhound** bus service (🖳 www.greyhound.ca). During summer months the **Brewster Bus** (🖳 www.brewster.ca) offers a daily service from Jasper to Lake Louise, Banff and Calgary.

Calgary

Affluent, self-confident, youthful and lively, Calgary is an attractive, compact city that is one of the fastest growing in Canada. Seen from a distance, its downtown core is a glittering island of glass and steel sitting in rolling grassland at the foot of the mighty Rocky Mountains. It is the accessibility of these mountains – less than an hour's drive away – that makes Calgary such an appealing place to visit, combining all the advantages of a modern city with on-your-doorstep wilderness. Also, one of the most famous events in Canada takes place here each July: the annual Calgary Stampede, featuring ten days of rodeos, country dancing and wild celebrations.

Although no longer served by national trains – the historic CPR passenger service stopped operating in 1989, and *The Canadian* goes via Edmonton, 294km north – the success of the privately run *Rocky Mountaineer* has revived Calgary's role as a railway city and today thousands of rail travellers pass through to travel on the old CPR route through the Rockies.

HISTORY

Fort Calgary

Calgary has one of the shortest histories of all Canada's cities, dating back to 1875 when a detachment of the North West Mounted Police (NWMP) built Fort Calgary at the confluence of the Bow and Elbow rivers. They'd been sent to establish order in a region disrupted by whisky traders and general lawlessness as the fur trade pushed west into the prairies. This area was home to thousands of Cree, Blackfoot and Stoney natives who lived off the vast numbers of buffalo that inhabited the region at that time; the Canadian government, however, had plans to settle the region with immigrants who would be transported west on the new transcontinental railroad under construction. Sending the NWMP was the first step in its plan to 'civilize' the region and create conditions that would encourage white settlement.

The CPR

Following the completion of the CPR railroad in 1885 hundreds of settlers arrived, principally from Britain, the Ukraine and Scandinavia, to claim land and farm it. Quickly, Calgary was transformed from the collection of rough wooden shacks it had been under the NWMP to a fledgling town with streets, stores and proper houses.

On 7 November 1884, Calgary was officially declared a town and, a decade later in January 1894, it was made a city. Throughout its early days, the role of the CPR was very prominent: not only did it bring settlers here by rail and export their produce to other markets, it also owned much of the land Calgary was built on and even named many of the new town's streets after CPR officials.

From ranching to oil

By the early 20th century, Calgary was a booming little city with an economy based firmly on ranching. This was supplemented by a second major industry in 1914 when the Turner Valley oil fields were discovered 35km south-west of the city. There was no looking back and in 1947 Calgary's importance as an oil and gas supplier was confirmed with the discovery of the spectacular Leduc oil field, followed by further discoveries throughout the province.

Today, Calgary houses the headquarters of many energy companies and is the nerve centre of Canada's oil and gas industries.

ARRIVING IN CALGARY

By air

Many international airlines have direct flights to Calgary, which is a popular arrival point in Canada. Getting to the city centre from the airport is easy on the Airporter Bus, which drops passengers at the main downtown hotels. It's a 20-minute ride into town, and the bus operates every half hour from 6.30am to 11.30pm. In addition, door-to-door minibus shuttles are provided by Airport Direct Ltd (☎ 403-291-1991) and Airport Shuttle Express (☎ 403-509-4799); ticket prices vary depending on where you're travelling to (roughly around $15). A taxi to downtown should cost no more than $25–30.

By bus

If you've come to Calgary to combine your trip on *The Canadian* with *The Rocky Mountaineer* train, the chances are you've arrived by bus from Edmonton. The **Greyhound** terminal is south-west of downtown at 877 Greyhound Way, from where free shuttle buses take passengers to the C-Train (see 'Getting Around' below) that goes into the centre. The **Red Arrow** terminal is more central at 205–9th Ave SE.

By train

The train station is right underneath the Calgary Tower at 131–9th Ave, in the heart of downtown. The Visitor Information Centre (see p156) is just one level above, so you can pick up maps and other tourist information while you're here.

GETTING AROUND

The downtown core is very compact and easily covered on **foot**. Several attractions, however, are out of the centre but can be reached by public transport, operated by Calgary Transit (☎ 403-262-1000). This consists of a network of

---

❏ **Calgary online**

💻 **www.tourismcalgary.com** Good, city-focused site produced by Calgary Convention and Visitors' Bureau. Questions can be emailed to 💻 destination@visitor.calgary.ab.ca.

💻 **www.discoveralberta.com** Information on the province by Tourism Alberta.

CITY GUIDES & PLANS

In-line skating
Certain areas of Calgary provide the perfect terrain for rollerblading, or **in-line skating** as it's known in North America. You can pick up a free leaflet from the Visitor Information Centre at the Calgary Tower Centre detailing the different pathways around town (basic to advanced). Alternatively, if you'd like to take a lesson, contact the City of Calgary Recreation on ☎ 403-268-3800. For more information, or for an online leaflet which you can download, go to the website 🖳 www.calgary.ca/parks and click on the section named Pathways. The in-line skating brochure can be found in the bottom right-hand corner of the page.

buses plus the **C-Train**, an overground light rail service running through the city centre along 7th Ave and out into the suburbs.

The downtown portion of the C-Train trip between 10th St and the City Hall is free. Otherwise, C-Train and bus fares are $2.25 for a single ticket (exact change required), $19.50 for a book of 10 tickets, or $5.60 for a day pass, available at some convenience stores or the Calgary Transit Customer Service Centre at 224–7th Ave SW. If you need to change buses, ask for a transfer when you buy your ticket. A reliable **taxi** company is Associated Cab (☎ 403-299-1111).

ORIENTATION

Calgary is divided into four quadrants: NW, NE, SW and SE. The dividing lines are the Bow River, running east to west, and Central St to Macleod Trail, running north to south. The quadrant is always included on addresses, and should be noted carefully to avoid going to the same address in the opposite quadrant. Most of downtown Calgary falls into the SW quadrant.

The focus of downtown is the pedestrianized stretch of 8th Avenue, known as **Stephen Avenue Mall** – it's not actually a mall but an attractive street lined with boutiques, bars and restaurants. Note that avenues run east–west and streets north–south.

SERVICES

Tourist information
The downtown **Visitor Information Centre**, run by the Calgary Convention and Visitors' Bureau, is on the ground level of the Calgary Tower Centre at Centre St and 9th Ave SE. In summer (mid-May to October) it's open daily 8am–8pm, and 8.30am–5pm for the rest of the year. Phone enquiries should be made to the Bureau's central office on ☎ 403-263-8510 or 1-800-661-1678.

Money
Downtown, you'll find plenty of banks with ATMs on Stephen Avenue Mall and the surrounding streets. Foreign exchange outlets include: Calgary Foreign Exchange, 307–4th Ave SW; Alberta Treasury Branch, 239–8th Ave SW; and Royal Bank, 339–8th Ave SW.

Consulates

Austria (☎ 403-283-6526) 1131 Kensington Rd NW
Denmark (☎ 403-245-5755) 1235–11th Ave
Germany (☎ 403-247-3357) 550–11th Ave SW, Suite 600
Hungary (☎ 403-252-4502) 1700–96th Ave
Italy (☎ 403-237-6603) Bay 9, 3927 Edmonton Trail NE
Netherlands (☎ 403-266-2710) Suite 708, 304–8th Ave SW
Norway (☎ 403-263-2270) Suite 1753, 708–8th Ave SW
Sweden (☎ 403-451-0354) 1039 Durham Ave SW
Switzerland (☎ 403-233-8919) 700 Sunlife Plaza, N Tower
USA (☎ 403-266-8962) Suite 1000, 615 Macleod Trail SE

Post, internet and laundry

The main **post office** is at 207–9th Ave. The best place to go for **internet access** is the public library at 616 Macleod Trail SE, or you could try Wired at 1032–17th Ave SW, Cinescape on the 2nd floor at Eau Claire Market, or at the Greyhound bus terminal (see p155). The most convenient **laundry** for downtown is Avenue Coin Laundry at 325B–17th Ave (☎ 403-262-8777)

WHERE TO STAY

Downtown accommodation is fairly thin on the ground in the mid-range bracket but many of the upmarket hotels offer discounts at weekends so it's worth checking in advance to see what deals are available. During Stampede (ten days in early July; exact dates at 🖳 www.calgarystampede.com) all accommodation is more expensive and needs to be reserved long in advance.

Budget accommodation

The *HI Hostel* (☎ 403-269-8239, 🖳 www.hihostels.ca) is at 520–7th Ave SE, three blocks east of the City Hall; take the free C-Train to the corner of 7th Ave and 3rd St then walk a couple of blocks east. The area is rather downtrodden and it might be best not to wander around alone at night but the hostel offers clean, comfortable dorm rooms, a bright and airy reading/internet room and a large kitchen. Beds cost $23 for members and $27 for non-members, although prices do increase slightly during the Calgary Stampede.

A couple of blocks away, the women-only *YWCA* (☎ 403-263-1559, 🖳 www.ywcaofcalgary.com) at 1301–5th Ave SE has immaculate singles with and without private bath ($55/$45); guests can also use the large pool and fitness centre and the location is decidedly more pleasant to walk around.

Mid-range hotels

Due to the recent closure of a few hotels in Calgary, the downtown mid-range market is rather bare. The best option is the highly recommended *Sandman*

❑ Accommodation prices quoted in this book are for **high season** (normally May or June to September). In low season many hotels offer substantial discounts.

Hotel (☎ 403-237-8626, 🖳 www.sandmanhotels.ca) at 888–7th Ave SW, literally straight off the free downtown C-train at 7th St. It has a smart, welcoming lobby, spruce rooms, a great indoor pool and fitness room and a fresh, modern feel to it. The hotel also boasts a business centre and a trendy bar, as well as Moxie's, a rather stylish grill and steakhouse. Doubles start at $125.

Otherwise, the **Bed and Breakfast Association of Calgary** offers a wide range of comfortable B&B accommodation, although many are out of the downtown area. For a complete list, see 🖳 www.bbcanada.com/associations/bbac.

Upmarket hotels

By far the most beautiful and romantic hotel in town is *The Fairmont Palliser* (☎ 403-262-1234, 🖳 www.fairmont.com), at 133–9th Ave, built by the CPR in 1914. The opulent lobby is a sea of marble, bronze and crystal and the rooms have a classic old-world charm. The hotel also boasts a superb restaurant and a lovely pool and spa – this is the place to stay if you're in search of some serious pampering. Doubles range between $149 and $429 depending on availability and day of the week (weekend rates are lower); be sure to check online for special offers.

Alternatively, you could try the *Westin* (☎ 403-266-1611, 🖳 www.westin. com), at 320–4th Ave SW, with a 24-hour fitness centre, a Starbucks coffeehouse on the premises and rooms from $285, or the *Calgary Marriott* (☎ 403-266-7331, 🖳 www.calgarymarriott.com), in a leafy and peaceful but wonderfully central location at 110–9th Ave SE – it's a smart, crisp, modern hotel where weekday rates are a steep $309 but weekend prices (Friday and Saturday nights) drop to around $159.

WHERE TO EAT

Calgary has a good spread of downtown restaurants including plenty of budget choices. Alberta beef ranks among the best in the world and a highlight of eating out in Calgary is sampling the locally produced prime ribs and steaks.

Budget food

The best place for a cheap, filling lunch is the **Eau Claire Market** by Prince's Island (see p161), which is packed with great-value restaurants and cafés as well as takeaway stalls serving everything from stir-fries to bagels. Another place for bargain food is the *Lazy Loaf and Kettle*, a few blocks off 7th Ave at 8 Parkdale Crescent NW, which serves fresh homemade soups, salads and light meals. For something more substantial, try the always-packed *Chianti*, a few blocks out of the centre at 1438–17th Ave SW. It serves excellent pasta dishes for around $10 and the atmosphere is good. The more centrally located *Divino's* at 817–1st St SW is a small, wood-panelled bistro serving delicious pizzas for around $15 among other more expensive choices.

If you're looking for a filling breakfast before a big day of sightseeing, head to the *Avenue Diner* on Stephen Avenue Mall (105A–8th Ave) where you can tuck into delicious omelettes and other great breakfast fare in a typical American-style diner.

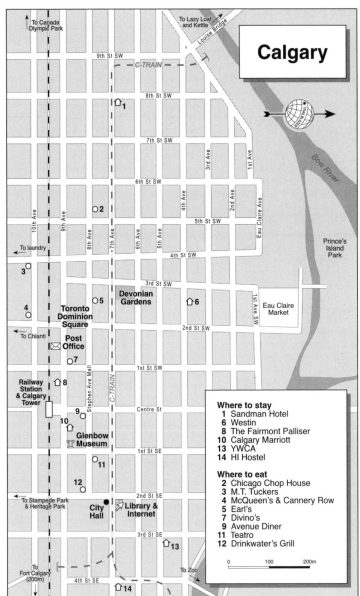

Calgary

To Canada Olympic Park

To Lazy Loaf and Kettle

Louise Bridge

C-TRAIN

9th St SW
8th St SW
7th St SW
6th St SW

Bow River

3rd Ave
1st Ave

9th Ave
10th Ave
8th Ave
7th Ave
6th Ave
5th Ave
4th Ave
2nd Ave

5th St SW
4th St SW

Eau Claire Ave

Prince's Island Park

To laundry

3rd St SW

Devonian Gardens

Eau Claire Market

1st Ave SW

Toronto Dominion Square

To Chianti

Post Office

2nd St SW

1st St SW

Railway Station & Calgary Tower

Stephen Ave Mall

C-TRAIN

Centre St

1st St SE

Glenbow Museum

To Stampede Park & Heritage Park

2nd St SE

City Hall

Library & Internet

3rd St SE

To Fort Calgary (200m)

4th St SE

To Zoo

Where to stay
1 Sandman Hotel
6 Westin
8 The Fairmont Palliser
10 Calgary Marriott
13 YWCA
14 HI Hostel

Where to eat
2 Chicago Chop House
3 M.T. Tuckers
4 McQueen's & Cannery Row
5 Earl's
7 Divino's
9 Avenue Diner
11 Teatro
12 Drinkwater's Grill

0   100   200m

Mid-range and upmarket restaurants

One of Calgary's most popular mid-priced restaurants is the large, bustling *Earl's* on 8th Ave between 2nd and 3rd streets, serving steaks, pasta, fish and more; the décor's pretty standard but the atmosphere's good and the cheesecake delicious.

A few blocks east at No 200, opposite Glenbow Museum, *Teatro* (☎ 403-290-1012) serves 'Italian market cuisine' in a splendid old building that was originally the Toronto Dominion Bank, boasting incredibly high ceilings and gleaming white pillars. It serves spectacular meat, fish and pasta dishes, like 'lasagne with lobster and scallops in a dill sauce'. Main-course prices range from $18 to $45 and there's also a tasting menu at $110 per person. Close by at No 237 (next to the City Hall), *Drinkwater's Grill* (☎ 403-264-9494) also occupies an historic building, this one with immense sky-blue pillars. It specializes in steaks and 'contemporary bistro food', with most mains around $20 to $30.

Another trendy place for steak is the *Chicago Chop House* (☎ 403-265-3000) at 604–8th Ave SW, impeccably chic with its stripped beech floor, stainless-steel open kitchen and bar in the middle of the dining room.

McQueen's seafood restaurant (☎ 403-269-4722) at 317–10th Ave SW also has a lot of style and has live blues and jazz at its piano bar. Most mains here are around $20–30. Downstairs, *Cannery Row* is larger, a lot cheaper and more hectic: it also serves a wide range of fish and shellfish, including delicious crab cakes. A short way down the road at 345–10th Ave SW is *MT Tuckers*, a big steakhouse with steaks from $15 to $20 and burgers for under $10.

WHAT TO SEE

Downtown

● **Calgary Tower** A good starting point for taking in the lie of the land and getting great views onto the mountains is this 190m-high tower (🖥 www.calgarytower.com) on the corner of Centre St and 9th Ave SW (it's also conveniently located next to the Visitor Information Centre). The observation tower has a large, vertigo-inducing glass floor which, I am reliably informed, 'can hold the weight of several elephants'. There's also a bar and grill for snacks and a revolving restaurant if you want to combine your visit with a meal. From June to November the tower is open 7am–11pm (last ride leaves at 10.30pm), and for the rest of the year 9am–11pm (last ride at 9pm). Tickets cost $12.95 or half price if you have a booking at the revolving restaurant.

● **Glenbow Museum** Right opposite the tower is the excellent Glenbow Museum (🖥 www.glenbow.org), a must-see while you're in town. The museum explores the Canadian West's history with a fascinating range of exhibits – displays include an enormous stuffed buffalo; fabulous native beadwork; old 'Mountie' uniforms; personal belongings of the first immigrants; indigenous art and crafts; a Blackfoot tepee, and a pioneer's log cabin. There's also a display on the CPR and its crucial role in shaping the West's development. Look out for the scale model of the Stoney Creek Bridge built in 1886, the highest on the line and still crossed today by *The Rocky Mountaineer* (see p230). Another interesting display is the 'Warriors' section, where visitors can walk through five centuries of war stories, weapons and armoury.

The museum is open daily 9am–5pm with the exception of Thursday (open until 9pm). Entrance costs $12.

● **Fort Calgary Historic Park** On the eastern edge of downtown, bordering 6th St SE, Fort Calgary Historic Park (🖥 www.fortcalgary.com) covers the land occupied by the original log stockade built in 1875 by the North West Mounted Police when they arrived to impose law and order on the region. They stayed there until 1914, when the buildings were demolished. You can now walk around an exact replica of the 1888 barracks complete with the canteen, recreation room and library. In addition there's a museum with reconstructions detailing life at the fort, along with stacks of memorabilia from Calgary's early days. Exhibits include NWMP uniforms, which you can try on and have your photo taken in; a reconstructed jail cell where you can try the handcuffs; a hospital room; a drugstore, and an old streetcar.

The museum and site are open daily 9am–5pm; entrance is $10.

● **Devonian Gardens** One of Calgary's biggest surprises is this luxuriant indoor garden on the top floor of the Toronto Dominion Square building, at 317–7th Ave. Opened in 1977 and covering two and a half acres, the garden boasts a glorious array of flowers and trees arranged around streams and waterfalls, making a relaxing place to stroll on a sunny afternoon or if you want to escape the crowds in the TD Mall. Open daily 9am–9pm with no admission fee.

● **Eau Claire Market and Prince's Island** Six blocks north of the Devonian Gardens, on the corner of 3rd St SW and 1st Ave SW, the colourful Eau Claire Market is packed with fresh produce stalls and little restaurants, as well as craft shops and interesting boutiques. This is one of Calgary's most appealing 'people's places' and has a lively, enjoyable atmosphere and a pretty location on the banks of the Bow River. The market also features a Latin-American dance studio where you can take lessons and learn to cha cha or tango or, if you've two left feet, just sit back and enjoy the entertainment and the atmosphere. Opposite the market a bridge leads across to Prince's Island, an attractive park and the site of evening outdoor performances of 'Shakespeare in the Park' during the summer months.

Out of Downtown
● **Canada Olympic Park** East of downtown at 88 Olympic Park Rd, the complex created to host the 1988 Winter Olympics is open to the public as an attraction. Bus tours for $15 (or self-guided tours for $7) take visitors up to look at the bobsleigh tracks and the ski-jump tower, from where they come down to the base on chairlifts. In summer you can try the public 'luge' for $6 a go.

There's also an extensive mountain-bike trail on the slopes of the park; you can hire bikes at the bottom, take them up on the chairlift and cycle down. For more details, check 🖥 www.canadaolympicpark.ca.

● **Heritage Park Historical Village** Sixteen kilometres south of the city centre, Heritage Park (☎ 403-268-8500, 🖥 www.heritagepark.ca) is a recreation of a 1910 prairie town, an 1880s' pre-railway settlement and an 1860s' fur-trading outpost, with over 150 meticulously restored buildings salvaged from other locations and brought here to be preserved.

Visitors to the **Calgary Heritage Park** are transported around the site in carriages dating from 1885, 1907 and 1912, with a former CPR conductor as a guide.
PHOTO © MELISSA GRAHAM

The three sites are fairly spread out and connected by a circular railroad served by steam trains. The three stops house original CPR log stations, including the first station erected at Laggan, now known as Lake Louise. Just behind Shepherd station you'll find a collection of beautiful old loco-motives and trains, including the splendid train constructed by the CPR to trans-port the Duke and Duchess of Cornwall (the future King George V and Queen Mary) on their tour of Canada in 1901; you can wander through their sleeping quarters and admire the luxury. You can also take a short cruise on *SS Moyie*, a beautiful steamboat which makes regular circular trips and has the added bonus of the Rocky Mountains as a backdrop.

Heritage Park is open from mid-May to early September daily between 9am–5pm, and then to mid-October weekends only. Entrance is $14 to walk around or $23 for unlimited access to the steam train, paddlewheeler and horse-drawn wagon. In summer, entrance before 10am includes a free pancake break-fast. To get here, take the C-Train towards Somerset/Bridlewood and get off at Heritage Station, then transfer to bus No 502.

● **Calgary Zoo** Calgary's zoo (🖥 www.calgaryzoo.com) is one of the best in Canada and quite progressive, with its animals in large areas that mimic their natural habitat as closely as possible. Of the 1200 animals, highlights include a family of gorillas in the Primates section; tigers and snow leopards in the Eurasia section; kangaroos and wallabies in the Australia section and lions, giraffes and hippos in the Destination Africa area. If you're not going to get the chance to see the real thing in the Rocky Mountains, you can see moose, bighorn sheep, Rocky Mountain goats and grizzly bears among other local wildlife in the Canadian Wilds area. The zoo also has beautiful botanical gar-dens and waterfalls and is currently working towards Project Discovery 2010, which will include a new habitat for the zoo's Asian elephants. The Calgary Zoo is a great family day out and is open daily 9am–5pm, with an admission fee of

$16 for adults ($10 for children between 13 to 17; $8 for children 12 and under). The zoo is very accessible from downtown Calgary: to get there take the C-Train towards Whitehorn and get off at the stop named Zoo.

FESTIVALS

● **Calgary Winter Festival**, late January to early February. Sporting and cultural events.

● **Calgary International Children's Festival**, May. Dozens of games and events for kids.

● **Shakespeare in the Park**, June to August. Outdoor performances of Shakespeare plays on Prince's Island in the Bow River.

● **Calgary Stampede**, around the first two weeks of July (check on ☎ 1-800-661-1767, or 🖥 www.calgarystampede.com). One of Canada's most famous events, with ten days of rodeos, chuck-wagon racing, pancake breakfasts, country dancing and much more.

● **International Native Arts Festival**, August. Exhibitions and sales of a wide range of native Canadian arts, from sculpture to leatherwork.

MOVING ON

By rail
The *Rocky Mountaineer* departs from the CPR station directly underneath the Calgary Tower at 131–9th Ave (☎ 403-294-9298 or 1-800-665-7245).

By bus
There are frequent departures from Calgary to Banff, Lake Louise, Edmonton, Vancouver and other destinations in western Canada. Most services are provided by **Greyhound** (☎ 403-265-9111), operating from 877 Greyhound Way, but if you're going to Edmonton note that **Red Arrow** (☎ 403-531-0350) buses are more comfortable with just three seats to an aisle: they leave from 205–9th Ave SE.

By air
To get to the airport from downtown, you can take the Airporter Bus (☎ 403-531-3909), which picks up at the main downtown hotels.

Door-to-door shuttles are provided by Airport Direct Ltd (☎ 403-291-1991) and Airport Shuttle Express (☎ 403-509-4799).

CITY GUIDES & PLANS

Vancouver

A great sleepiness lies on Vancouver as compared with an American town; men don't fly up and down the streets telling lies, and the spittoons in the delightfully comfortable hotels are unused; the baths are free and their rooms are unlocked.

Rudyard Kipling, *From Sea to Sea*, 1900

Vancouver just doesn't have to try. In front is the ocean, behind are the snow-capped mountains and in between is this bustling city full of cafés, restaurants, boutiques and healthy, long-limbed people. It is utterly seductive.

The city is situated on a peninsula in the south-west corner of British Columbia. It has a mild, temperate climate and its inhabitants have a reputation for taking a laidback attitude to life (it is said that Vancouver is more Californian than Canadian). Its easygoing ambience, however, conceals a vigorous commercial, financial and industrial sector that has made it the economic hub of western Canada. Its port handles 65 million tonnes a year, real estate in the city is undergoing a massive boom and its population is the fastest-growing in North America. Meanwhile, large amounts of energy and cash are being injected into the city's tourist sector as Vancouver prepares to host the 2010 Winter Olympics with nearby Whistler.

HISTORY

Early visitors

It is thought that Coast Indian tribes inhabited the area as early as 5000BC and developed a number of fishing communities. The first European to visit the site where Vancouver now stands was the Spanish sailor, José Navéz, in 1791. The following year the English explorer, Captain George Vancouver, made a fleeting one-day visit on his way to search for the North West Passage. The site was then largely ignored by Europeans until the 1858 Fraser River gold rush brought fortune-seekers to the area.

Gastown

Of these fortune-seekers, three intrepid Englishmen decided to stay and set up (rather curiously) a brickyard on the shore of the Burrard Inlet. The venture failed, but a more astute entrepreneur moved in to establish the highly successful Hastings Saw Mill. A small settlement soon sprang up and became known as Gastown after a garrulous local bar-owner named 'Gassy' Jack Deighton. In 1869 it was incorporated as a town under its official name of Granville, only to go up in flames later that year.

CPR terminus

The rapidly rebuilt Granville would probably have remained a small coastal town if it hadn't been for Van Horne's decision, on a visit to the area in 1884, to

Vancouver's Chinese immigrants

When Andrew Onderdonk began work on his section of the transcontinental rail line through the Fraser Valley, he knew he had a serious labour shortage on his hands. British Columbia's population was very small and Onderdonk needed at least 10,000 men. The solution was found in the large numbers of Chinese labourers in California who had worked on the Union Pacific Railway and were more than willing to come and work for Onderdonk at a cheaper rate than the locals. When still more workers were needed they were shipped over from Canton – between 1881 and 1885 more than 15,000 Chinese came to work on the railway.

Once the line was completed many of these stayed on to the disgust of British Columbians, who regarded the Chinese with contempt. In an attempt to curb immigration the Chinese 'head tax' imposed on new arrivals was increased to a drastic $100 in 1900. Two years later, as anti-Chinese feelings reached hysterical proportions, a Royal Commission on Chinese and Japanese Immigration produced a report which concluded that Asians were 'obnoxious to a free community and dangerous to the state' and, accordingly, 'unfit for full citizenship'.

In 1903 the head tax was raised to $500 and the Immigration Act of 1923 effectively banned Chinese immigration (the day the act was passed is known as 'Humiliation Day' by Canadian Chinese). Amazingly, it was not until 1947 that this appalling legislation was repealed, and it was not until 1967 that the final restrictions on Chinese immigration were removed.

make it the terminus of the new transcontinental railway instead of Port Moody (about 20km away). He also decided that Vancouver would be a more fitting name than Granville. Thus, Vancouver officially came into existence on 16 April 1886 and the first through train from Montreal arrived on 23 May the following year. The railway brought a massive boom to the town, which by the end of the century outstripped Victoria in size and commercial importance. Before long it had also replaced Winnipeg as the most important city in western Canada.

Vancouver today

Vancouver's commercial success has been built on its fishing, lumber and minerals industries and on its huge port which is today the largest on the west coast of North America. Most exports are bound for Asia and include wheat, timber, ore and cellulose. In little more than a hundred years Vancouver has grown from a tiny outpost to Canada's third-largest and fastest-growing city. Some 600,000 people live in the city proper, and over 2.1 million live in Greater Vancouver.

ARRIVING IN VANCOUVER

By air

Vancouver International Airport is 12km south of the city centre – about a 20-minute drive. From 6am until midnight an Airporter shuttle bus runs between the airport and a number of downtown hotels; there are three routes, so check with the driver which is best for your hotel. The bus departs from Level 2 of the airport and one-way tickets cost $13. The same ride by taxi will cost around $23–26.

> ❏ **Vancouver online**
> 🖥 **www.tourismvancouver.com** Tourism Vancouver's attractive site, with information on the city and day trips to the surrounding area.
>
> 🖥 **www.travel.bc.ca** A look at the whole province with Tourism British Columbia. Emails can be sent to 🖥 snbc-res@sympatico.ca.

By rail
Trains arrive at the stately Pacific Central Station in a slightly insalubrious corner of town. It's a bit of a walk from downtown but is directly linked to the centre by the Sky Train (Vancouver's fully automated light-rail transit – fares are $2.25 or $8 for a day-pass). Otherwise there are plenty of taxis at the station (about $10 to downtown).

GETTING AROUND

Local transport is operated by BC Transit (☎ 604-953-3333, 🖥 www.translink. bc.ca). In addition to their vast network of buses they run a **ferry service** (known as the SeaBus) across the Burrard Inlet between downtown and North Vancouver, and the state-of-the-art driverless **Sky Train** between Vancouver and the suburb of Surrey. Single zone fares are $2.25 for all three modes of transport. You can buy day passes for $8, available at many convenience stores, the Vancouver Tourist InfoCentre and the SeaBus terminal and SkyTrain station. BC Transit produces an excellent free pocket guide which tells you how to get to all Vancouver's attractions by public transport; pick it up in the Vancouver Touristinfo Centre.

You can hire **bikes** and **rollerblades** from a number of rental outlets around the corner of Denman and Georgia, including Spokes Bicycle Rental & Espresso Bar (☎ 604-688-5141) and Bikes 'n' Blades at 718 Denman St (☎ 604-602-9899). For **taxis** try Black Top Cabs (☎ 604-731-1111) or Yellow Cabs (☎ 604-681-1111)

ORIENTATION

Downtown Vancouver sits on a small peninsula framed by Burrard Inlet to the north and False Creek to the south. Stanley Park covers the western tip and the city centre pretty much fills the rest of the peninsula, spilling south onto the other side of False Creek. The main downtown artery is Robson St; the focal point of the waterfront is Canada Place. Be sure to avoid Hastings St East, Vancouver's skid row and certainly not a safe place to be after dark.

SERVICES

Tourist information
The excellent **Vancouver Touristinfo Centre** (☎ 604-683-2000, 🖥 www.touris mvancouver.org) is on the Plaza Level at 200 Burrard St, close to the waterfront. As well as providing the usual information the office has a foreign exchange and accommodation booking service. It's open daily 8.30am–6pm.

Money

There's no shortage of downtown banks, with a cluster around Georgia at Burrard and Howe. Foreign exchange offices include American Express at 1040 West Georgia St, International Foreign Exchange at 1169 Robson St, Custom House Currency Exchange at 375 Water St and Thomas Cook Foreign Exchange at Suite 130, 999 Canada Place.

Consulates

Austria (☎ 604-683-5808) Suite 1380, 200 Granville St
Belgium (☎ 604-684-6838) Suite 570, 688 West Hastings
Britain (☎ 604-683-4421) Suite 800, 1111 Melville St
Denmark (☎ 604-684-5171) Suite 755, 777 Hornby St
Finland (☎ 604-688-4483) 1100–1188 West Georgia St
France (☎ 604-681-2301) Suite 1100, 1130 West Pender St
Germany (☎ 604-684-4258) Suite 704, 999 Canada Place
Ireland (☎ 604-683-9233) Suite 1400, 100 West Pender St
Italy (☎ 604-684-7288) Suite 705, 1200 Burrard St
Japan (☎ 604-684-5868) Suite 900, 1177 West Hastings St
Netherlands (☎ 604-684-6448) Suite 821, 475 Howe St
New Zealand (☎ 604-684-7388) Suite 1200, 888 Dunsmuir St
Norway (☎ 604-682-7977) Suite 1200, 200 Burrard St
Sweden (☎ 604-683-5838) Suite 1100, 1188 West Georgia St
Switzerland (☎ 604-684-2231) Suite 790, 999 Canada Place
USA (☎ 604-685-4311) 1095 West Pender St

Post, internet and laundry

Vancouver's main **post office** is 349 West Georgia. The cheapest **internet access**, at just $1.50 per hour, is at 119 Computer World, just around the corner from the HI Hostel at 1221 Thurlow St. You'll also find internet access at Kinko's Copies & Internet (open 24 hours a day) at 789 West Pender; Lingo Cyberbistro at 547 Seymour St; and Websters Internet Café at 340 Robson St.

The most central downtown **laundries** are Davie Laundromat at 1061 Davie St (on the corner with Thurlow) and The Clothesline Laundry at 1070 Davie St.

WHERE TO STAY

Budget accommodation

Vancouver boasts three HI hostels (🖳 www.hihostels.ca). The excellent *HI Vancouver Downtown Hostel* (☎ 604-684-4565) is at 1114 Burnaby St in a quiet, leafy corner of town. Beds are in small shared rooms for up to four people, with single-sex bathrooms on each floor. One of the highlights of staying here is the free continental breakfast served each morning between 8am and 9.15am, consisting of bagels, cereals, fresh fruit and juices. A dorm bed costs between $23.50 and $26.50 for members and $27.50 and $30.50 for non-members, and there are a few private en-suite doubles at $55 for members and $64 for non-members; free linen and towels are included in the price. The new *HI Vancouver Central Hostel* (☎ 604-685-5335) at 1025 Granville St has an even

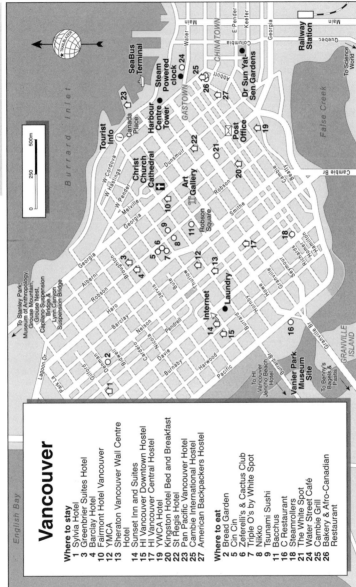

Vancouver

Where to stay
1 Sylvia Hotel
3 Greenbrier Suites Hotel
4 Barclay Hotel
10 Fairmont Hotel Vancouver
12 YMCA
13 Sheraton Vancouver Wall Centre Hotel
14 Sunset Inn and Suites
15 HI Vancouver Downtown Hostel
17 HI Vancouver Central Hostel
19 YWCA Hotel
20 Kingston Hotel Bed and Breakfast
22 St Regis Hotel
23 Pan Pacific Vancouver Hotel
25 Cambie International Hostel
27 American Backpackers Hostel

Where to eat
2 Bread Garden
5 Cin Cin
6 Zeferelli's & Cactus Club
7 Triple O's by White Spot
8 Nikko
9 Tsunami Sushi
11 Bacchus
16 C Restaurant
18 Steamrollers
21 The White Spot
24 Water Street Café
25 Cambie Grill
26 Bakery & Afro-Canadian Restaurant

❏ Accommodation prices quoted in this book are for **high season** (normally May or June to September). In low season many hotels offer substantial discounts.

more central location, though it's consequently less leafy and peaceful. The hostel does, however, offer a free shuttle service to and from the train station and organizes a weekly pub crawl every Monday night in association with the HI Downtown hostel. Rates are the same as in HI Downtown, with continental breakfast included in the price.

The original *HI Vancouver Jericho Beach Hostel* (☎ 604-224-3208), at 1515 Discovery St, is a little more basic but the location, right by Jericho beach, is fantastic. Beds here are $20 for members and $24 for non-members; to get there take the No 4 bus from Granville St.

Centrally located at 300–310 Cambie St, in the historic Gastown area, *Cambie International Hostel* (☎ 604-684-6466, 🖳 www.cambiehostels.com) is one of three Cambie hostels in Vancouver and Vancouver Island. With dorm beds from $20 and a few private rooms available for $54 (or $61 with a private bathroom), the hostel offers clean rooms, laundry facilities and a free coffee and muffin each morning from the bakery next door.

A little scruffy but very cheap is the *American Backpackers Hostel* (☎ 604-688-0112, 🖳 www.ameribackpackers.com) at 347 Pender St where dorm beds cost a mere $10, single rooms $25 and double rooms $35. Though not in as inviting an area as the other hostels, the rates are certainly appealing if you're travelling on a tight budget.

Mid-range hotels

Definitely more hotel than hostel, the immaculate *YWCA Hotel* (☎ 604-895-5830, 🖳 www.ywcahotel.com), at 733 Beatty St, has a range of rooms, from singles with shared bathrooms for $64 right up five-bed rooms with private bathroom for $155 (a double with private bath costs $119). The YWCA has its own cosy coffee shop, internet and laundry facilities and there's air conditioning and mini fridges in all the rooms. More old-fashioned but great value is the *Kingston Hotel Bed and Breakfast* (☎ 604-684-9024, 🖳 www.kingstonhotelvancouver.com), at 757 Richard St, which styles itself as a European-type B&B. Its rooms are cheerful and well maintained, with singles from $55 (shared bath) and doubles from $65 (shared bath). Continental breakfast is included and other facilities include sauna, coin-operated laundry and a secure underground car park.

For a step up in comfort, the *St Regis Hotel* (☎ 604-681-1135, 🖳 www.stre gishotel.com), at 602 Dunsmuir St, is another good choice, with smart standard rooms ranging from $129 to $169, including breakfast. A similar establishment, the *Barclay Hotel* (☎ 604-688-8850, 🖳 www.barclayhotel.com) is excellently located at 1348 Robson St, seconds from the shops and cafés and a short walk to Stanley Park. It has pleasant rooms at fair rates, with singles/doubles from $75/$95. Across the road at No 1393, on the corner with Broughton, is the newly renovated *Greenbrier Suites* (☎ 604-683-4558, 🖳 www.greenbrierhotel.com), with spacious self-catering apartments, all with kitchenettes and full bathrooms, from $129 in high season – some with lovely views across the harbour.

With similar rates, the *Sunset Inn and Suites* (☎ 604-688-2474, 🖳 www.sunsetinn.com) is another apartment-hotel, this time in peaceful, leafy Burnaby St at number 1111. Rooms range from standard studio suites with full kitchen, dining area, wireless internet access and private bathroom (from $129) to large one-bedroom suites with balconies (starting at $159). Down at English Bay, a stone's throw from the beach, *Sylvia Hotel* at 1154 Gilford St (☎ 604-681-9321, 🖳 www.sylviahotel.com) is a charming, ivy-covered hotel offering pleasant rooms from $109 to $179, depending on size.

Upmarket hotels

Vancouver's most flamboyant place to stay is undoubtedly the five-diamond *Sheraton Vancouver Wall Centre Hotel* (☎ 604-331-1000, 🖳 www.sheratonvancouver.com). This 35-storey building is sheathed in glass from top to bottom; each of the 744 rooms has floor to ceiling windows that can be opened and $300,000 worth of BC art is scattered around the building. It's at 1088 Burrard St and standard high-season rates range between $259 to $299, though 'Super Saver' rates are sometimes available and there are often discounts if you book online. The hotel features a jazzy restaurant called Indigo where guests are seated on chairs individually draped with different colours of the rainbow. Another glitzy five-diamond job is the *Pan Pacific Vancouver Hotel* (☎ 604-662-8111, 🖳 www.vancouver.panpacific.com) down in Canada Place, with spectacular waterfront views and an elevated reception area on the 3rd floor (which you reach by escalator). There's a wonderful, airy atmosphere to the building; high-season rates start at $510 for a city view and $560 for a harbour view.

On a more traditional note, the beautifully refined *Fairmont Hotel Vancouver* (☎ 604-684-3131, 🖳 www.fairmont.com) can be found at 900 West Georgia St, at the corner with Burrard. Opened in 1933 for the arrival of King George V and Queen Elizabeth I, who stayed here while in Vancouver, this old CPR railway hotel is now a heritage building and is one of the most elegant establishments in the city. As well as a large indoor pool, a charming lounge (where 'high tea' is served between 2pm and 4pm) and stylish bedrooms, the Fairmont Hotel Vancouver even has its own mascot in the friendly form of Mavis the dog, who can often be seen wandering around the reception area. Rates can be anywhere between $250 and $400.

WHERE TO EAT

Vancouver offers a huge choice of places to eat, from dirt cheap to super-extravagant, and the number of people who eat out ensures that there's usually a lively atmosphere in the majority of them.

Most popular and common is Asian food (particularly Chinese, Japanese, Vietnamese and Korean) and 'West Coast' cuisine, which is a sort of fusion between Asian and Mediterranean food, with an emphasis on fresh, locally available produce and beautiful presentation.

Budget food

A good spot for a quick lunch is *Steamrollers* at 437 Davie, a tiny place with a take-away counter and a sit-down bar serving steamed burritos and a selection of tasty wraps for under $10.

Also good for lunch are the many sushi bars around town: a couple to try are *Tsunami Sushi* at 1025 Robson, where diners choose their food from a con-veyor belt in front of their seats (a plate of mixed sushi here costs around $10), and *Nikko*, over the road at No 1008, which does enormous lunch boxes for similar prices.

A little bit too close to the seedy part of town but worth hunting out is the *Cambie Grill*, below the hostel of the same name at 300 Cambie St. Claiming to be Vancouver's oldest pub, it's a real spit-and-sawdust place with cheap, fill-ing bar food. Next door there's a good bakery selling sandwiches and salads and, further along at No 324, you'll find the *Afro-Canadian Restaurant*, with healthy meals, including some great African dishes, for around $10.

Healthy, attractive food is also on offer at the *Bread Garden* chain of local sit-down delis; branches include 1040 Denman St and 812 Bute St, both of which stay open until midnight through the week and until 2am at the weekend. Rather more predictable but very filling food is available at *The White Spot*, a popular local chain with a large branch at Georgia 580, serving burgers, milkshakes, sand-wiches and grills. A friendly diner complete with 'Guys' and 'Gals' toilets and owned by White Spot is *Triple O's by White Spot* at 803 Thurlow St. Breakfast dishes and burgers are around $3–6 and you can enjoy your meal whilst humming along to classic Fifties and Sixties tunes playing on the jukebox. Great fun.

Enjoying a choice location at 2503 West Broadway, with a patio looking onto English Bay beach, is *Benny's Bagels*, a pleasant place for sandwiches, 'melts' and bagels by the ocean – but be warned that it gets busy and you may have to wait awhile to get served.

Mid-range and upmarket restaurants

Milestones is a very popular mid-priced local chain serving fairly standard meat, fish and pasta dishes in colourful surroundings; there are downtown branches at 1145 Robson and 1210 Denman, which both get packed out on Friday and Saturday nights. There's a proliferation of restaurants along Robson St, one of the best being *Cin Cin* at No 1154, serving Italian/West Coast (and rather pricey) food in a rustic-style dining room with a lovely outside terrace. *Zeferelli's*, nearby at No 1136, is also 'West Coast' and very good. A cheaper option is the *Cactus Club Café* below Zeferelli's; it's very lively and the Tex/Mex menu isn't bad at all. Gastown's another place with plenty of eating spots, including *Water Street Café* (mains around $15–18) with its very pleas-ant outdoor terrace which looks onto the steam clock.

Vancouver's high-end restaurants are well worth a splurge. One of the best in the city is *C Restaurant* (☎ 604-681-1164) at 1600 Howe St, looking across the water to Granville Island. As well as lovely views, it boasts a stylish, mini-malist interior, a buzzing crowd and superb seafood – try the grilled octopus with foie gras, or Alaskan sable fish. Another first-rate restaurant is award-winning

Pastis, a short cab ride from downtown at 2153 West 4th Ave (☎ 604-731-5020) which specializes in southern French cuisine. Diners are greeted with a pastis cocktail when they arrive and the atmosphere manages to be both informal and classy. Centrally located *Bacchus* (☎ 604-608-5319) at 845 Hornby St is definitely a place for dinner rather than lunch, with its dark corners and low lighting. The choice of food is agonizing, ranging from 'risotto of saffron and blueshell mussels' to 'pine-nut and parsley crusted rack of lamb'. For a post-dinner digestif, the adjoining bar is one of the most appealing in town.

Finally, mention must be made of those restaurants that boast outstanding views. *Top of Vancouver* (☎ 604-669-2220), the 167-metre-high, revolving restaurant at the Harbour Centre, is undeniably touristy but you're unlikely to care when you can look across your dinner plate to a range of snow-capped mountains rising from the ocean. Most mains here are in the $20–35 range; diners don't have to pay for the ride up in the elevator.

Grouse Nest (☎ 604-980-9311), at the top of Grouse Mountain (see p179), boasts superb views and is the sort of place where marriage proposals are regularly made. The most romantic place to sit is the smaller, corner room attached to the main dining room; you can request (but aren't guaranteed) a window seat when you reserve. The prices are fairly reasonable for such a privileged location (main dishes from $20 to $35) and those with a dinner reservation get a free ride up in the cable car.

NIGHTLIFE

Vancouver's nightlife scene is extremely lively, offering a huge choice of bars, pubs, live music, jazz venues, nightclubs and much more. Among the current favourites, *La Bodega* at 1277 Howe (near Davie) is a colourful tapas bar with great sangria and Spanish and Latin music.

On Granville Island at 1585 Johnston, *The Arts Club Theatre Backstage Lounge* makes a more mellow alternative, with live blues and jazz at the weekend and views across the water. A couple of upmarket, stylish places for a drink are *Gerard's* at 845 Burrard, featuring lots of dark wood and leather armchairs, and *Bacchus* at 845 Hornby, which has a roaring fire when the weather turns chilly. Both places have live piano music at the weekend and are popular with a slightly older, professional crowd. A little younger and rowdier is the *Yaletown Brewing Company* at 1111 Mainland St, a large pub-restaurant which brews its own beer on the premises.

The self-proclaimed oldest pub in Vancouver, *The Cambie*, at 300 Cambie St, is very rustic and always busy night and day. For live music, one of the most enduringly popular venues is *The Railway Club* at 579 Dunsmuir (at Seymour), which puts on a different act (from folk to rock to jazz) every night except Sunday, when there's a movie showing instead. Among the city's nightclubs, you could try the eternally popular *Luv-a-Fair* at 1275 Seymour (at Davie) or the hyper-trendy *Mars* at 1320 Richards.

WHAT TO SEE

Vancouver is a relaxing place to spend time in. It's not packed full of museums and obligatory sights. The best thing to do here is just wander round and take in the atmosphere in the city's many 'people's places' (to use Vancouver-speak).

A fun way to get a quick overview of the city is to take a tour aboard one of the Vancouver Trolley Company's replica turn-of-the-century trolley buses. The tours take in 24 stops, including Gastown, Chinatown and Stanley Park, and as tickets are 'hop-on/hop-off', you can jump off at any point along the way and then join the tour again later on in the day, with trolleys running every 20 minutes. Tickets ($33) can be purchased from drivers or at the ticket booth in Gastown (157 Water St), and are valid for two consecutive days; for more information contact ☎ 604-801-5515 or 🖥 www.vancouvertrolley.com.

Robson St to English Bay

Another good way to get a feel for the city is to take a walk down Robson, starting at Robson Square. Nicknamed 'Rodeo Drive of the North', it's Vancouver's liveliest street and is lined with clothes boutiques, bookstores, record shops, cafés and restaurants. By night it's packed with young people out on the town.

If you turn left off Robson down Denman (more cafés and restaurants) you'll end up at English Bay Beach. The views from here are lovely and it's a very relaxing place to go and lie with a book in summer. The walk to English Bay from Robson Square takes about half an hour; the No 5 bus follows the same route.

Vancouver Art Gallery

Close to Robson Square, the Vancouver Art Gallery (🖥 www.vanartgallery. bc.ca) is well laid-out and worth a visit. The highlight of the permanent display is the excellent collection of works by Emily Carr, whose swirling greens and blues depict the landscape and Indian communities of the West Coast. There's also an extensive collection of contemporary visual art, with contributions from Stan Douglas and Ian Wallace to name just two. Otherwise, the museum is given over mainly to temporary exhibitions, either visiting or from the gallery's own collection.

Located at 750 Hornby St, the Vancouver Art Gallery is open 10am–5.30pm Monday, Wednesday and Friday–Sunday, and 10am–9pm on Tuesday and Thursday. Entrance is $15 (with pay-as-you-wish on Tuesday 5–9pm).

Christ Church Cathedral

Should Vancouver's busy streets become too much, there are a number of downtown churches where you can gather your thoughts and enjoy some peace and quiet. Close to the Vancouver Art Gallery at 690 Burrard St, Christ Church Cathedral was built as an Anglican church in 1888 and features 32 beautiful stained glass windows, a magnificent cedar ceiling and a most impressive organ. It sits just across from the Fairmont Hotel Vancouver and was attended by King George and Queen Elizabeth during their visit to Vancouver in 1933. As well as holding services throughout the week, it opens to visitors from 10am to 4pm from Monday to Friday, with extended hours at weekends during the summer (Saturdays 9.30am–12.30pm, Sundays 12.30–5pm).

Canada Place and Harbour Centre Tower

Canada Place, down by the waterfront, was built as the pavilion for Expo '86. The complex, with its roof of billowing sails, was designed to resemble a large ship and is worth visiting if just for its excellent vantage point over the harbour.

You can get an even better view, though you have to pay $11 for it, from the 177-metre-high observation platform at the nearby **Harbour Centre Tower** (🖳 www.vancouverlookout.com) at 555 West Hastings St. On clear evenings the views over the surrounding mountains, streaked with pink, are absolutely stunning. The tower is open daily 8.30am–10.30pm from May to mid-October and 9am–9pm for the rest of the year (last ride up 20 minutes before closing time).

Gastown

Named after 19th-century entrepreneur 'Gassy Jack', whose nickname derives from his talkative nature rather than his digestive system, Vancouver's oldest quarter was given a huge facelift in the 1970s and today is one of the most popular spots in town. With its cobbled streets lined with gift shops and cafés, Gastown is shamelessly tourist-orientated but it's a lively, fun place to take a stroll, especially Water St, the core of the area. Not to be missed is the hilarious spectacle of tourist crowds silently waiting – breath held, cameras poised – for the **steam-powered clock** on Water St to start chiming and hissing vapour, which it obligingly does every 15 minutes.

Another Gastown highlight was the excellent Storyeum (🖳 www.storyeum. com) at 142 Water St, which recounted Vancouver's history with the help of singing, dancing and lots of audience participation, until it ran out of funds and closed its doors in late 2006. It's seeking new sponsors, though, so it's definitely worth checking to see if it's reopened by the time you visit.

Chinatown

Chinatown is a frenetic tangle of streets packed with restaurants, markets, bakeries, herb shops and thousands of Chinese people. The main thoroughfares are Pender and Keefer streets (a 20-minute walk from Robson Square, or a short bus ride on the No 19 or 22 eastbound on Pender; if you're walking to Chinatown from Gastown, try to avoid crossing the rundown area of East Hastings St).

If the relentless bustle gets too much for you, the **Dr Sun Yat-Sen Classical Chinese Garden** (🖳 www.vancouverchinesegarden.com) will sort you out. Modelled on the Ming Dynasty gardens in the city of Suzhou and incorporating the Taoist philosophy of yin and yang, the garden is an oasis of harmony and tranquillity. In summer, live Chinese music is often performed in the gardens; for information call ☎ 604-662-3207. It's located at 578 Carrall St, next to the Chinese Cultural Centre. Entrance is $8.75 and opening hours are daily 10am–6pm May to mid-June, 9.30am–7pm mid-June to late August and 10am–4.30pm October to April (closed on Mondays between November and May). Tea and a 45-minute tour are included in the price of the ticket.

Science World

A few blocks south of the Chinese Gardens, near the train station at 1455 Quebec St, this fascinating centre (🖳 www.scienceworld.bc.ca) is full of hands-on exhibits allowing you to crawl through a beaver lodge among other things. It's also home to the world's largest Omnimax Dome cinema. Entrance to the

---

🚂 VISITING VICTORIA, VANCOUVER ISLAND

It would be a great shame to visit Vancouver and not take the opportunity to travel across to beautiful Vancouver Island, only a one-and-a-half-hour ferry ride away. **Victoria**, its biggest city and the capital of British Columbia, sits on the south coast of the island and can easily be visited as a day-trip. An important British centre during colonial times, it still sports the air of an old-fashioned English seaside town, with its quaint streets, genteel tearooms and fine Victorian architecture – a fact the tourist industry exploits to the full. Commercialism aside, Victoria's laidback ambience and picturesque setting make it a very enjoyable place to visit.

Getting there
BC Ferries (☎ 250-381-1401, 🖳 www.bcferries.com) operates frequent crossings from Vancouver's Tsawwassen dock to Swartz Bay near Victoria; tickets cost $11 each way for foot passengers. To get to the ferry terminal from downtown Vancouver take the 98B bus from the corner of Howe and Davie to the Airport station and then the No 620 bus to Tsawwassen dock (the bus fare is $4.50 weekdays or $2.25 at weekends; make sure you ask for a three-zone transfer). The bus ride to the terminal will take about 1 hour 30 minutes and then the ferry crossing is a further 1 hour 35 minutes. When you get to Vancouver Island, pick up the No 70 bus from the ferry terminal to downtown Victoria, which takes about an hour to reach (the bus fare is just under $9).

A simpler option, you could take a coach tour: Pacific Coach Lines (☎ 604-662-8074, 🖳 www.pacificcoach.com) do great deals, with hourly departures during summer. Tickets cost $34.50 single, $67 return, including the ferry crossing – buy tickets in advance at Pacific Central Station, or from the bus driver when you board.

Tourist information
Tourism Victoria's **Visitor Centre** (☎ 250-953-2033, 🖳 www.tourismvictoria.com) is centrally located on the harbourfront at 812 Wharf St. It's open daily, from May to September 8.30am–8.30pm and for the rest of the year 9am–5pm.

Where to stay
You could easily visit Victoria as a day-trip from Vancouver but if you want to spend the night here there's plenty of accommodation to choose from. The best budget option is the *HI Victoria Hostel* at 516 Yates St (☎ 250-385-4511, 🖳 www.hihostels. ca), five minutes from the waterfront in a great downtown location. Dorm beds start at $18 for members and $22 for non-members, with a few private en-suite rooms available as well ($48–58).

If you'd prefer to pull out all the stops and spend an evening in total luxury then there's only one place to do it: *The Fairmont Empress*, overlooking the harbour at 721 Government St (☎ 250-384-8111, 🖳 www.fairmont.com). With its beautiful gardens and ivy-covered exterior, it certainly is an impressive building; high-season rooms go for around $450. If you can't afford to stay here, then drop by for **afternoon tea** instead (noon onwards; from $26) and you'll be treated to an exquisite selection of sandwiches, scones and clotted cream. Reservations are required so be sure to book ahead on ☎ 250-389-2727. *(Continued on p176)*

❏ **VISITING VICTORIA, VANCOUVER ISLAND**   (*continued from p175*)

Where to eat
Victoria has some great restaurants, bars and cafés, many of them very reasonably priced. All you really need to do is wander along by the harbour and see what takes your fancy. A firm local favourite, sitting right on the harbour at 500 Fort St, is *The Keg*, with a lively atmosphere and delicious steaks. Alternatively, at 555 Johnson St, two streets up from the wharf and directly behind Willie's Bakery, *Il Terrazzo* offers affordable Italian cuisine with a fantastic outdoor patio.

What to see
One of the most popular activities on Vancouver Island is **whale-watching**, with a number of companies offering excursions, such as The Prince of Whales (☎ 250-383-4884, or toll-free 1-888-383-4884, 🖳 www.princeofwhales.com) on the harbourfront, directly below the Visitor Centre. Three-hour trips cost from $85 but it's worth every penny – there's nothing quite like being a few metres away from a pod of orcas (though sightings are not guaranteed), and you'll also get to see sea lions and seals.

Back on dry land, the most appealing thing to do is just wander around the **harbourfront** and **Old Town** area, and soak up the atmosphere. Of the individual attractions, the three stand-outs are the Royal British Columbia Museum, the Parliament building and the out-of-town Butchart Gardens.

● **Royal BC Museum**
At 675 Belleville St, the Royal BC Museum (🖳 www.royalbcmuseum.bc.ca) takes you through British Columbia's history with a range of outstanding galleries and exhibits. Check out a replica of a section of Captain Vancouver's 18th-century ship, *HMS Discovery*; walk through a turn-of-the-20th-century town complete with silent movie-theatre, Chinatown alley and railway station; admire a series of native totem poles and ceremonial masks; and visit a First Nations longhouse and learn about shaman practices. The museum is open daily 9am–5pm (and until 10pm on Fridays and Saturdays from June to September); admission is $14.

● **Parliament Buildings**
An imposing edifice overlooking the harbour, Victoria's Parliament Buildings was designed by a 25-year old architect in 1893 in honour of Queen Victoria's sixtieth year on the throne. Completed in 1915, the stately domed building was the subject of much controversy due to its hefty construction costs. Today, the Parliament Buildings are open to the public for regular tours led by staff in period costume, with a visit from a youthful 'Queen Victoria' herself. Tours are free and take place every 30 minutes in the summer between 9am and 5pm, with the last tour leaving at 4.30pm. The building is particularly striking at night when it's illuminated by hundreds of tiny light bulbs.

● **The Butchart Gardens**
Established in the early 20th century, what was originally a hobby for Jennie Butchart has today become a gardener's paradise attracting over a million visitors each year (🖳 www.butchartgardens.com). Located on an old limestone quarry, Jennie's 'Sunken Garden' is simply breathtaking with its stunning flowerbeds and different types of shrubs spreading out as far as the eye can see. In summer the gardens stay open late on Saturday nights and feature a fireworks display. The gardens are a forty-minute bus-ride from town; take the No 75 bus from downtown (Blanchard St at Fairfield). Opening hours are 9am–10.30pm from mid-June to early September and 9am–5pm for the rest of the year; entrance is $23.

centre is $14.50, or $19.50 with an Omnimax film thrown in. The building is open daily from 10am to 6pm; Omnimax hours change depending on what film is currently being shown.

Granville Island

Southwest of the downtown core, across False Creek, Granville Island was developed as an industrial site in 1915, largely to provide space for the railway yards of the Canadian Northern Railway and the Great Northern Railway. After years of disuse it received a handsome redevelopment package from the federal government in 1972 and was soon transformed into a colourful and lively centre of cafés, artists' workshops and boatyards. The area works much better than Gastown, partly due to the fact that it's as popular with locals as with tourists. While you're here, don't miss the lively Granville Market, packed with fresh vegetables, fruit and pasta and some delicious baked goods.

To get here by public transport, take either the No 50 bus south down Granville St or a ferry from False Creek Ferries' dock on Sunset Beach Park, at the southern end of Thurlow St (🖳 www.granvilleislandferries.bc.ca). Ferries run from 7am to 10.30pm in high season and single tickets are $2.50. Alternatively, the Vancouver Trolley stops off here (see p173).

Vanier Park museum site

Close to Granville Island, the Vanier Park museum site is home to three of the city's main museums: the Vancouver Museum, the HR Macmillan Space Centre and the Maritime Museum. The grounds are very pretty and there's an attractive coast path leading from the park to **Kitsilano Beach**. To get there by bus, take the No 2 or 22 from Burrard St and get off at the first stop after the bridge, or you can take a False Creek Ferry (see above). If you're travelling on the Vancouver Trolley, there's a designated stop at the museum site.

● **The Vancouver Museum** Concentrating on local history, this museum (🖳 www.vanmuseum.bc.ca) takes you through the city's initial settlement and later development with exhibits ranging from clothes and canoes to photographs and replicas of turn-of-the-20th-century shops. The displays are well presented and the accompanying text is thoughtfully written but the museum has a very parochial air to it and is, on the whole, a bit disappointing.

The museum is open daily 10am–5pm (Thursdays till 9pm); closed Mondays from September to June. Entrance is $10.

● **HR Macmillan Space Centre** The centre (🖳 www.spacecentre.ca) combines flight-simulators and displays on space exploration with a planetarium specializing in astronomy and rock laser shows (for showing times call ☎ 604-738-7827; tickets cost $14 for adults and $10.75 for children). It also has an observatory next door where you can look at the stars under the guidance of astronomers.

● **Vancouver Maritime Museum** In addition to the usual wooden models and old photos, the Vancouver Maritime Museum (🖳 www.vancouvermaritimemuseum.com) is home to the *St Roch* – a gem of an exhibit. This two-masted arctic patrol ship, built in 1928, was only the second vessel to navigate the treacherous North West Passage and the first to do it in both directions; there are guided tours around the ship every half hour. In recent years the museum has acquired more fascinating artefacts, such as the clock from *HM Bark Resolute*, one of six ships that went in search of Sir John Franklin when he went missing in the mid-19th century (see p223). From May to September the museum is open daily 10am–5pm and for the rest of the year the hours are: Tuesday to Saturday 10am–5pm and Sunday noon to 5pm; entrance is $10.

Stanley Park

Visit Stanley Park and you begin to see why Vancouverites look so happy: they have a thousand acres of green space on their doorstep to unwind in. Situated on the tip of a peninsula, most of the park is surrounded by ocean.

You can walk all the way round its edge on the 10km seawall promenade or take a free bus on the road running parallel. From the eastern side are excellent views over Vancouver's downtown skyline and from the west are equally fine views of the mountains looming over West Vancouver across the Burrard Inlet. To get to Stanley Park, take the No 19 bus from West Pender St (at Burrard).

Points of interest to look out for include: the **Lost Lagoon**, home to Canada geese, ducks and swans; a collection of magnificent **totem poles**; **Prospect Point** (excellent views) and the **Hollow Tree**, an incredible red cedar thought to be up to 1000 years old, with a circumference that would take three or four adults holding hands to circle it. Another highlight is the beautiful **Rose Gardens** featuring an array of immaculate flowerbeds filled with different types of roses.

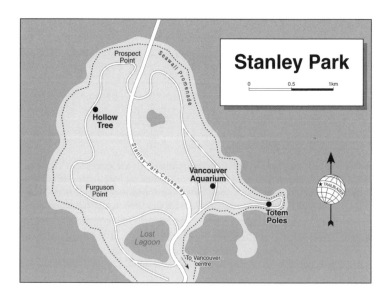

Stanley Park

Also inside the park is the excellent **Vancouver Aquarium** (🖳 www.vanaqua. org). Entrance is a steep $18.50 (seniors and students $13.95) but with 8000 marine species represented, including sea otters, beluga whales, sea lions and sharks, it's a fascinating place. There's also the opportunity to book either a Trainer Tour or a Beluga Tour which allows you to get up close and personal with whales and sea otters (call ahead on ☎ 604-659-3474). The aquarium is open daily 9.30am–7pm during July and August and 10am–5.30pm for the rest of the year.

UBC Museum of Anthropology

Located out of town on the university campus, this outstanding museum (☎ 604-822-3825, 🖳 www.moa.ubc.ca) is well worth the trip. Its modern, award-winning buildings house a vast collection of artefacts with an emphasis on cultures of BC's Pacific Coast Natives. Exhibits include masks, jewellery, textiles, ivory carvings and a fine collection of totem poles. Particularly arresting is *The Raven and the First Men*, an enormous cedar sculpture designed by Haida artist Bill Reid.

In summer (mid-May to early September) the museum is open daily 10am–5pm and on Tuesdays until 9pm; outside these months it's open Wednesdays to Sundays 11am–5pm, Tuesdays 11am–9pm. Entrance is $9 (free on Tuesday evenings between 5pm and 9pm).

To get to the museum take the southbound No 4 or 10 bus from Granville to its final stop near the campus.

Grouse Mountain and Capilano Suspension Bridge

Rising up from North Vancouver, just across Burrard Inlet, the 1250-metre summit of **Grouse Mountain** can be easily reached by the Skyride cable car, giving sweeping views for miles around. The ride up is exhilarating but very expensive at $29.95 although your ticket does include a number of different activities from ice skating and sleigh rides in the winter to visits to a Refuge for Endangered Wildlife in the summer. Admission to Grouse Mountain is free with advance dinner reservations at the restaurant at the top (well worth considering; see p172). Alternatively you can hike up the thigh-killing Grouse Grind trail in about one and a half to two hours, and in winter (November to April) you can ski down. To get to Grouse Mountain, take the SeaBus across to Lonsdale Quay and then bus No 236. Opening hours are 9am–10pm 365 days a year.

The same bus also passes the entrance to the 137-metre-long **Capilano Suspension Bridge** (☎ 604-985-7474, 🖳 www.capbridge.com) which wobbles precariously over a narrow gorge and river some 70m below. Crossing the bridge certainly gets your heart pounding but you have to pay a staggering $25.95 (students $7.95, seniors $10.75) for the thrill (prices are slightly cheaper at $21.95 from November to early May); note that a ticket up Grouse Mountain gets you $1.50 off the entrance to the bridge. Entrance to the Capilano Suspension Bridge also includes some interesting pathways through surrounding woodland and you have the opportunity to head up into the trees and amble along a series of raised walkways, known as the **Treetop Adventure**. The bridge is open daily 8.30am to 8pm from late May to early September and 9am–5pm for the rest of the year.

Lynn Canyon Suspension Bridge and Park

A more economical alternative to the Capilano Suspension Bridge is the very similar Lynn Canyon Suspension Bridge (🖳 www.lynncanyonparkguide.bc.ca), which is free, and a 20-minute bus ride (No 229) from Lonsdale Quay. An added bonus of visiting this bridge is the adjoining 617 acres of walking trails in lush forest. The park is open 7am–9pm in summer, 7am–7pm in spring/autumn, and 7am–6pm in winter.

FESTIVALS

● **International Dragon Boat Festival**, late June. Lively three-day event featuring boat races, music and theatre shows.
● **International Jazz Festival**, late June to early July. Balmy summer evenings of jazz and blues – a highly pleasurable festival (🖳 www.jazzvancouver.com).
● **Firework competition**, early August. A sponsored music and firework extravaganza.
● **International Comedy Festival**, early August. Usually has an excellent line-up; great location, too, on Granville Island.
● **Vancouver Fringe Festival**, usually first two weeks in September. Excellent range of material encompassing drama, comedy, dance and musicals. Very popular.

MOVING ON

By rail

The Canadian leaves Vancouver's Pacific Central Station for Toronto on Tuesdays, Fridays and Sundays; the journey takes three days and three nights. You can get to the station from downtown on the Sky Train, which terminates a few minutes' walk from the train station. Alternatively, a taxi should cost no more than about $10.

There's also an Amtrak connection from Vancouver to Seattle (☎ 1-888-842-7245) leaving from the same station.

The Rocky Mountaineer trains, on the other hand, leave from *The Rocky Mountaineer* station, a short distance away from the VIA station at 1755 Cottrell St, just off Terminal Avenue.

The Whistler Mountaineer leaves from North Vancouver station; passengers are taken there by shuttle bus from a number of downtown hotels.

By air

The Vancouver Airporter bus (☎ 604-946-8866) runs from the bus station inside the main train station as well as major downtown hotels to Vancouver International Airport. Note that you will be stung for an airport improvement fee when flying out of Vancouver: this is $5 for destinations within BC, and $15 if you're travelling outside North America.

Useful numbers include Air Canada: ☎ 604-689-0300 and American Airlines: ☎ 1-800-368-1955.

Churchill

History

There have been Inuit settlements in this area for thousands of years, though sadly there's little trace left of them today. The first Europeans arrived when the Danish navigator Jens Munk led an expedition in search of the North-West Passage (1619–20). Forced to winter his ship near the mouth of the Churchill River, out of a crew of 48 only he and two others survived.

Later, in 1717, the Hudson's Bay Company established a fur-trading post here which remained active for the next 150 years. To judge by the entry for 16 July in the journal of Captain James Knight, it was not a popular posting: 'I never did See such a Miserable Place in my Life'. When the post was no longer used, Churchill became virtually obsolete until the grain boom on the prairies at the beginning of the 20th century. Politicians and farmers campaigned for a port on Hudson Bay and eventually one was established at Churchill, connected to Winnipeg by the new railway line.

Churchill today

The town is as bleak as its sub-arctic surroundings but the residents are friendly and welcoming. Their hospitality, however, cannot mask the fact that there is a distinct feeling of dereliction about the place and unemployment is fairly high amongst its 1000-strong population, especially among the natives. Churchill's principal attraction is its wildlife, especially the polar bears that gather close to town in October while waiting for Hudson Bay to freeze over. But once you've visited the Eskimo Museum, there's very little to do in the town itself.

Tourist information

The railway station houses a small **tourist information office** known as Parks Canada and is generally open 1pm–4.30pm, although staff are also there when *The Hudson Bay* arrives on Tuesday and Friday mornings.

Where to stay

Accommodation gets booked up very quickly (and prices rise sharply) during the wildlife seasons so you're advised to book ahead. Places to try include the friendly ***Seaport Hotel*** (☎ 204-675-8807; 🖳 www.seaporthotel.ca) at 299 Kelsey Boulevard, about 100 metres from the train station, which offers clean, comfortable rooms in a very central location. The hotel has its own fully licensed restaurant serving food throughout the day and there's also a complimentary airport shuttle service. Rooms range from $85 to $105.

Another popular hotel in town is the ***Polar Inn*** (☎ 204-675-8878; 🖳 www. polarinn.com), further along the road at number 153, which not only offers clean, comfortable guest rooms but also has kitchenette suites and one-bedroom apartments. Rates start from $98 to $135.

Just off Kelsey Boulevard, at 34 Franklin St, the *Tundra Inn* (☎ 1-800-265-8563; 🖥 www.tundrainn.com) is another friendly hotel with 31 spacious rooms. A continental breakfast is included between December and September and the hotel also has a fully licensed dining room serving great meals. Rates go from $95 to $195.

Where to eat
Despite the influx of tourists each autumn, Churchill has only a small selection of restaurants and cafés. The *Trader's Table Restaurant* (☎ 204-675-2141), at 124 Kelsey Blvd, has warm, filling fare, while *Gypsy's Bakery* is a popular café/restaurant that lies further along Kelsey Boulevard past the Seaport Hotel. If the cold weather gets too much, it's the perfect place to warm up over a cup of hot coffee and enjoy a home-baked pastry.

What to see
The main activities for visitors to Churchill are wildlife viewing and dogsled rides. The best months for wildlife:
● Polar bears: mid September to November.
● Beluga whales: mid June to August. Tours are expensive at around $80 but from the boats you'll also get to see **Fort Prince of Wales**, built in the 18th century and now a National Historic Site.
● Birds: April to June.
● Iceberg tours: June.
● Dogsled rides: November to May.

Other wildlife you might spot here includes arctic fox, ptarmigan, and caribou. If you visit between January and April you are also likely to see the **northern lights**, while botanists can enjoy the arctic wildflowers from late June to early August.

Local tour operators, most of whom offer a spread of activities, include:

● **Great White Bear Tours** (☎ 204-675-2781, 🖥 www.greatwhitebeartours. com).
● **Sea North Tours** (☎ 204-675-2195, 🖥 www.seanorthtours.com).
● **Tundra Buggy Tours** (☎ 204-675-2121 between 1 July and 30 November; ☎ 1-204-949-2050; 🖥 www.tundrabuggytours.com).
● **International Wildlife Adventures** (☎ 204-949-2050, or 1-800-593-8881, 🖥 www.wildlifeadventures.com)

Other places of interest in this small town include **St Paul's Anglican Church**, which overlooks Hudson's Bay and is popular with visitors due to a stained-glass window which was originally presented to the York Factory in 1887 by Lady Franklin in memory of her husband (see p223). The factory was the HBC's headquarters in the region and their main supply base and port. Founded in the late seventeenth century, it lay approximately 100km southeast of Churchill, and remained in operation right up to 1957. The site is now maintained by Parks Canada as a National Historic Site. The glass window remains in one piece despite being airlifted from the York Factory to Churchill in the

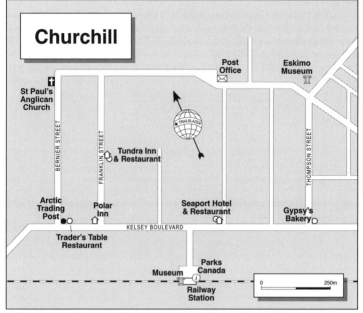

1960s. If you'd like to learn more about the Inuit in Canada then head to the **Eskimo Museum**, just off Kelsey Blvd at the end of Selkirk St. The museum has been around since 1944 and is filled with fascinating artifacts and a lifesize replica of a polar bear! The opening hours vary depending upon the time of year though it's always open 1–4.30pm from Monday to Saturday, year-round. You can buy good value souvenirs here.

The railway station also has its own fun **museum**, too, which is free and displays the history of Churchill and the York Factory. The staff are most helpful and can provide lots of information regarding the local wildlife.

Finally, if you'd like to take home something to remind yourself of northern Manitoba, head to the **Arctic Trading Post** on Kelsey Boulevard, a charming store with equally charming staff, selling everything from Inuit jewellery to furs to local crafts and produce.

MOVING ON

By rail
The Hudson Bay leaves Churchill on Tuesdays, Thursdays and Saturdays at 8.30pm, arriving at Winnipeg thirty-five and a half hours later (Thursdays, Saturdays and Mondays) at 8.05am.

By air

If you can't face the journey back by train, Calm Air International offers regular two-and-a-half-hour flights from Churchill to Winnipeg – currently three daily on week days and one daily on weekends, costing from around $680 per person (or from around $930 for a return ticket from Winnipeg to Churchill). For up-to-date schedules and prices check out ▭ www.calmair.com, or call them on ☎ 204-675-8858, or toll-free on 1-888-225-6247. There's no bus service to Churchill's airport but some hotels and tour companies offer a shuttle service; alternatively book a taxi with Churchill Taxi on ☎ 204-675-2345 (approximately $17).

PART 5: ROUTE GUIDE AND MAPS

Using this guide

You can follow your route on the strip maps in this guide and read about the points of interest along the way in the accompanying text.

Where something of interest is on only one side of the track, it is identified by the letters N (north), S (south), W (west) and E (east). Note that in some cases these compass directions are only approximate. Since the direction of travel from Toronto to Vancouver is due west, when you're on this journey north is on the right-hand side of the train.

Railway subdivisions

Each line is divided into subdivisions. These are usually about 125 miles long which was the average distance a steam train could travel in 12 hours when the railways were built. If you take the train all the way from Halifax to Vancouver, you'll pass through 20 subdivisions.

These are shown as —— **RAILWAY SUBDIVISION** —— in the text.

Mile markers

The mileage within each subdivision is indicated by mile markers at the side of the track. Subdivisions run from east to west or south to north, so Mile 0 will

---

❑ **Speed calculations**
You can work out how fast you're travelling by measuring the time it takes the train to get from one mile marker to the next one, then consulting this table.

Seconds	kph	mph	Seconds	kph	mph
36	170	100	80	72	45
38	153	95	85	68	42
40	145	90	90	64	40
42	138	86	95	61	38
44	132	82	100	58	36
46	126	78	105	55	34
48	121	75	110	53	33
50	116	72	115	50	31
52	111	69	120	48	30
54	108	67	130	45	28
56	103	64	150	39	24
58	100	62	160	37	23
60	96	60	170	34	21
65	88	55	210	27	17
70	82	51	240	24	15

> **Miles or kilometres?**
> While travelling through Canada you may well be struck by the odd mix-
> ture of kilometres and miles, feet and metres in use throughout the country.
> Conversion to the metric system from the British Imperial system began here in 1971
> and while the process is more or less complete, many traces of the old method of
> measurement remain. The result can be a little confusing; for instance, VIA's timeta-
> bles give all distances in kilometres, but the CN subdivisions are still broken down
> by miles and marked by mileposts at the side of the track.

always be at the eastern or southern terminal of a subdivision. When you reach
the end of a subdivision the next one begins. This is known as a railway divisional point and the miles go back to '0'. The mile markers are usually white
rectangular boards on metal posts or telegraph poles. They can be on either side
of the track.

Signal masts
You'll also notice numbers marked on signal masts along the way. You can
work out which mile you're at by inserting a decimal point before the last
digit. For instance, if the number on the signal mast is 562 that means you're
at Mile 56.2.

Station names
Of course the foolproof way to find out where you are is to look out for the
names of the stations you're passing. These are conveniently announced on
signposts a mile before each station. The names of sidings or junctions are often
displayed by the track as well.

Stops
Most of the stops are for only a few minutes, giving the crew just enough time
to whisk passengers on and off. Longer stops are always indicated in the
timetable and are shown in this guide in brackets after the station name. You'll
notice that some of the stops in the timetable have asterisks after them; these are
'flag stops' which means the train will stop here only when someone wants to
get on or off. Flag stops are also marked by an asterisk in this guide, eg
Clearwater*.

Time zones
Most of the routes described take you through at least two time zones; *The
Canadian* takes you through four. When you enter a new time zone this will be
indicated in the text using the following abbreviations: AT (Atlantic Time); ET
(Eastern Time); CT (Central Time); MT (Mountain Time); PT (Pacific Time).
See p43 for more on time zones.

ROUTE GUIDE & MAPS

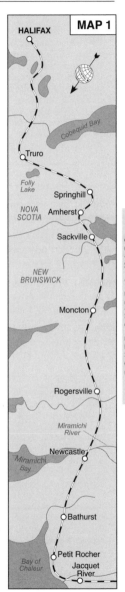

MAP 1

HALIFAX

Cobequid Bay

Truro

Folly
Lake

Springhill

NOVA
SCOTIA

Amherst

Sackville

NEW
BRUNSWICK

Moncton

Rogersville

Miramichi
River

Newcastle

Miramichi
Bay

Bathurst

Petit Rocher

Jacquet
River

Bay of
Chaleur

ROUTE GUIDE & MAPS

The Ocean:
Halifax to Montreal

The Ocean follows the meandering lines of the old
Intercolonial Railway; indeed the line loops around
so much, swinging off to tiny villages, that it was
said the contractors were paid by the mile.

It's a line with a history – the first passenger
train ran from Halifax to Lévis, opposite Quebec
City, back in 1876. The train following this route has
been known as *The Ocean* since 1904, making it the
longest-running service in Canada.

The line takes you through three provinces and
two time zones and, as you might expect, past a
good deal of water: you'll see plenty of lakes, har-
bours, bays and rivers, including the great St
Lawrence, which the train follows for a large portion of the journey. The trip from Halifax to
Montreal takes 19 hours.

[MAP 1]
Mile 0: Halifax [AT]   For a detailed guide to
Halifax, see pp69-81.

Mile 4 (S): The train passes **Fairview Cemetery**
where 125 victims of the *Titanic* tragedy are buried.
There's also a large common grave here for the
unidentified men and women who died in the
Halifax Explosion (see p79).

Mile 18–27: As you leave the city you move into a
landscape of spruce forest and lakes. Look east at
Mile 18 for a view of Kinsac Lake, and west
between Mile 24 and 27 for lovely views over
Shubenacadie Lake.

Mile 63: Truro There was an Acadian settlement
here as early as 1701 but these unfortunate people
were forced to make way for New England settlers in
1755. Since then it's become a major railway centre
and a thriving farming, lumbering and dairy area. It's
a pretty town though the station, set in the middle of
an ugly shopping mall, would suggest otherwise.

The expulsion of the Acadians

Acadia (or Acadie) was the name given to the original French settlements on the Atlantic Coast that date from around 1610. This land was also claimed by the British who renamed it Nova Scotia. They finally acquired Acadia in the Treaty of Utrecht in 1713, though they more or less left it alone until 1750–60 when thousands of New England settlers were moved in to colonize the area.

Britain demanded of the Acadians an oath of unconditional allegiance to the British Crown but the French refused, vowing neutrality instead. In response, the Acadian population was rounded up, herded onto ships and forcibly deported. Up to 10,000 of these people were expelled between 1755 and 1762 and the event has gone down as one of the greatest tragedies of the French-speaking people of Canada.

———————————— **RAILWAY SUBDIVISION** ————————————

Mile 11: Just after crossing the Debert River the train swings around a great, sweeping curve of track known as the **Grecian Bend**, apparently laid at the behest of an influential local ironworks owner.

Mile 23(N): Folly Lake Formed by a melting glacier 10,000 years ago, it's supposed to be a watering spot for moose and bear.

Mile 25: For the next five miles the train rides high above the Wallace River, along the Wentworth Valley. As you leave the valley behind, look south for a view of Sugarloaf Mountain in the distance.

Mile 59: Springhill Jct* Springhill used to be an important coal-mining centre but its pits were dogged by tragedy: in 1891 125 miners were killed in an explosion; 39 died in an accident in 1956; just two years later a tunnel collapsed

---

Nova Scotia

Nova Scotia is Canada's second smallest province, covering just over 55,000 square miles. It sits in the North Atlantic Ocean on a lobster-shaped peninsula, surrounded by 7579km of coastline. One of the three Maritime Provinces, practically everything about Nova Scotia – its history, its climate, its industries, its people – is intricately bound up with the sea. The first Europeans in the area were fishermen, lured over by the legendary supplies of cod here, and the first towns were set up as ports, first by the French and then by the British. The biggest, Halifax, was and remains an important naval base as well as being the province's capital.

It's an area of great natural beauty, particularly around the coast with its incredible variety of fjords, bays, coves, inlets, mudflats, sand dunes, beaches, lagoons and salt marshes. This rugged terrain, added to the province's isolation from central Canada, lends a remote and slightly sleepy feel to the place – qualities that draw significant numbers of tourists here each year. Nova Scotia's population is 873,000; about 75% of these are of British extract, and 11% of French descent (with German and Dutch origin making up the rest). The average income per capita is less than 80% of the national average but Nova Scotians generally claim, with good reason, to enjoy a fine quality of life in an unspoilt environment.

ROUTE GUIDE & MAPS

New Brunswick
The official name of this province is New/Nouveau Brunswick. Over a third of its population of 715,000 is French-speaking and New Brunswick is Canada's only officially bilingual province. It was originally administered as part of Nova Scotia but when its population expanded with the arrival of about 14,000 English Loyalists after the American War of Independence, it was made a separate province in 1784. It's bordered by Quebec to the north and Maine (USA) to the west and is connected to Nova Scotia by the Chignecto Isthmus.

In the early decades of Confederation, New Brunswick was the most prosperous region of Canada. Its economy was based on the massive boatbuilding industry centred in Saint John, which exploited the enormous quantity of timber available from the province's interior forest land. However, when ships started to be built from steel its fortunes declined rapidly and have never properly recovered, due in some part to Canada's national policies which restrict individual provinces from setting their own competitive tariffs. New Brunswick is one of the Maritime Provinces, along with Nova Scotia and Prince Edward Island. Its capital is Fredericton.

killing a further 74 men. Today the pits are all shut down but the bravery of the men who once worked there is still honoured in the **Springhill Miners' Museum**.

Mile 76: Amherst The town was once a booming industrial centre of Nova Scotia but large numbers of the population left for New England after World War I and the local economy has never recovered its former success.

Mile 80: Here you cross the Missaquash River which separates Nova Scotia from New Brunswick.

Mile 81(N): On top of the hill you can see **Fort Beauséjour**, built by the French between 1750 and 1755, then promptly captured by the British the year it was completed. This low-lying building doesn't exactly dominate the skyline, so keep your eyes peeled if you want a glimpse of it.

Mile 86: Sackville This is a small, pretty town with old timbered houses and, surprisingly for its size, a university, Mount Allison, founded over 150 years ago. What's more, this university was the first in Canada to grant degrees to women, when Grace Anne Lockhart was made a Bachelor of Science here in 1875. Sackville is surrounded by the saltwater **Tantramar Marshes**. Keep a look out for Canada geese, marsh hawks, blue-winged teal, black ducks and numerous other waterfowl; the area is a national wildlife reserve and is one of the densest breeding grounds in the world for many species.

Mile 125: Moncton   [20-minute stop]
The original name of this town was The Bend; sadly it was renamed Moncton (losing a 'k' along the way) in 1855, in honour of General Robert Monckton, a British commander who became lieutenant-governor of Nova Scotia. Efforts to officially respell the town's name in the 1920s were vigorously opposed by the locals, and Moncton it remained. Today about a third of the population is French-speaking. The 20-minute stop provides a good opportunity to stretch your legs.

> 'From Moncton, westward, there is much along the line worthy of description, but thousands of Railway tourists will see it all with their own eyes in a year or two – the deep forests of New Brunswick, the noble Miramichi River with its Railway bridging on a somewhat gigantic scale, the magnificent highway scenery of the Baie des Chaleurs, the Restigouche and the wild mountain gorges of the Matapédia.'
> **Rev Grant**, *Ocean to Ocean* (1873)

─────────── **RAILWAY SUBDIVISION** ───────────

Mile 62: Here you cross the **Miramichi River** and then, immediately after, the Little Miramichi. Anglers reportedly flock to these waters from all over the world, lured by their silver Atlantic salmon.

Mile 66: Newcastle The local economy revolves around the town's thriving salmon fisheries. It also boasts a large radio station which met its moment of glory during World War II when it was selected as the British government's receiving station. It's no longer a main stop.

Mile 110: Bathurst This small copper-mining and fishing town marks the beginning of the Caraquet coast. The sandy beaches and old Acadian fishing villages along this coast have made the area a popular tourist resort.

Mile 120: Petit Rocher* This small seaside village is a popular summer resort. Villagers celebrate the Acadian National Holiday every year here on August 15.

Mile 138: Jacquet River* This town was founded by a Mr J Doyle in 1790 who, according to local legend, was its only inhabitant for many years. To the north is the Bay of Chaleur; the train will hug its shores for the next 35 miles. The views over the bay are particularly pretty between miles 165 and 170.

[MAP 2]

Mile 154: Charlo* This little fishing and forestry town has its own local airport with regularly scheduled flights to Montreal.

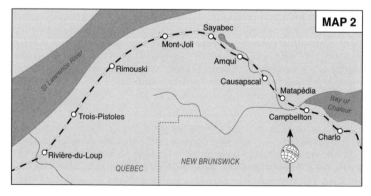

Mile 173: Campbellton The town was originally settled by the dispossessed Acadians back in 1757, but they were once more forced out of their homes by the English a few years later.

The skyline at Campbellton is dominated by the 300-metre high Sugarloaf Mountain – a huge lump of volcanic rock – but it may be too dark to get a good look by the time you arrive.

───────────── **RAILWAY SUBDIVISION** ─────────────

Mile 12: Matapédia (ET) Matapédia gets its name from a Micmac word which means 'The river that breaks into branches'. You are now in Quebec Province.

The **Micmac** (sometimes spelt Mi'kmaq) occupy the coastal regions of the Gaspé and Maritime Provinces. It is not certain how long they have been there, though it could be anything up to 10,000 years. Their settlements were traditionally located around bays or rivers, and their community and economy revolved around fishing and hunting. As with most native tribes, however, their society was virtually dismantled with the arrival of the Europeans. Attempts by the government to integrate Micmacs with white Canadians resulted in few advantages for the natives and the loss of most of their land, villages and customs. Today there are about 20,000 people of Micmac origin living in this part of Canada.

Mile 47: Causapscal* A lumbering and farming village touched by romance. It was here that Donald A Smith of the CPR (see p58) fell in love with and married his beautiful Indian bride.

Mile 60: Amqui Again, this place name is derived from a Micmac word, this time intriguingly meaning 'Place of amusement'.

───────────────────────────────

Quebec

Quebec is Canada's largest province, covering 1.65 million sq km. The UK would fit into this vast area seven times over but Quebec's population is a fraction of the UK's at 6.5 million. The province stretches right up to the Hudson Strait, not far from the Arctic Circle, but most of the land is covered by the Canadian Shield (see p31) and is virtually uninhabitable. Subsequently, almost all Quebeckers live in the fertile valley of the St Lawrence River, with over a third in Montreal alone.

Quebec is unique in North America in being an almost wholly French-speaking region: over 90% of its people have French as their mother tongue. Its distinctness from the rest of Canada has given rise to a vigorous separatist movement over the last few decades and Quebec has been teetering on the brink of independence in recent years (see p36).

In 1995 a referendum was held in which Quebeckers voted to stay with Canada by just 1%, a figure that proves that the uncertainty of Quebec's future is far from over – though the strong feelings concerning the sovereignty issue do seem to have died down somewhat since then. If Quebec were to become a separate nation it would break up the rest of Canada into two blocks, as the province separates Ontario from New Brunswick, Nova Scotia, Newfoundland and Prince Edward Island. Quebec also borders four American states: Maine, New Hampshire, Vermont and New York.

ROUTE GUIDE & MAPS

Mile 76: Sayabec* The train passes through this town late at night but, if you haven't gone to bed yet, you may be able make out the striking silhouette of Sayabec's church (E), standing on a hillside.

Mile 105: Mont-Joli The moose- and deer-hunting capital of Quebec, this little town is also known as 'Gateway to the Gaspé'.

Mile 123: Rimouski With a population of around 30,000, this is the first sizeable town since Moncton. The Roman Catholic cathedral is the centre of the diocese. Much of the town was destroyed by a fire in 1950 but there are few signs of this left today.

Mile 161: Trois-Pistoles No one knows for sure how this village got its name but legend has it that a sailor sent to fetch water from a stranded ship lost the silver goblet he was carrying, which was worth three gold *pistoles* (a French coin).

These days Trois-Pistoles is a popular whale-watching spot: beluga, blue and finback whales are all common in this part of the St Lawrence.

Mile 188: Rivière-du-Loup This town used to be called Fraserville but the large packs of wolves that once gathered around the river gave the place its more poetic name.

———————————————— RAILWAY SUBDIVISION ————————————————

[MAP 3, p193]

Mile 41: La Pocatière This town of about 5000 people is home to a modern, avant-garde cathedral containing works by an eminent Quebec sculptor.

Mile 78: Montmagny* Probably the most noteworthy feature of this biscuit-manufacturing town is its curious ten-sided church.

———————————————— RAILWAY SUBDIVISION ————————————————

Mile 8: Charny Now that *The Ocean* no longer stops at Lévis, on the opposite bank of the St Lawrence from Quebec City, this is where passengers wanting to visit Quebec City get off the train. From here, a minibus will take you on the half-hour ride into town (for $9.20; tickets bought inside the train station), where it'll drop you at the Gare du Palais in the city's Basse-Ville (see p84).

As you pull out of Charny the train crosses a wide bridge over the Chaudière River. The river takes its name from the 'boiling waters' of its falls, the tallest being forty metres high. Once out of Charny you move into a rural landscape of forests or pastures dotted with tiny villages, pretty church spires and farms.

This fertile land stretches most of the way from here to Montreal. Most of the trees that you pass along this stretch are maple trees, used to produce that great Canadian staple, maple syrup. A hole is bored in each tree so that the sap can be removed, drop by drop; this is then heated under controlled temperatures

———————————————————————————————————————

(Opposite) In fall the forests of maple put on a glorious display of reds and golds. (Photo © Jim Manthorpe).

and the sap turns into syrup. It's then transferred to a cute glass bottle that ends up on your breakfast table next to your pancakes.

Mile 98: Drummondville Note the huge hydro-electric station the train passes just before you get to this busy industrial town.

Mile 40: St-Hyacinthe The mileage suddenly goes down to Mile 40 following a railway junction just before the town. The great gothic building to the south is the St-Hyacinthe Seminary, supposedly modelled on Amiens Cathedral. It is said of St-Hyacinthe that until very recently it had a higher concentration of religious institutions than any other town in the world. It's also the birthplace of Canada's greatest organ builder, Joseph Casavant.

Mile 50: There's a dramatic change of scenery as two of the **Monteregian Hills** suddenly loom up. These huge volcanic mounds were formed 120 million years ago when the area was covered by sea. Particularly impressive is the dark and somewhat menacing Mont Rouge, towering over the track at **Boloeil** (Mile 56). Altogether there are seven of these hills, the westernmost being Mont Royal in Montreal.

Mile 55: As you cross the Richelieu River, spare a thought for the victims of the terrible rail accident at this spot in 1864. A Grand Trunk train carrying mainly German and Polish immigrants was unable to stop for the rising drawbridge and went plunging between the gap into the river; 100 passengers died.

Mile 70: *The Ocean* crosses the St Lawrence Seaway into greater Montreal, stopping briefly at the suburb **St-Lambert**. Look north as you cross the bridge for excellent views of Montreal's skyline. A few miles on from St-Lambert you're in Montreal's Central Station. For more information about **Montreal**, see pp94-109.

(Opposite) **Top**: Montmorency Falls (see p93), near Quebec City, are one and a half times the height of Niagara Falls. **Bottom**: Halifax (see pp69-81) contains many eye-catching examples of the brightly-painted clapboard houses typical of eastern Canada.

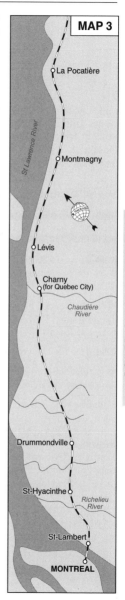

MAP 3

La Pocatière

St Lawrence River

Montmagny

Lévis

Charny
(for Quebec City)

Chaudière River

Drummondville

St-Hyacinthe

Richelieu River

St-Lambert

MONTREAL

ROUTE GUIDE & MAPS

The Corridor route:
Montreal to Toronto

VIA's modern LRC (Light, Rapid & Comfortable) trains travel along the old Grand Trunk inter-city route, following first the St Lawrence River (which drifts in and out of sight) to its source at Lake Ontario, and then the shores of the lake as far as Toronto. The journey takes four hours on the non-stop express and $4^{1}/_{2}$ to $5^{1}/_{2}$ on other trains.

[MAP 4]

Mile 0: Montreal [ET] See pp94-109.

Mile 11: Dorval The train makes a brief stop just outside Montreal, near the southern international airport. Moving out of Dorval the tracks run parallel to the highway (Route 20) which will remain in view for the next hour or so.

Mile 21 and 23: Here you cross the Ottawa River. Look north for fine views down the river to the Lake of Two Mountains studded with little islands. In the distance you can see the Laurentian Highlands.

Mile 25: Around here the urban landscape peters out and the train moves into a rural setting. The land is as flat as a pancake and the only things to look at are trees and farms.

Mile 41: The train crosses the boundary between Quebec and Ontario.

Mile 58: The peculiar igloo-shaped buildings you can see standing by the track are used by the government to store sand to sprinkle on the roads in the winter.

Mile 65–105: The track running along this stretch was re-laid in the late 1950s when the original track was submerged by the artificial widening of the St Lawrence River. This was part of the construction of the huge **St Lawrence Seaway**, a system of canals and locks connecting the Atlantic Ocean to the St Lawrence River and the Great Lakes. The biggest section is the one you're now running alongside (though it's just out of sight), linking Montreal with Lake Ontario; it can take vessels of up to 222.5m long and 23.2m wide. The railways

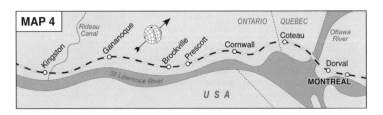

MAP 4

Rideau Canal

Kingston

Gananoque

Brockville

Prescott

Cornwall

ONTARIO | QUEBEC

Coteau

Ottawa River

Dorval

MONTREAL

St Lawrence River

U S A

weren't the only thing submerged by the Seaway: over 500 homes and 6500 people had to be relocated to two newly built towns; you'll pass one of them, **Ingleside**, at Mile 80.

Mile 68: Cornwall Site of one of the province's oldest courthouses (1833) and a restored 'Regency Cottage' museum.

If you look south here you can make out the original route of the track before it was re-laid.

Mile 109 (S): Over the trees you can see a huge bridge; this is the International Bridge linking Canada with the US. Right by the bridge are several enormous grain elevators.

Mile 112: A large water-storage tower announces your arrival at **Prescott**. In stark contrast to this modern edifice is Prescott's beautiful stone station, about 150 years old.

Mile 125: Brockville (or 'Gateway to the Thousand Islands') Between here and Kingston the St Lawrence River is dotted with hundreds of little islands, covered with rock and trees. The area, an extension of the Canadian Shield, is very beautiful and has attracted tourists since the early 1800s but unfortunately not much of it can be seen from the train.

Mile 135–145: The rolling pastures suddenly give way to ten miles of beautiful limestone rock and wild-looking trees – a brief glimpse of the scenery covering the Thousand Islands just to the south.

Mile 155: Gananoque The other 'Gateway to the Thousand Islands.' It also has a bridge across the St Lawrence to the US.

Mile 169: The train crosses the **Rideau Canal** that links Kingston with Ottawa. The canal was completed in 1832 and was originally designed (following the War

Ontario
Sandwiched between Quebec and Manitoba, Ontario sprawls over a million sq km, from the Great Lakes in the south up to Hudson Bay in the north. A large part of this area is Shield country, with its boreal forest, granite outcrops and countless lakes. 'Ontario' is an Iroquoian word meaning 'Shining waters', a most appropriate name since the province contains a full quarter of the world's fresh water.

It is the most populated province in Canada (with nine million people) and has been so since the first census was taken in 1871. It is also the wealthiest, with the highest degree of urbanization and industrialization, and the most diversified economy. Its manufacturing sector is particularly important, with about half of all goods produced in Canada coming from Ontario. Another major source of revenue is the rich mineral deposits discovered with the construction of the railroad across the Canadian Shield.

Ontario attracts many tourists each year, being home to the nation's capital (Ottawa), its largest city (Toronto) and the Niagara Falls. Its charms are not exclusively urban, however, and popular wilderness retreats include Georgian Bay, the Thousand Islands and Algonquin Park (a mecca for canoeists, with its 1600km of water trails).

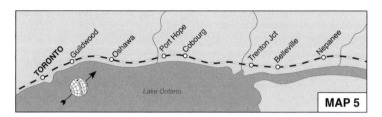

of 1812) to guarantee a supply route north of the US border in the event of another war. In winter this canal turns into a busy skating rink and is used by many locals to skate to work.

Mile 176: Kingston This town's claims to fame include being the former capital of the Province of Canada (1841–67) and the birthplace of Sir John A Macdonald, Canada's first Prime Minister.

Mile 180: As the train passes attractive Collins Bay with all its pleasure yachts bobbing in the water, you get your first glimpse of Lake Ontario.

Mile 182: A big water tower stands by the track (N) with 'Amherst View' written on it. About a mile further on you can snatch a bit of this view for yourself – the beautiful Amherst Island on Lake Ontario (S).

[MAP 5]

Mile 199: Nepanee Just before you get here look south as you cross the river and you'll see a series of pretty waterfalls. The picturesque view continues with Nepanee's beautiful town hall (S) and then its charming old railway station.

Mile 220: Belleville This town has been, in its time, an important fur-trading, saw-milling and cheese-making centre. Like Nepanee it boasts an attractive, well-preserved station dating from the 1850s.

Mile 233: Trenton Jct This little town was chosen as the base for the Royal Canadian Air Force during World War II and was the training centre for Commonwealth pilots.

Back in the 1920s, however, not content with the usual saw-milling and lumbering industries, Trenton tried to establish itself as a film production centre. Unfortunately the glamorous plan didn't really take off and only a handful of films were produced here.

Mile 260 (S): Over the next few miles there are lovely views of Lake Ontario.

Mile 265: Cobourg Among this small town's architectural highlights is a court which is a replica of London's Old Bailey. You may also be interested to know that Cobourg was the site of one of Canada's oldest railways – a 48km track to Peterborough across Rice Lake.

The line was not a success; right at the beginning most of the construction team was wiped out by cholera, and then when the track was finally laid in the mid-1850s the 5km Rice Lake Bridge proved rather unstable. When the Prince of Wales visited the area in 1860 it was considered best that he shouldn't cross the bridge in case it collapsed – and collapse it did less than one year later, leaving Cobourg with an inoperable and bankrupt railway.

Mile 268: By now the train is running right alongside the lakeshore; the views are stunning so keep your cameras at the ready.

Mile 270: Port Hope This town has one of the best preserved turn-of-the-20th-century main streets in Canada. You won't see much of it from the train but its beautiful little railway station is equally well kept.

Mile 271: More superb views of Lake Ontario – sandy beaches, clay bluffs and holiday homes dotted along the shore.

Mile 300: Oshawa This manufacturing city (predominantly of motor cars) was the birthplace of industrial unions in Canada, following a 4000-men strike at General Motors in 1937. The controversy surrounding the company's and the government's response to the strike resulted in two cabinet ministers resigning. Eventually the company gave in to the strikers' demands – this was the first union victory in the country. You can see the GM site on the other side of the rail tracks from the station.

Mile 315: Once more the tracks sweep right by the edge of the lake. Take your fill of the beautiful views before the train heads off into Toronto's suburbs where a stop is made at **Guildwood** at Mile 321.

Mile 333: Toronto Your journey ends at Union Station. For more about Toronto, see pp110-25.

ROUTE GUIDE & MAPS

The Canadian:
Toronto to Vancouver

This epic journey of 4424km takes three days and three nights. You'll travel through some of the most diverse landscape contained within a single country. The highlight of the journey is without question the ride through the Rocky Mountains; the stretch between Jasper and Kamloops takes you through some of the most spectacular scenery in the world.

TORONTO TO WINNIPEG

[MAP 6]

Mile 1–50 [ET]: For the first half hour or so the train chugs through the dismal Toronto suburbs before the landscape gives way to the fertile pastures and picturesque farms that characterize southern Ontario. Travelling this way in 1872, Rev Grant noted: 'The first half of the journey, or as far as Lake Simcoe, is through a fair and fertile land; too flat to be picturesque, but sufficiently rolling for farming purposes. Clumps of stately elms, with noble stems, shooting high before their fan-shape commences, relieve the monotony of the scene.' (*Ocean to Ocean*).

Mile 99: Washago* Sounding alarmingly like a shampoo, this tiny village is situated on the northern shores of Lake Couchiching. The name is actually taken from the native 'Wash-a-go-min' which means 'Sparkling waters.' To the west you can see the beautiful **Georgian Bay**, an arm of Lake Huron, one of the Great Lakes. The waters are studded with islands and holiday cottages are dotted around the shore.

Mile 100: *The Canadian* now crosses the Severn River which flows into Hudson Bay. The river was used by fur traders in the 17th and 18th centuries as a route between the bay and Lake Winnipeg. Beyond the river the landscape alters dramatically as you move into the wild, rugged terrain of the **Canadian Shield** (see p31). For the next few hours the train winds its way between great outcrops of pink and grey granite, surrounded by a dazzling array of lakes, waterfalls and streams. The scenery is utterly beautiful.

Mile 150: Parry Sound* This town has a peculiar history. The land was bought in the mid-19th century by a Mr W H Beatty who laid out a settlement and encouraged families to move there. As it grew into a successful logging centre, Mr Beatty's son became a sort of self-appointed squire. He was known by everyone as 'The Governor,' enforced prohibition on the villagers and even began to circulate his own money! These days Parry Sound is a bustling tourist resort in the summer. It's known as 'Gateway to the Thirty Thousand Islands' on Lake Huron – the world's largest concentration of islands. You can see some of these (S) over the next few miles.

Mile 215: After crossing the Pickerel River, the train crosses the **French River**, part of a historic fur-trading route. It's still popular with canoeists who share its shallow waters with large numbers of bass, pike and muskellunge.

Mile 260: Sudbury Jct* As you approach Sudbury look south for a view of the towering 381-metre INCO smokestack. The region's rich nickel and copper deposits were discovered during the construction of the trans-Canada railway and since then Sudbury has become the largest nickel-mining centre in the world. The mining and smelting were responsible for ravaging the surrounding landscape, earning the area the nickname 'Lunar garden', but extensive reforestation and redevelopment projects have improved the environment.

[MAP 7]

Mile 276: Capreol **[25-minute stop]**
Besides being a railway divisional point, this small town serves as a distribution centre for Sudbury's

> ❑ For a distance of 600 miles there stretched away to the north-west a vast tract of rock-fringed lake, swamp and forest; lying spread in primeval savagery, an untravelled wilderness.
> **Butler**, *The Great Lone Land* (1872)

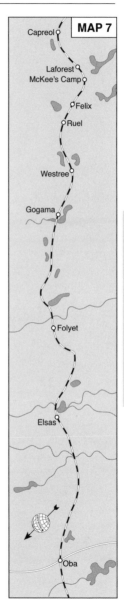

ROUTE GUIDE & MAPS

MAP 8

Hornepayne

Hillsport

Caramat

Longlac

Nakina

Auden

Jackfish Creek

Ferland

Lake Nipigon

Mud River

Armstrong

mining industry. *The Canadian* now enters what is known as the 'thousand mile gap' cutting through the Canadian Shield.

─────────── **RAILWAY SUBDIVISION** ───────────

Mile 5: Moving out of Capreol the train enters the increasingly remote interior of northern Ontario. It's mind-boggling to think that the exposed bedrock you can see is 500 million years old. You can begin to understand why it took more than 20,000 men to get the track from here to the prairies: the train is forced to weave and loop around numerous lakes, all the while cutting through the rock or bogland of the Shield. The communities that have sprung up along the track remain isolated and sparsely populated (Farlane, for instance, has fewer than 40 inhabitants) and most of the stops between here and Winnipeg are flag stops. Only the occasional trapper, fisherman or lumberjack is likely to get on or off.

Mile 86: Gogama* This is a typical logging village. The area between here and **Folyet** (Mile 150) is renowned for moose and bear but it'll probably be too dark to see anything as you travel through.

Mile 258: Oba* A railway junction amidst the wilderness! The trans-Canada line crosses the tracks of the Algoma Central Railway (from Sault Ste Marie to Hearst), hence the little railway hotel in this village of a hundred people.

[MAP 8]
Mile 295: Hornepayne   **[35-minute stop]**
Once a gold-mining town, Hornepayne now relies on its pulp mill to keep its workforce employed. It has about 1500 inhabitants.

─────────── **RAILWAY SUBDIVISION** ───────────

Mile 76: Caramat* Like many sites along the line, Caramat sprang up as a logging town and then almost vanished once the area was logged and the workmen moved on.

Mile 100: Longlac* This former gold-mining settlement sits on the northern banks of Long Lake which drains into Lake Superior. The lake is forty-five miles long and just two miles wide. Almost half the village's population (of over 2000) is French-speaking.

Mile 131: Nakina* This little fur-trapping town also boasts an airfield and a radio station.

Mile 210: *The Canadian* goes over a viaduct high above Jackfish Creek. Look south for fine views over Lake Nipigon, the fourth largest lake in Ontario.

Mile 219: Mud River* Another viaduct takes you across the murky waters that give the village its name.

Mile 243: Armstrong* The landscape by now is monotonous: trees, trees and more trees. This continues for several hours but you'll think fondly of them as you cross the treeless prairies. To the south are fine views of Lake Nipigon, almost 100km in length.

[MAP 9]

Mile 264: Collins* [CT] You've now crossed over into Central Time.

———————— RAILWAY SUBDIVISION ————————

Mile 67: Flindt Landing* This fishing resort is situated on a little island. Look north to see the cabins and huts.

Mile 78: Savant Lake* Another long, narrow lake, 25 miles long and just five miles wide. This settlement is visited mainly by people out fishing.

Mile 139: Sioux Lookout   **[25-minute stop]**
Sioux Lookout sounds as if it's going to be interesting but it's not. There are a few banks and shops across the road from the train station (a once opulent mock-Tudor building which is now falling into disrepair) but nothing much to see around the platform. The place was far more glamorous in days gone by: it was the home of the Ojibway natives who used the nearby hills as a lookout during an attack by Sioux Indians.

———————— RAILWAY SUBDIVISION ————————

Mile 12: Hudson* This tiny settlement was once the main centre for flights to the far north during the gold-rush years.

Mile 90: Canyon* The train skirts the shores of Canyon Lake for about ten miles.

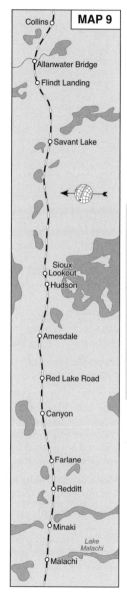

ROUTE GUIDE & MAPS

> ### Manitoba
> Manitoba is in the very centre of Canada, and borders Ontario to the east and Saskatchewan to the west. It covers 650,000 sq km but is sparsely populated with about one million inhabitants – over half of them in its capital city, Winnipeg. Its northern regions are covered by the frozen tundra of the Hudson lowlands but the province's dominant geographic feature is the Canadian Shield, spreading over half the land. To the south is the flat, fertile wheat belt that provides Manitoba with most of its wealth.
>
> This vast territory was originally part of Rupert's Land, owned by the Hudson's Bay Company who used the intricate system of lakes and rivers for their fur-trading activities. After this land was purchased by the first Canadian government, Manitoba became a separate province largely due to the efforts of the rebellious Louis Riel (see p35). When it was incorporated in 1870 it was known as the 'postage stamp province' because its area was so tiny, covering little more than a small rectangle around Winnipeg. It quickly grew, especially following the completion of the transcontinental railroad which allowed wheat to be exported and brought in thousands of settlers from eastern Canada and eastern Europe. Today it's one of the most ethnically diverse provinces of Canada, with thousands of Manitobans of Ukrainian, German, French, Italian, Dutch, Polish, Hungarian and Scandinavian origin.

Mile 113: Farlane* Look south for a view of Farlane's pretty rail station. This tiny settlement was once a favourite fishing resort of Winnipeg's affluent middle class.

Mile 137: Minaki* This used to be a fashionable riverside tourist resort in the 1920s and '30s. The CNR built the elegant Minaki Lodge which you can see (N) as you cross the Winnipeg River.

Mile 153: Malachi* Look south for a beautiful view over Lake Malachi. The attractive hamlet by the lake is still popular with tourists.

[MAP 10]

Mile 160: Rice Lake* Just short of the Ontario/Manitoba border, Rice Lake is a popular fishing destination. You're now in **Whiteshell Provincial Park**, a wilderness area with over 200 lakes. One of these, West Hawk Lake, is 111 metres deep and is supposed to have been created by a giant meteorite. Keep your eyes open for the black bear, deer, moose, coyotes and beavers that live in the park.

Mile 180: Brereton Lake* The last of the lakes. The trees begin to thin out here, giving way to fields and farms.

Mile 197: Elma* Look south as you approach this little hamlet for a view of a Ukrainian church with its striking, onion-shaped dome. This is typical of the ethnically diverse settlements dotted across the prairies; immigrants were encouraged to come here from all over the world to populate the region once the railway was built and a large number came from eastern Europe.

Mile 244: Transcona* Just before arriving in this Winnipeg suburb you cross the Red River Floodway on a viaduct 275 metres long. The canal was built to divert floodwaters around Winnipeg following the massive flood of 1950 which forced 100,000 Winnipegers to evacuate their homes.

Mile 252: Winnipeg **[60-minute stop]**
A welcome hour-long break to stretch your legs. You could call in at the Winnipeg Railway Museum, located in the train station, or visit 'The Forks' (the market/café/people-watching centre of Winnipeg), directly behind the station. If you're staying in Winnipeg, see pp127-37 for a guide to the city.

———————— RAILWAY SUBDIVISION ————————

WINNIPEG TO EDMONTON

Mile 15: As you pull out of Winnipeg the train rolls into some of the most fertile land in Canada. Enormous fields stretch all around, the flatness broken only by farms and grain elevators standing by the rail track.

Mile 55: Portage-la-Prairie* A portage is the connecting overland stretch of a water route. For the fur traders, this area was a portage between the Assiniboine River and Lake Manitoba. The activities pursued at Portage-la-Prairie today are not quite so exotic: it's a food-processing centre specializing in mushrooms and frozen foods.

Passing through in 1872, Rev Grant noted: 'Portage la Prairie is the centre of what will soon be a thriving settlement and, when the railway is built, a large town must spring up. On the way to the little village we passed, in less than ten miles, three camps of Sioux – each of them with about twenty wigwams ranged in a circular form. The three camps probably numbered three hundred souls. The men were handsome fellows, and a few of the women were pretty. We did not see many of the women, however, as they kept to the camps doing all the dirty work, while the men marched along the road, every one of them with a gun on his shoulder.'

MAP 10

ONTARIO
MANITOBA

Rice Lake

Ophir

Brereton Lake

Elma

Red River Floodway

Transcona

WINNIPEG

Portage-la-Prairie

Brandon North

Rivers

ROUTE GUIDE & MAPS

Mile 128: Brandon North* Brandon is Manitoba's second largest city (about 39,000 people) – you can just about make it out, five miles south of the station.

Mile 143: Rivers* You approach this little town on a 27-metre-long bridge high above the Minnedosa (Cree for 'Swift waters') River. Look out for the colourful grain elevators alongside the track.

[MAP 11]

Mile 180: For the next 25 miles the train follows the **Qu'Appelle Valley**. Look south for lovely views over the lakes and waterways threading through the emerald-green land. The name is derived from the French translation of an Indian legend which told of a young man who, on hearing his name called as he crossed the valley, cried out 'Qui appelle?' ('Who calls?') The only reply was the echo of his voice: 'Qu'appelle....qu'appelle....' He later discovered that the voice he had heard was his lover crying out for him at the moment of her death. A cheery little story to ponder on as the train chugs into the shadows of dusk.

Mile 213: Manitoba/Saskatchewan border As the train moves into the Saskatchewan prairies the land gets flatter and flatter. VIA's scheduling thankfully has you travelling through most of Saskatchewan in the dark (in both directions) – presumably to avoid the risk of 'prairie madness' breaking out on the trains.

'The broad, open valley of the Qu' Appelle stretched out along to the west, making a grand break in what would otherwise have been an unbroken plateau of Prairie. Three miles to the south of this valley, and therefore opposite us but farther down, two or three small white buildings on the edge of the plateau were pointed out as Fort Ellice. To the north of the Qu'Appelle, the sun was dipping behind woods far away on the edge of the horizon, and throwing a mellow light on the vast expanse which spread around in every direction.'
Rev Grant, *Ocean to Ocean* (1873)

Saskatchewan
Saskatchewan is true prairie country – over two thirds of its land is part of the Great Plains, largely composed of fertile, arable soil. It's known as 'the bread basket of Canada' owing to its prodigious wheat production, which meets 60% of the nation's consumption and 12% of total world demand. Saskatchewan has also carved a niche for itself in the manufacturing and distribution of agricultural implements, which it exports around the world. To add to its economic feathers are a range of abundant mineral deposits including uranium, copper, gold and potash.

The region belonged to the Hudson's Bay Company for two centuries and was not settled by Europeans until the 1870s. Up until then it had been largely the preserve of the Plains Indians (whose tribes included Cree, Assiniboine, Chipeweyan and Blackfoot) and vast herds of buffalo. After Confederation, the area was first administered by the government as part of the Northwest Territories (most of western Canada) and it wasn't until 1905 that Saskatchewan became a separate province, along with Alberta. Its name was derived from the Cree word for the Saskatchewan River, meaning 'Swiftly-flowing water'. Its capital is Regina and its population is now just over one million.

Mile 280: Melville This town (it's officially a city but the word seems inappropriate for a prairie community of 5000 people) was established by the Grand Trunk Pacific Railway in 1908. It was named after Charles Melville Hays, the GTP president who died in the sinking of the *Titanic*.

———————————— RAILWAY SUBDIVISION ————————————

Mile 129: Watrous* This town sprang up on the banks of Manitou Lake to house the thousands of visitors who came by rail to bathe in the lake's mineral-rich (and supposedly curative) waters. The buoyancy of these waters is greater than that of the Dead Sea.

Mile 189: Saskatchewan River A 457-metre bridge brings you into the 'City of Bridges', Saskatoon.

Mile 191: Saskatoon   [25-minute stop]
Saskatchewan's second city (with a population of 185,000) started out as a Temperance Colony in 1882. The Temperance Movement aimed to curb or eliminate the consumption of alcohol in pursuit of a better society. The growth of Saskatoon was slow until the Grand Trunk Pacific brought its northern transcontinental tracks here in 1906. Today it's a small but very prosperous prairie city, its economy revolving around oil and wheat.

For those spending time here, attractions include the **Ukrainian Museum of Canada**, the **Western Development Museum** and **Wanuskewin Heritage Park**. However, both eastbound and westbound trains arrive here in the middle of the night and the station is seven miles out of town – so unless you've got your heart set on visiting Saskatoon, getting off here involves far too much effort and hassle. If you do, however, you ought to book your first night's

MAP 12

Biggar

Unity

SASKATCHEWAN

ALBERTA

Wainwright

Battle River

Viking

Holden

accommodation in advance. You could try the *Patricia Hotel* (☎ 306-242-8861) at 345 2nd Ave – the rooms are pleasant and reasonably priced at around $50–80 a night. A taxi from the station to downtown will cost you around $15.

[MAP 12]
Mile 247: Biggar 'New York is big, but this is Biggar!' is this little town's slogan. It sprang up when the Grand Trunk Pacific decided to locate a railway divisional point here. As well as being a railway centre, Biggar is the tractor-manufacturing capital of Saskatchewan.

——————— RAILWAY SUBDIVISION ———————

Travelling across this area in 1872, Butler was moved to write: 'No solitude can equal the loneliness of a night-shadowed prairie: one feels the stillness, and hears the silence, the wail of the prowling wolf makes the voice of solitude audible, the stars look down through infinite silence upon a silence almost as intense.' (*The Great Lone Land*).

Mile 57: Unity* The first attempt to mine potash in Canada took place in Unity. It wasn't an overly successful venture but the subsequent mining of salt was a huge success and continues today.

Mile 101: [MT] Saskatchewan/Alberta border As you move into Alberta you also move into the Mountain Time Zone.

Mile 140: Wainwright* This town was created by transplanting another settlement, Denwood, 4km from its original location. Everything was moved – houses, stores, the church – and the settlement was

❏ 'After breakfast we entered on a vast plain that stretched out on every side to the horizon. This had once been the favourite resort of the buffalo, and we passed in the course of the day more than a score of skulls that were bleaching on the prairie. All the other bones had of course been chopped and boiled by the Indian women for the oil in them.'
Cumberland, *The Queen's Highway* (1887)

> ### Alberta
> Alberta is one of Canada's most prosperous and attractive provinces, stretching across the rolling prairies in the east and centre to some of the most dramatic Rockies scenery at the province's western border. Jasper National Park, the biggest of the four Rocky Mountain parks, lies entirely within Alberta, and the most heavily visited parts of Banff National Park sit inside the province.
>
> Alberta is just over one hundred years old, created in 1905 along with Saskatchewan. (These provinces are, incidentally, the only two in Canada not to have any salt-water coast.) It was named after Queen Victoria's fourth daughter, Princess Caroline Alberta, who was married to a former Governor-General of Canada. The two mainstays of Alberta's economy are wheat and oil, the latter bringing a great boom to the two main cities, Calgary and Edmonton, in the 1970s. These cities have been engaged in fierce rivalry for many years, and while Edmonton scored the coup of being made the province's capital, Calgary has managed to win hands down in most other areas. Alberta's population is 2.5 million and it is the fourth largest province in Canada.

promptly rechristened Wainwright in honour of William Wainwright of the Grand Trunk Pacific.

A huge, brightly coloured grain elevator towers by the railway station; the train always stops here so keep your camera at hand for that classic grain elevator shot. There's a peregrine falcon breeding centre near Wainwright; keep your eyes peeled for a sighting.

Mile 147: As you move out of Wainwright the relentless flatness of the land starts to give way to gently rolling plains. Look north for an impressive view over the mile-wide Battle River Valley. The river looks like a little stream as it snakes along, far below the train. You soon cross it on an 884-metre-long steel trestle, giving you fine views on both sides.

Mile 184: Viking* This small town was settled at the beginning of the 20th century by Scandinavians, hence its name. Not far from the town are **The Ribstones**, two massive rock carvings created by the Plains Indians about one thousand years ago, depicting a buffalo backbone and ribs.

Mile 205(N): The train passes **Holden**. The town's onion-domed Ukrainian Church looms dramatically on the horizon.

Mile 240(S): Look out for moose and elk in North Cooking Lake.

Mile 260: Edmonton   [45-minute stop]
The train crosses the North Saskatchewan River on a 500-metre-long bridge, taking you into Edmonton. Your approach to the city is heralded by the enormous oil refineries that have brought Edmonton its wealth. For Edmonton, see pp138-46.

ROUTE GUIDE & MAPS

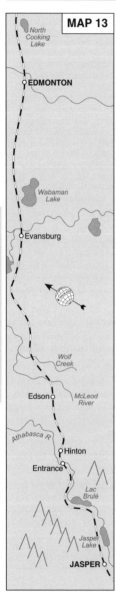

EDMONTON TO JASPER

[MAP 13]

Mile 32(N): The train passes another ornate Russian Orthodox church. Strangely, these buildings are as much a part of the prairies as the grain elevators.

Mile 44(S): The train skirts the shores of Wabamun Lake for the next ten miles. Wabamun is the Cree word for 'mirror'.

Mile 45(N): The tranquillity of the scene is interrupted by the huge power stations on the lakeshore. These are coal-fired power generators; the biggest one is called the Sundance Power Plant.

Mile 67: The train crosses the Pembina River, once used as a water route to the Cariboo gold fields.

Mile 68: Evansburg* A small coal-mining village named after Harry Evans, a former mayor of Edmonton.

Mile 73–122: The train crosses five bridges over a series of rivers and creeks. The most impressive crossings are at Mile 121 (over Wolf Creek) and Mile 122 (over McLeod River); both bridges are 40m high.

Mile 130: Edson* This little lumbering town was established as a railway divisional point in 1910 by the Grand Trunk Pacific. It was named after Edson J Chamberlain, the company's vice-president.

Mile 136(N): Look down for an attractive view of Sundance Creek.

Mile 150: The terrain is becoming increasingly hilly and you can feel the train begin to climb higher. To the south are sweeping views over the McLeod River valley.

Mile 165: At last – the Rocky Mountains! Look towards the front of the train for your first view of the distant snow-capped peaks. The excitement on board is palpable, as all the passengers start 'oohing' and 'aahing' and pressing their faces to the windows.

Mile 184: Hinton* As you pull out of this busy town the views of the mountains suddenly become quite breathtaking.

> 'Looking west, I beheld the great range in unclouded glory... An immense plain stretched from my feet to the mountain – a plain so vast that every object of hill and wooded lake lay dwarfed into one continuous level, and at the back of this level, beyond the pines and the lakes and the river courses, rose the giant, solid, impassable, silent – a mighty barrier rising midst an immense land, standing sentinel over the plains and prairies of America, over the measureless solitudes of this great lone land. Here, at last, lay the Rocky Mountains.'
>
> **Butler**, *The Great Lone Land* (1872)

Mile 190: The train passes a little village, charmingly named **Entrance**. It marks, of course, your official entrance into the Rocky Mountains.

Mile 192(N): The **Athabasca River** comes into view. On a sunny day its waters are a beautiful jade-green. The train follows its course from here to Jasper.

Mile 197: For the next eight miles the train skirts **Lac Brulé**, named after Etienne Brulé, the famous 17th-century explorer who was the first Frenchman to live among native Canadians.

Mile 200: By now the train is right in the middle of the mountains; they tower above you on both sides of the track. To the north is the Bosche Range and to the south the Miette Range.

Mile 206: Here you cross the boundary of **Jasper National Park**. It's staggeringly vast, covering over 10,880 sq km, with peaks as high as 3747 metres. It's the biggest of Canada's mountain national parks, and also one of the best for wildlife.

Mile 215: Now known as the **Devona Siding**, this was once the site of Jasper House, a supply post used by travellers crossing the mountains for the fur trade. It was built in 1817 by a merchant called Jasper Hawe whose name has proved a more enduring feature of the region than his store.

Mile 216(S): Jasper Lake This lake is less than one mile wide and is getting narrower and narrower because of the silt deposits carried here from the mountains by the Athabasca River.

Mile 225: Henry House Elk are a common sight along this stretch of the Athabasca Valley.

Mile 235: Jasper [75-minute stop]

For more information on Jasper see pp147-53. If you hadn't planned to stop over in Jasper, you might well change your mind during the next 75 minutes. If you've already been to Banff, you'll be amazed by the complete absence of taxi drivers, tour guides and general clamour at the train station of this quieter, calmer town.

JASPER TO KAMLOOPS

[MAP 14]

Mile 17 [PT]: You're now going through the **Yellowhead Pass** which provides a gap through the **continental divide**. The continental divide is the line following the main ranges of the Rocky Mountains; on one side of the line rivers flow west to the Pacific, on the other side they drain into the Arctic or the Atlantic. It is also the border between Alberta and British Columbia and is the point at which you move from Mountain Time into Pacific Time.

Mile 22(S): The shimmering **Yellowhead Lake** appears, framed by Mount Fitzwilliam and Mount Rockingham. It's one of the most beautiful views of the journey.

Mile 24(S): Here you get your first glimpse of the **Fraser River**. It was named after Simon Fraser who in 1808 was the first European to journey the 1368km to the river's mouth.

As you follow the course of the Fraser River, spare a thought for the millions of salmon who don't have such a smooth ride on their way to the Pacific and back again. The headwaters of the river's tributaries are the spawning ground of millions of Pacific salmon. Around March the newly-hatched fry begin their migration down the Fraser River to the Pacific Ocean. Only a quarter will make it. The survivors spend the next two and a half years swimming around the North Pacific where quite a few more will meet their end. Then the ones that are left begin their incredible journey back to the place of their birth, where they will spawn and die. They swim (upstream) at an average speed of 30km per day and literally leap over the obstacles in their path. This amazing cycle takes place once every four years.

ROUTE GUIDE & MAPS

British Columbia

This is Canada's most westerly province and quite possibly its most beautiful. Just short of a million square km in area, British Columbia embraces gentle ranch land, towering peaks, arid desert land and lush rainforest. About 70% of the province is covered by mountains, with most of this area unpopulated. British Columbians, numbering about three million, tend to live near the south-west coast, the majority of them concentrated in Vancouver. BC's population is the third highest in Canada after Ontario and Quebec. It is also the third largest province in surface area, after Quebec and Ontario. Only one American state, Alaska, is bigger than British Columbia.

The province is home to an incredibly diverse range of communities, from the great British enclave in Victoria to the young and cosmopolitan crowd of Vancouver; and from the lumberjacks and miners of the interior to the North-West coastal tribes. The latter, which include the Haida, Kwakiutl and Nootka, are among the most culturally distinct native groups in Canada. Their art is currently undergoing a big renaissance, particularly the carving of totem poles.

Mile 36 (S): Moose Lake The pale green waters of this lake reflect the passing train and surrounding peaks. The lake is full of rainbow trout and is said to be a popular watering spot for moose.

The Travelling Reverend was much taken with the place in 1872 and wrote: 'Moose Lake that we struck last night but only got a tolerable view of today, is a beautiful sheet of water, ten or eleven miles long, by three wide...The survey for the Railway is proceeding along the north side, where the bluffs, though high appear not so sheer as on the south. The hillsides of the country beyond support a growth of splendid spruce, black pine and Douglas fir, some of the spruce the finest any of us had ever seen. So far in our descent from the Pass, the difficulties in the way of the railroad are not formidable nor the grades likely to be heavy. Still, the work that the surveyors are engaged on requires a patience, hardihood, and forethought that few who ride in Pullman cars on the road in after years will ever appreciate.'

Mile 50 (S): Look out for a quick glimpse of the roaring waterfall at Glacier Creek.

Mile 52–60(N): Good views of **Mount Robson**, the tallest peak in the Canadian Rockies at 3954m. The native name for this mountain is 'Yuh Hai Has Hun' or 'Mountain of Spiritual Road.'

Mile 66: The tracks veer south and the snow-capped mountains of the **Premier Range** come into view (W). The eleven peaks are named after Canadian and British prime ministers. The dominant peak is Mount Sir Wilfrid Laurier, covered by a huge glacier which also spreads onto Mount Mackenzie King and Mount Arthur Meighen.

Mile 73(S): The mountain you're passing is the **Terry Fox Memorial Mountain**, named in honour of the brave man who attempted to run across Canada to raise money and awareness for cancer research. Fox had already lost one leg to cancer when he set out on his 'Marathon of Hope' from St John's in April 1980; 5373km further on, in Thunder Bay, it was discovered that the cancer had spread to his lungs and he was forced to abandon the run. He died in June the following year, having raised $24 million.

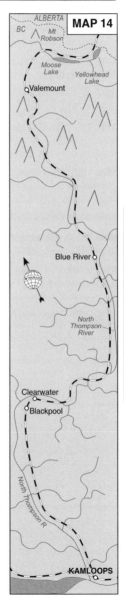

MAP 14

ALBERTA
BC
Mt Robson
Moose Lake
Yellowhead Lake
Valemount
Blue River
North Thompson River
Clearwater
Blackpool
North Thompson R
KAMLOOPS

ROUTE GUIDE & MAPS

Mile 74: Valemount* This little lumber town (population 1000) nestles in a wide valley between the Rocky, Cariboo and Monashee mountain ranges, at an elevation of 1100 metres.

Mile 91: Look west for a stunning view of the **Albreda Icefields Glacier**, over 10,000 feet thick.

Mile 106: The train meets the North Thompson River and follows it for 26 miles to Blue River.

Mile 113 (S): The sparkling **Pyramid Falls** tumble 90 metres from a lake on Mount Cheadle, falling in tiers towards the railtrack, enveloped in clouds of diaphanous spray. It's quite a spectacle and a great photo opportunity.

Mile 132: Blue River* This former railway centre has developed into a thriving outdoor resort, specializing in heli-skiing in the Monashee Mountains at the cost of some $500 a day.

——————————————— RAILWAY SUBDIVISION ———————————————

Mile 5: As you leave Blue River the landscape begins to change from one of mountains and lakes into a distinctly more rugged terrain.

Mile 8 (E): For the next eight miles the **North Thompson River** narrows into a stretch of turbulent, treacherous rapids known as **Little Hell's Gate** or Porte

Place names
The names of many places or geographic features in Canada are taken from native languages, especially on the west coast. The translations of these are often highly evocative. Take, for example, Yoho ('Awesome'); Kitimat ('People of the snow'); Skeena ('River of mists'); Cowichan ('Mountain warming its back'); Squalix ('Restful'), Toketic ('Beautiful place'); Chaumox ('Too hot'); Shawnigan ('Great battle') and Nanaimo ('Big strong tribe') – all in British Columbia. Manitoba takes its name from the Ojibwan words 'manito waba' which, referring to the rapids of Lake Manitoba, means 'The sound of the great spirit Manitou.' Its capital, Winnipeg, is derived from the word *win-nipi*, meaning 'murky waters'.

Other interesting Indian place names include Nipigon (Ontario) meaning 'Clear, fast water'; Oakshela (Saskatchewan), meaning 'Child'; Sintaluta (Saskatchewan) which means 'Tail of the red fox'; Shubenacadie (Nova Scotia) meaning 'The place where potatoes grow'; Stewiacke (Nova Scotia) meaning 'Oozing from dead water' and Nappan (Nova Scotia) which means 'Good place for wigwam poles.'

There are also some interesting English and French names. In Quebec there's Rivière-du-Loup (after the wolves that once gathered around the water); Chaudière (describing the rapids as a 'Boiling kettle'); Pointe-aux-trembles (after a host of trembling trees) and Grandmère (after a rock in the river looking like a crouching old woman). English names range from the poetic (eg Moonlight in Ontario) to the bizarre, such as Eyebrow in Saskatoon and Joe Batt's Arm and Come by Chance in Newfoundland. Naturally, you don't get a country with as much water as Canada without a wide variety of place names dedicated to the stuff, including Swift Current, Clearwater, Floods, Wolf Creek, Moose Lake, Canoe River, Mud Bay, Seal Cove and Ocean Pond, to name but a few.

d'Enfer. The train skirts the river until it joins up with the Fraser River near Lytton, making numerous crossings from one bank to the other, following the path forced by engineers down the canyon.

Mile 15–20: Looking onto the mountainside across the river (S) you can see the large swathes of forest devastated by the great forest fire of 1998.

Mile 20–21: Note the slide detectors along the wall of the mountain. Rock slides are common in this spot.

Mile 42: To the west you can make out the **Mad River Rapids**.

Mile 67: Clearwater* This logging and farming town provides a base for visitors to Wells Gray Provincial Park, one of the most beautiful wilderness and recreational areas in British Columbia.

Mile 72(W): An osprey nest balances on a telegraph pole. These birds cause so much trouble with the telegraph lines that false lines are erected where they can build their nests without disrupting the telecommunications network.

Mile 74: Blackpool Named, apparently, because of the dark waters in this stretch of the river, and not after the great city of lights in the north of England.

Mile 86: Before the highway came, the village of **Little Fort** used to operate a cable ferry across the Thompson River, powered only by the river's waters. You can still see the cables.

Mile 114: Fishermen used to stretch nets across the rapids you can see (W) to catch salmon. They're known as Fishtrap Rapids.

Mile 139: Kamloops [35-minute stop]
Kamloops is one of BC's biggest cities, with a population of 83,000. It's the province's most important cattle centre. It has also served as a busy centre of the fur trade, with trading bases established by the Pacific Fur Company in 1812 and the Hudson's Bay Company in 1821. The earliest inhabitants of the area were the Shuswap tribe who named their settlement 'Cume-loups', meaning 'Meeting of waters': the North Thompson and South Thompson rivers meet here.

KAMLOOPS TO VANCOUVER

The portion of the journey between Kamloops and Vancouver takes place mostly overnight on both westbound and eastbound VIA trains. For a detailed description of this route, see *The Rocky Mountaineer* route guide on pp231-3.

'As we drew near Kamloops, characteristics of a different climate could be noted with increasing distinctness. A milder atmosphere, softer skies, easy rolling hills; but the total absence of underbrush and the dry grey grass everywhere covering the ground were the most striking differences to us, accustomed so long to the broad-leaved underbrush and dark green foliage of the humid upper country. We had clearly left the high rainy ground and entered the lower arid region.' **Rev Grant**, *Ocean to Ocean* (1873)

ROUTE GUIDE & MAPS

The Skeena:
Jasper to Prince Rupert

The Skeena takes you through some of the most beautiful wilderness in British Columbia – through the Rocky Mountains, into BC's Interior Plateau and up the Skeena Valley to Prince Rupert. On the way you'll pass snow-capped peaks, glaciers, fjords and waterfalls, and Indian villages with their famed totem poles. The service now operates as a two-day, daylight-only journey, with an overnight stop in Prince George. The travelling time from Jasper to Prince George is 5 hours 15 minutes, and from Prince George to Prince Rupert just over 12 hours.

[MAP 15, p215]

Mile 0–44: The train follows the same track as *The Canadian* between Jasper and Redpass Junction – see pp210.

Mile 44: Redpass Junction Here *The Skeena* parts company with the route followed by *The Canadian*.

As you head north-west, look out towards the rear of the train (E) for superb views of **Mount Robson**, the highest peak in the Rockies at 3954 metres (12,972ft). The views are particularly stunning around Mile 10. Look out for bears and moose; it was here that I made my only bear-sighting from any train.

Mile 14.5: The train passes Swiftwater, an old Grand Trunk Pacific stop so named for the racing waters of all the glacial streams nearby.

Mile 17: Here the train crosses the **Fraser River**. To the west are the 10-metre-high Rearguard Falls. In summer you might be able to spot spawning salmon trying to leap over the falls to continue their epic journey up the river.

Mile 20: Taverna This marks the end of an extremely short railway division.

———————————— **RAILWAY SUBDIVISION** ————————————

Mile 4: Tête Jaune This little hamlet is named after Pierre Hatsinaton, an early 19th-century trapper who was known by all as Tête Jaune because of his famed golden locks (also celebrated in the name of the Yellowhead Pass).

The village was a stop on the route of the famous **Overlanders**, the name now given to a group of about 150 people who, in 1862, set out from Ontario to make their way to the British Columbian gold fields. The trans-Canada railway had not, of course, been built by then; the Overlanders had to take steamships and American railways to get to Fort Garry (Winnipeg). This marked the end of public transport; from here they continued their arduous journey using horses and carts. They set off from Fort Garry at the beginning of June and arrived in

Fort Edmonton on 21 July. This is where the going got really tough; they had to trade in their carts for pack horses and hire Indian guides to show them the paths through the Rockies.

The travellers arrived at Tête Jaune in late August. From here some rafted up the Fraser River to Fort George (Prince George); of these only six survived. Others rafted down to Kamloops, including the only woman of the party, Mrs Catherine Shubert, who was pregnant at the time! The day following the party's arrival in Kamloops, Mrs Shubert gave birth to her fourth child.

Mile 63: McBride This village stands on a high plateau in the shadow of the Rocky Mountains. It's named after Richard McBride, British Columbia's youngest ever premier (he was 33 when he was elected in 1903).

While the Grand Trunk Pacific was being built, this railway divisional point was a busy and booming little town. These days there are only about 700 people left – though the little town recently enjoyed a burst of fame when it took part in a TV show called Hockeyville, where towns across Canada competed to see which showed the most spirit and support for the home hockey team.

McBride is the last scheduled stop before Prince George. There are several flag stops dotted along the desolate stretch of track in between but few people get on or off.

—————— RAILWAY SUBDIVISION ——————

Mile 69: Penny* This tiny hamlet, with a population of just over 30 people, is typical of the sparsely populated communities along this section of the line.

Mile 79: Longworth* Unlike Penny this settlement doesn't even have a station; just a little shack marking the stop.

Mile 122: Giscome* This is a village come down in the world; it once had the biggest sawmill in northern British Columbia but this was shut down in 1974.

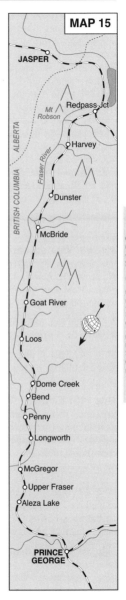

Mile 146: Prince George   [overnight stop]

The train goes over a half-mile-long bridge across the Fraser River on approaching Prince George. The city, with a population of 67,000, is British Columbia's third-largest and is situated at the junction of the Nechako and Fraser rivers, just under 800km north of Vancouver. Simon Fraser established the Fort George fur-trading post here in 1807. The place really took off when the GTP made it an important railway divisional point. Today the main industries are logging and mining.

There's an obligatory overnight stop in Prince George when travelling on *The Skeena*. The train station is conveniently located downtown. Hotels not too far away include the fairly basic ***Downtown Motel*** (☎ 250-563-9241 or ☎ 1-800-663-5729), 650 Dominion St at 6th Ave, and the smarter and more expensive ***Ramada Hotel Downtown Prince George*** (☎ 250-563-0055 or ☎ 1-800-663-6620), at 444 George St. There should be plenty of **taxis** at the train station but if not order one on ☎ 250-564-4444.

———————————— RAILWAY SUBDIVISION ————————————

[MAP 16]

Mile 69: Vanderhoof This little town is named after Herbert Vanderhoof who was hired by the GTP to devise a huge advertising campaign to persuade Americans to move up and settle in the Canadian North West. Apparently his efforts were very successful, though it's hard to believe it travelling through the region today.

Mile 93: This is where the last spike was driven on the Grand Trunk Pacific Railway on 7 April 1914.

Mile 94: Fort Fraser* Like Prince George, this was originally a fur-trading post established by Simon Fraser. Today it's a lumbering village of about 400 people.

Mile 115: Endako With a population of just 100, Endako is a tiny railway divisional point. Its economy revolves around the mining of molybdenum (a metallic element with a very high melting point that's used to strengthen iron and steel). This strange substance is Canada's third most valuable metal after copper and gold.

———————————— RAILWAY SUBDIVISION ————————————

Mile 33: The train skirts Burns Lake (W); note the little island in the middle of the lake. This has been known as **Deadman's Island** ever since an explosion on the track during the construction of the railway caused the death of thirty men, fifteen of whom were standing on this island.

Mile 35: Burns Lake Settlers established a town here in the 1870s when the Overland Telegraph line to Alaska and Siberia was being built (the line was never completed). When the GTP arrived it began to grow quite rapidly and is

ROUTE GUIDE & MAPS

still flourishing today with four mines, including a molybdenum mine, and two large saw mills.

Mile 51(E): Rose Lake's waters flow in two different directions: east through the Endako and Nechako rivers and west to the Bulkley River. The train now follows the Bulkley westwards.

Mile 85: Houston
Originally called Pleasant Valley, the settlement was renamed in 1910 after John Houston who established Prince Rupert's first newspaper. About 4000 people live here today, most of them employed in the town's sawmill or pulp mill.

Mile 105: Look north as the train travels up the Bulkley Valley for your first view of the snow-capped **Skeena Mountains**.

Mile 116: Telkwa* Another small settlement established by the Overland Telegraph as it advanced towards Alaska.

Mile 125: Smithers
Nestling in the Bulkley Valley and surrounded by four mountain ranges, this busy little town (pop about 5000) has an idyllic setting. The mountains behind the station are part of the Skeena Range, and opposite the station you can see the Hudson Bay Range.

――――――― RAILWAY SUBDIVISION ―――――――

Mile 3(E): This lake used to be called Chicken Lake but this was deemed inappropriate by the GTP who changed it to the somewhat duller Lake Kathlyn.

Mile 5: For some time the train has been getting closer and closer to Hudson Bay Mountain (W); at this point you get a superb view of the Kathlyn Glacier on the mountain – a giant slab of ice more than one hundred metres thick.

Mile 13: The train now takes you through a long tunnel after which it starts to climb high above the Bulkley River.

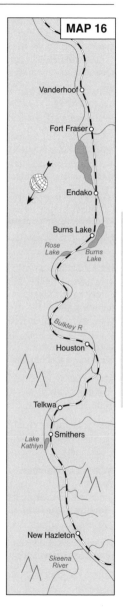

MAP 16

Vanderhoof

Fort Fraser

Endako

Burns Lake

Rose Lake

Burns Lake

Bulkley R

Houston

Telkwa

Lake Kathlyn

Smithers

New Hazleton

Skeena River

ROUTE GUIDE & MAPS

Mile 28–36: Some wonderful, soaring trestle bridges ahead: one over Boulder Creek at Mile 28, then another over Porphyry Creek at Mile 31. Both bridges sweep round to the north giving excellent views along the train.

At Mile 36 you cross a further trestle over Mud Creek – with magnificent mountain views on all sides.

Mile 40: *The Skeena* goes through a 630-metre-long tunnel, the longest of the journey. It's followed by two more tunnels; as the train travels between them look down for a quick glimpse of the Bulkley Gate, a huge 'gate' of rock jutting out into the river.

Mile 45: New Hazleton There are three Hazletons in the area: South Hazleton, New Hazleton and Hazleton. They all have a rich collection of totem poles. It is just after New Hazleton that the train finally joins up with the Skeena River.

Mile 50: Here the train crosses the Sealy Gulch bridge. It's 275 metres long and soars sixty metres above the water.

Once over the bridge the train makes its way into the Skeena Valley. The scenery is breathtaking from here to Prince Rupert.

[MAP 17]

Mile 73: Kitwanga* The translation of Kitwanga is 'The people of the place of plenty of rabbits'. No doubt the GTP were unaware of this or they would surely have changed it to something more seemly. This interesting Indian village is famous for its row of enormous, beautifully-preserved **totem poles**, some as high as eighteen metres. These poles are not visible from the train, but if you look south just after passing the station you can see some other less ornate ones. If you're going to Vancouver be sure to visit the art gallery where you can see some excellent paintings by Emily Carr of the totem poles in this region.

Mile 75: As you leave Kitwanga the view to the south is dominated by the striking Seven Sisters mountain. The jagged peaks remain in view for the next 20 miles or so.

Mile 81: Cedarvale* Founded in the 1880s by a missionary who successfully converted all of the resident natives and turned the village into a hive of Christianity.

Mile 101: Dorreen* Dorreen has no road access so the railway provides a vital link for the few people who live in this remote community. It was an important site during the Omenica gold rush and a few locals still pan the rivers for elusive specks of gold.

Mile 107: Pacific* A former railway divisional point, Pacific was emptied almost overnight when the division was transferred to Terrace. For a long while it was an abandoned and derelict ghost town but it has begun to be repopulated.

Mile 119: Usk* Look out for Usk's ferry which uses the force of the waters to power the boat back and forth across the Skeena River.

Mile 121–123: The riverbanks give way to the solid rock of the Kitselas Canyon which the train cuts through in four tunnels. Just before you enter the first tunnel, look down to the river to see a whirlpool at the canyon's mouth.

Mile 131: Terrace With a population of over 10,000, Terrace is the first community for a long while that can safely be called a town. It was known by local natives as Kitimat but was renamed Terrace by white settlers because of the flat terraces of land lining the banks of the river.

---------------------------------- RAILWAY SUBDIVISION ----------------------------------

Mile 45: Travelling through the **Coast Mountains**, the train moves into what is probably the most stunning landscape of the journey. To the south the **Skeena River** is dotted with numerous little islands. Immediately north are the fern-covered mountainsides, just a few metres from the track. Waterfalls plunge down the rock of the mountains, the most abundant and beautiful occurring between miles 46 and 50. Look out also for the bald eagles that are very common in this area: about six swooped and circled around our train for almost a mile around this point.

Mile 48: Kwinitsa* This very picturesque station is located in a dangerous avalanche spot – note the snowsheds on the side of the mountain.

Miles 65–70: The views across the river (S) are extremely beautiful. The vivid green islands seem to loom out of the swirling mists of the Skeena, an Indian word meaning 'River of mists'. The whole thing looks like a travel brochure for the Norwegian fjords.

Mile 83(S): Smith Island was the location of a remote settlement at the turn of the 20th century, which stands as an abandoned ghost town today.

Mile 87: The train goes over the Zanardi Rapids and on to Kaien Island. Prince Rupert is located a few miles away.

Mile 92: Just before you get to Prince Rupert you pass the ferry terminals (S) from where passengers depart on their journey up to Alaska on the Alaska Marine Highway or down to Vancouver Island with British Columbia Ferries.

Mile 94: Prince Rupert
You'll notice the drop in temperature as soon as you get off the train: Alaska is, after all, just 40 miles away. The town (population around 16,000) is surround-

ROUTE GUIDE & MAPS

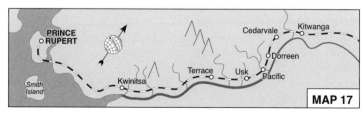

ed by deep-green mountains which seem to rise right out of the sea. The two tallest peaks are over 600 metres. There's not much to do here but it's a beautiful place to do nothing in.

● **Prince Rupert – Where to stay** Accommodation isn't too hard to come by in Prince Rupert, though many places fill up with ferry arrivals in high season so it's worth booking ahead.

An excellent choice is the ***Inn on the Harbour*** at 720 1st Ave (☎ 250-624-9107 or ☎ 1-800-663-8155) with modest but comfortable rooms (some with sea views) from around $50 to $80 a double. Similarly priced and another dependable option is the ***Aleeda*** at 900 3rd Ave (☎ 250-627-1367).

For more luxury, try the ***Best Western Highliner Inn*** at 815 1st Ave West (☎ 250-624-9060 or 1-800-668-3115), where doubles go from around $100. Alternatively, seek advice on accommodation in Prince Rupert from VIA (☎ 250-624-5637) or Tourism BC (☎ 250-624-5637).

● **What to see** Points of interest in town include the **Kwinitsa Station Railway Museum**, steps from the Via train station down at the harbourside and the **Museum of Northern British Columbia**, currently annexed to the **Infocentre** (☎ 250-624-5637) on the corner of 1st Ave and McBride but due to be relocated. Check at the Infocentre for this and any other tourist information.

● **Moving on from Prince Rupert** For those in a hurry, **Air BC** (112 6th St, ☎ 250-624-4554 or 1-800-663-3721) flies daily to Vancouver, as does **Canadian Regional** (office in Rupert Square Mall on 2nd Ave, ☎ 250-624-6292 or 1-800-665-1177). By far the most appealing options, however, are the ferries that head south to Vancouver Island and north to Alaska. The ferry terminal is at Fairview Dock, 2km south of Prince Rupert, and most easily reached by taxi.

BC Ferries' (☎ 250-386-3431 or 1-888-223-3779 from anywhere in BC) services to Port Hardy on the north tip of Vancouver Island leave three or four times a week from June to mid-October and once a week during the rest of the year. It's a 15-hour journey through spectacular fjordland; tickets cost around $100 in summer, and around $60 in winter. **Alaska Marine Highway Ferries** (☎ 250-627-1744 or ☎ 1-800-642-0066) to Skagway in Alaska run four to six times a week from May to mid-October and twice a week in winter (around $120, much less in winter). The journey takes about 36 hours.

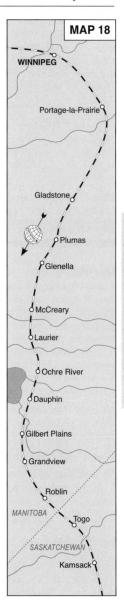

MAP 18

WINNIPEG

Portage-la-Prairie

Gladstone

Plumas

Glenella

McCreary

Laurier

Ochre River

Dauphin

Gilbert Plains

Grandview

Roblin

MANITOBA

Togo

SASKATCHEWAN

Kamsack

ROUTE GUIDE & MAPS

The Hudson Bay:
Winnipeg to Churchill

What possesses people to travel one thousand miles by train through bleak, monotonous landscape to Canada's freezing sub-arctic? Especially when they know they've got to get on the same train and make the same long journey back again. There's not much to see (lakes, trees and tundra) but there's something curiously exciting about travelling through such desolation, going somewhere you can't get to by car, reaching the ultimate end of the line. Apart from this, Churchill is a fascinating place to spend some time if you're interested in wildlife.

The railway, built at great expense over many years and completed in 1929, was intended to transport grain up to Hudson Bay where it would be shipped off to Russia. The bay, however, is frozen over for nine months of the year which somewhat restricts ocean-going activity.

The line runs at an enormous loss and is probably one of VIA's biggest headaches but closure would be highly controversial as the train is the only connection with the outside world for the many native communities along the line. Still, it's hard to know how long the service will survive, so take the opportunity to go on this wonderful dinosaur of a journey while you can.

[MAP 18]

Mile 0: Winnipeg You set out around 10pm from Winnipeg's Union Station (see p129 for details).

Mile 55: Portage-la-Prairie At this point *The Hudson Bay* leaves the tracks used by *The Canadian* to begin its lonely trek north.

Mile 91: Gladstone Dubbed 'Happy Rock' by the train's crew, this little town was originally called Palestine when it was settled by Ontario farmers in the 1870s. Today it's famous in the region for its large cattle auction.

Mile 121: Dauphin This prosperous distribution and transportation centre is one of the oldest Ukrainian settlements in Canada (they established an agricultural community here in the 1890s). The Ukrainian influence continues to be strong and Dauphin hosts Canada's annual National Ukrainian Festival which has been going since the 1960s. Dauphin lies in a fertile valley between Riding Mountain and Duck Lake provincial parks.

———————————— RAILWAY SUBDIVISION ————————————

Mile 62: Roblin Situated on the banks of Goose Lake near the Manitoba/Saskatchewan border, this small agricultural town was founded by the Canadian Northern Railway after the arrival of the first train from Dauphin in 1903. One of Manitoba's first co-operative grain elevators was built here by local farmers.

Mile 79: Togo* Just on the other side of the Manitoba/Saskatchewan border lies this little mixed farming village.

Mile 100: Kamsack Named after a prominent local Indian, this village (population about 2500) was on one of the fur-trading routes for many years.

[MAP 19]

Mile 108: Veregin This town was founded by the Doukhobors in 1899 and named after the movement's leader, Peter Vasilevish Veregin. The Doukhobors were Russians who dissented radically from the Orthodox Church, believing that God is found not in churches but within each man. They rejected secular governments, advocated pacifism and believed that the Bible should be communicated orally rather than through the written word.

Following periodic persecution in Russia the Doukhobors were permitted to emigrate to Canada in 1898–99, in some part thanks to the efforts of Leo Tolstoy and the Quakers. Over 7000 sailed over, most of these settling in western Canada which the government was doing its best to populate at the time.

Mile 124: Canora Take the first two letters of each word in 'Canadian Northern Railway' and what do you get? Thus the town was established and named by the aforementioned company in 1904 when they located a divisional point here.

———————————— RAILWAY SUBDIVISION ————————————

93: Hudson Bay You've still got a long way to go before you get to the bay itself; this town was named by the Canadian Northern Railway in 1908 to commemorate the first phase of the Hudson Bay Railway.

———————————— RAILWAY SUBDIVISION ————————————

Mile 88: The Pas [40-minute stop]

This town provides a welcome chance to get off the train just after breakfast to stretch your legs and get some fresh air. The Pas lies on the south bank of the Saskatchewan River and has been, in its time, an Indian settlement, a fur-trading centre and a fishing and lumbering town. The town-site was bought in 1906 from the Cree inhabitants who now live on the northern banks of the river.

Take a look at the attractive **Anglican Church of the Messiah**, dating from 1840. Some of the furniture inside was carved by members of a rescue party searching for **Sir John Franklin** and his fellow explorers who'd disappeared on their search for the North-West Passage. European explorers had been looking for a water route through North America to the Orient ever since it was discovered that this continent blocked the way to Asia. Franklin's expedition was hoping to discover a route through the Arctic when it went missing in 1845; what followed was one of the largest ever rescue operations of its kind. Franklin was never found, and efforts to solve the mystery continued well into the 20th century. The bodies of some crew members were discovered buried on Beechy Island, perfectly preserved by the permafrost. In 1986 these were temporarily exhumed and analysed by scientists: they discovered evidence of scurvy and probably cannibalism among the men.

An earlier famous explorer in search of the elusive North-West Passage was **Henry Hudson** who set out to find it back in 1610. He took his expedition into the huge bay and sailed down the eastern coast, where he was forced to winter his boat.

When the ice broke up Hudson set about continuing the exploration to the dismay of his crew. A mutiny broke out and the rebels packed Hudson, his son and other supporters into a boat and set them adrift on the bay to die. It is in honour of this unfortunate leader that Hudson Bay is named.

As the train pulls out of **The Pas** look north as you cross the river at the Otineka Mall, part of the Indian Reserve and renowned for its finely crafted goods.

———————— **RAILWAY SUBDIVISION** ————————

Mile 9: This is where the lakes start. The first one you can see is **Tremaudan Lake** (E). Next, at Mile 13 (W), is **Clearwater Lake**. Then at Mile 31 you can see **Cormorant Lake** (W). This is an important nesting habitat for waterfowl; keep your eyes open for geese, teal and crow-ducks. You'll pass many more lakes along this stretch. If you're travelling during spring or summer, look out for the numerous wild flowers growing alongside the track: tiger

ROUTE GUIDE & MAPS

lilies, brown-eyed Suzies, pink lady's slippers and honeysuckle are particularly abundant. The ground is also punctuated by curious limestone rock formations.

Mile 29: The little village of Budd was named after Henry Budd, the first native in western Canada to be ordained as an Anglican Minister (in 1853).

Mile 37: The train passes two large osprey nests on the top of telegraph poles right by the side of the track (E).

Mile 41: Cormorant This was one of the first settlements to spring up along the line once the railway was completed. There'll probably be quite a few people getting on or off here, mainly Indian or Inuit families. Note that the word 'Eskimo' is not a polite way to refer to an Inuit – it means 'Eater of raw flesh' in the Algonquian language. 'Inuit', on the other hand, simply means 'People'.

Mile 55: Rawebb You'd be forgiven for thinking Rawebb was an Indian place name. The village was named after a former mayor of Winnipeg, Ralph Webb.

Mile 81: Wekusko This tiny settlement of around 50 people is located on one of the few roads in the region, a 35-mile link to the nearby town of Snow Lake.

[MAP 20]

Mile 90: The limestone rock gives way to *muskeg* (an Algonquian word meaning 'grassy bog'). Muskeg is organic terrain which produces peat deposits. Where there's muskeg there's often permafrost, which the train will be moving into presently.

Mile 136: Wabowden Situated between tiny Bowden and Rock Island lakes, Wabowden serves as a supply centre for the communities in northern Manitoba. Between here and Thicket Portage look out for pelicans and bald eagles.

Mile 177: Hockin This village was named in honour of Corporal CH Hockin of the North West Mounted Police who was killed in 1897 in a shoot-out with a Cree outlaw known as **Almighty Voice** (or Kah-kee-say-mane-too-wayo). Almighty Voice had been imprisoned for stealing a cow and when he escaped from jail he killed a mountie in the process. Police hunted him for almost two years before cornering him with a couple of young relatives. The Indians were up against a hundred police and civilians but they put up a fierce fight, killing three men (including Hockin). In the end the fugitives were killed, and the incident has become a symbol of the tragically violent confrontation between the Indians and the whites in North America.

Back in 1872, Butler wrote: 'Terrible deeds have been wrought out in that western land; terrible heart-sickening deeds of cruelty and rapacious infamy – have been I say? No, are to this day and hour, and never perhaps more sickening than now in the full blaze of nineteenth century civilization. If on the long

ROUTE GUIDE & MAPS

(Opposite) Top: Grain elevators tower over the rail track all the way across the prairies. It has been said that they are the only indigenous form of Canadian architecture. **Bottom**: Winnipeg Railway Museum (see p134) is well worth a visit and usually open when *The Canadian* takes its hour-long break here. **(Overleaf)**: Lake Louise, Banff National Park.

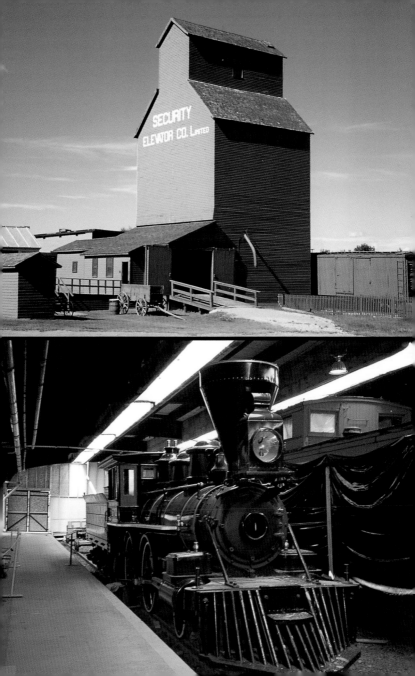

line of the American frontier, from the Gulf of Mexico to the British boundary, a single life is taken by an Indian, if even horse or ox be stolen from a settler, the fact is chronicled in scores of journals throughout the United States, but the reverse of the story we never know. The countless deeds of perfidious robbery, of ruthless murder done by white savages out in these Western wilds never find the light of day. The poor red man has no telegraph, no newspaper, no type, to tell his sufferings and his woes. My God, what a terrible tale could I not tell of these dark deeds done by the white savage against the far nobler red man!' (*The Great Lone Land*).

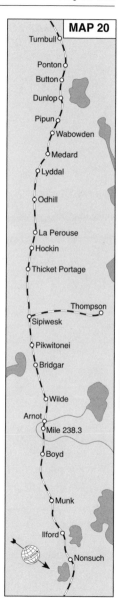

Mile 184: Thicket Portage Fur traders used this as a land crossing between the lakes and streams which connect Lake Winnipeg to the Nelson River (which goes up to Hudson Bay).

One of the crew told me that back in the '70s the mayor of Thicket Portage was given a large sum of money to have a road constructed in the area. Instead, he took off to Hawaii with his friends for a holiday. The locals were furious and practically lynched him on his return. For a while he was reduced to trapping and selling furs to earn his crusts but when it became clear that no one else was willing to do the job, he found himself reinstated as mayor!

Mile 200: At Sipiwesk the train leaves the main line to follow a 30-mile branch to Thompson and back.

Mile 30: Thompson   **[90-minute stop]**
This busy industrial city of 15,000 people is something of a surprise after all the remote communities and stretches of wilderness you've been going through. It was created from scratch following the discovery of abundant nickel deposits in 1956 and named after John F Thompson, the chairman of INCO.

Unfortunately the railway station is a few miles from the city so there's very little to do here in the 90-minute stop unless you're prepared to take a taxi into town and back. The attractions aren't, however, worth the risk of being left behind by the train.

(Opposite) If you go to Churchill between October and May you can try out a sled ride (see p182). Each dog is capable of hauling up to 180 pounds.

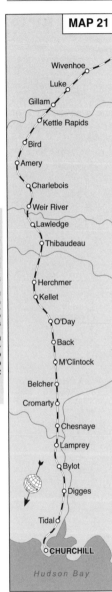

MAP 21

ROUTE GUIDE & MAPS

Mile 200: Four hours later you're back in **Sipiwesk** – a depressing lack of advancement.

Mile 213: Pikwitonei This name is taken from the Cree word meaning 'Broken mouth' though no one seems to be sure why. Perhaps another bust-up between mounties and natives?

Mile 230: Wilde This place name definitely does come from another Indian-NWMP confrontation, this time in 1886. Sergeant WB Wilde was killed in the incident and the village name commemorates him.

Mile 238.3: This flag stop is known simply by its mileage. By the time you get here it'll probably be nighttime again.

Mile 269: Munk Named after Jens Munk, the first European to discover what is now Churchill. The Danish navigator arrived in September 1619 with two ships carrying forty-eight men. They were forced to spend winter there and suffered an outbreak of scurvy. Only three men survived; Munk was one of them.

Mile 295: Nonsuch This village is named after the famous ship owned by the Hudson's Bay Company.

[MAP 21]

Mile 326: Gillam With a population of nearly 2000, this is the biggest community since Thompson. The town's economy is based on its three hydroelectric power stations on the Nelson River.

Mile 350: Around here the train leaves the Laurentian Plateau and moves into the Hudson Bay lowlands. From here onwards the muskeg is permanently frozen, a condition known as permafrost. The frost extends about 12 metres down, making engineering work extremely difficult. The telegraph wires have to be supported by three poles forming a tripod.

Mile 440–80: When morning breaks you'll probably be travelling through the Barren Lands. Pull up your blinds and prepare to be dazzled by snow (for most of the year, anyway). The trees have nearly all vanished, and the ones that are left are stunted and shrivelled. You've gone beyond the tree line into the sub-arctic tundra. Look out for arctic ptarmigan and silver fox.

Mile 509: Churchill At long, long last!

The Rocky Mountaineer

The privately owned *Rocky Mountaineer* runs along three different routes: the **Kicking Horse** route from Vancouver to Banff/Calgary; the **Yellowhead route** from Vancouver to Jasper; and the newly introduced **Fraser Discovery route** from Whistler to Jasper. All of them are two-day daylight-only journeys with overnight accommodation in a hotel included in the package.

Trains on the Kicking Horse route and Yellowhead route follow the same track from Vancouver to **Kamloops**, in the Rockies, where passengers spend the night. After Kamloops, Jasper-bound trains take the northern route through the Rockies via the Yellowhead Pass (along the same track as *The Canadian*), while travellers going to Banff or Calgary take the original, southern route on CPR tracks. This is the only passenger train to travel along part of Canada's first transcontinental line, completed in 1885.

The Fraser Discovery route follows the old Pacific Great Eastern (which later became BC Rail) tracks along what was called the 'Cariboo Dayliner' line to Prince George, where it joins the tracks used by *The Skeena* between Prince George and Jasper.

Note that journeys can be taken in either an eastbound or westbound direction: in this guide, we describe the Kicking Horse and Yellowhead routes in a westbound direction, in common with all the VIA Rail routes described in this guide; however, the Fraser Discovery route is described in a northbound direction (ultimately heading east) following the direction of construction and the mile markers within each subdivision.

KICKING HORSE ROUTE: CALGARY/BANFF TO VANCOUVER

Calgary/Banff to Kamloops
[Map 22, p229]

Mile 0: Calgary (MT) For more information on Calgary see pp154-63. Home of cowboys, stampedes and oil-wells, Calgary is Canada's most famous prairie city. It's also the city closest to the Rocky Mountains that has an international airport, with plenty of scheduled and charter flights arriving from all over the world.

Mile 16(S): Look to the front of the train for your first glimpse of the Rocky Mountains, which are about 70km away.

Mile 24: Cochrane Just beyond the station is the Cochrane Landmark, a bronze statue of a cowboy riding his horse.

Mile 45: The peaks loom closer and closer as the train advances towards the mountains. To the north you can see Saddle Peak and Orient Peak and to the south you can see Heart Mountain.

Mile 54: Kananaskis The name of this village is Indian for 'Man with a tomahawk in his head' and is named after a local native who survived this experience.

Mile 66(S): The Three Sisters Mountain was given this name by the brother of Major AB Rogers, the explorer who discovered Rogers Pass, because he thought its peaks looked like three nuns.

Mile 71: Banff National Park At this point the train crosses the eastern boundary of Banff National Park. It was originally known as the Rocky Mountain National Park when it was founded in 1887 (when there were just two other national parks in the world).

It was when the railway was being constructed that Banff's famous hot springs were discovered, prompting immediate claims to the land by men hoping to reap a profit. The Canadian Government decided that the area must be protected from commercial development and established the park. Today it encompasses 6640 sq km and is Canada's most heavily visited national park, attracting almost three million visitors each year.

Mile 73(S): For the next eight miles the train skirts the towering **Mount Rundle**.

Mile 81: Banff The station was originally known as 'Siding 29' by the railway men building the line; it was renamed in 1880 by Donald Smith of the CPR.

Today the town (population 4600) is a busy (and some would say overcrowded) base for thousands of tourists, providing them with an impressive quantity of hotels, restaurants and shops.

Its most famous hotel is the exclusive *Banff Springs Hotel*, formally opened by William Cornelius Van Horne for the CPR back in 1888. You can see the green turrets of its copper roof as you pass it on the train at Mile 82 (S).

Mile 99(N): There are excellent views of **Castle Mountain**, with its broad, flat top from here. The mountain was originally named in the 1850s by the explorer, James Hector, but it was officially changed to Mount Eisenhower in 1946. This change of name was strongly resisted by local people who lobbied to have it changed back. In 1979 the government duly restored the mountain's original name, allotting Eisenhower Peak to its highest point.

Mile 116(S): Watch out for a quick flash of **Victoria Glacier**. You can't see much of it from the train but fear not: you will see its image rising over Lake Louise thousands of times on thousands of postcards, calendars and tea towels before you get out of Canada.

Mile 116.5(S): Lake Louise station This is no longer used by the railways; the beautifully preserved log building now serves as a restaurant.

Mile 122: Stephen [PT] At 1625 metres above sea level, this is the highest point on the CPR line. It's also the point at which the train crosses the Continental Divide.

ROUTE GUIDE & MAPS

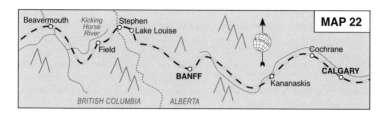

Mile 128: Spiral Tunnels Here the train goes through the extraordinary Spiral Tunnels. When the CPR decided to build the track through the Kicking Horse Pass they hadn't quite reckoned on the steepness of the drop on the western side of Mount Stephen. There was no time or money for building tunnels, so the track plunged straight down for eight miles at a dizzying 4.5% gradient – more than twice the grade normally permitted by the government.

This hazardous stretch of track was known as the **Big Hill**. Trains made it to the top only with the help of four specially designed locomotives with 154-tonne engines; two pulled at the front, and another two pushed from behind. Most dangerous, though, was the trip down the hill. All passenger trains stopped at the top so that the brakes could be thoroughly checked before the heart-stopping descent began. Safety switches were operated to divert runaway trains onto uphill tracks. Nonetheless, many lives were lost as a result of trains getting out of control.

The danger was finally eliminated when the **Spiral Tunnels** were built in 1909, reducing the gradient to 2.2%. This was achieved by curving the track 250 degrees through the Upper Spiral, and then 230 degrees through the Lower Spiral. The train loops around in a sort of figure of eight, in such a way that the rear of the train crosses over the front of the train, several feet below.

Mile 136: Field Once a busy railway divisional point, Field's economy now revolves around the tourism industry in Yoho National Park.

─────────────── **RAILWAY SUBDIVISION** ───────────────

Mile 20: The train, following the course of the **Kicking Horse River**, enters the Kicking Horse Canyon. The river takes its name from an incident in which Dr James Hector, a member of the Palliser expedition commissioned to explore western Canada in 1857–60, was thrown off his horse when he rode it into the river's rushing waters. Hector was badly injured by a kick from the frightened horse, but he continued with the expedition.

Mile 35: The Kicking Horse River meets the Columbia River. To the south you can see the Beaverfoot Range and to the north the Van Horne Range.

Mile 62: Beavermouth This is the site of the riots by a group of striking railwaymen, desperate for their long-overdue wages in the middle of the CPR's financial crisis of 1884. It's reputed to be a good place for sighting bears.

[Map 23]

Mile 70: Photo opportunities abound as the train crosses a series of high bridges. First is the 183-metre-long **Mountain Creek Bridge**. Then, at Mile 74, is a bridge over **Surprise Creek**, over 50 metres below. Finally you reach the climax, the crossing of the highest bridge on the CPR line: **Stoney Creek Bridge** at Mile 76. It's 147 metres long and curves 99 metres over the water. For the next twenty miles you'll be surrounded by breath-taking mountain vistas as you travel through the heart of the Selkirks.

Mile 80: The train enters the five-mile-long **Connaught Tunnel**, built to avoid the dangerous avalanches that plagued the route over Rogers Pass. It was completed in 1916 and until 1988 was the longest tunnel in North America. This record is now held by the **Mount McDonald Tunnel**, nine miles long and built underneath the Connaught Tunnel. It is used by westbound freight trains.

Mile 94: Note the concrete snowsheds above the train (N); there are frequent avalanches in this area.

Mile 125: Revelstoke This small city of around 8000 people was named after Lord Revelstoke, an English banker who helped bail the CPR out of their financial difficulties in 1884.

──────────────── **RAILWAY SUBDIVISION** ────────────────

Mile 5: The train is now on its way up the last big climb, this time up the Monashee Mountains which it will cross via Eagle Pass. There are waterfalls at this point on both sides of the train.

Mile 28: Craigellachie No fanfare marked the occasion when, on 7 November 1885, Donald Smith drove in the last spike of the CPR trans-Canada railway here in **Eagle Pass**. The only monument to that triumphant completion is a plaque on a cairn by the side of the track (N).

Mile 44: For the next 25 miles the train skirts the Salmon Arm of **Shuswap Lake**, which boasts prodigious quantities of Dolly Varden and kokanee salmon. Note the colourful houseboats moored in the lake.

Mile 82: Look south for a glorious view over Shuswap Lake.

Mile 100: At this point the train starts to move away from the forested mountains into a landscape of gently rolling hills.

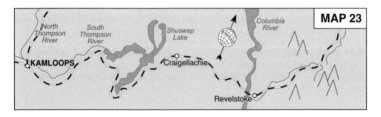

Mile 103(N): Look out for the **hoodoos** standing on the hillside. These fantastic pillars of rock have been eroded into strange shapes by wind, rain and running water.

Mile 111(S): If you're wondering what's growing in these fields it is, in fact, ginseng. Once grown only in Korea and Manchuria, this plant is now thriving in British Columbia.

Mile 114: This is the site of Bill Miner's least successful train robbery. Miner, known as the Gentleman Bandit, was a famous Canadian train robber in the early 20th century. In 1904 he had robbed a CPR train near Mission (BC) of $7000 but when he tried to pull off the same stunt at this spot two years later he got the wrong train and ended up with only $15 and a bottle of pills.

The robber, getting on for 60 by now, was obviously losing his touch: he was captured by police and sent to jail for 25 years. He did, however, manage to escape a year later taking off to the US where he spent the rest of his days robbing more trains.

Mile 128: Kamloops This is where you get off *The Rocky Mountaineer* for your overnight stay at a nearby hotel. A brief description of Kamloops is on p213.

———————————————— RAILWAY SUBDIVISION ————————————————

Kamloops to Vancouver   **[Map 24, p232]**

Mile 1: The train follows the South Thompson River (S) as far as Lytton, 97 miles away. The track is carved into the rocky cliffs of the Thompson Canyon and switches back and forth across the river.

The colours of the canyon walls are muted reds and browns and the desert-like landscape contrasts sharply with the lush mountains you passed on your previous day's journey.

Mile 49: Ashcroft* This is one of Canada's driest towns, with an average annual rainfall of just 18 centimetres.

Rev Grant was not charmed by the place when he was here in 1872 and wrote: 'The country about Ashcroft is sparsely peopled, and men accustomed to the rich grassy plains on the other side of the mountains might wonder at first sight that it is peopled at all. In appearance, it is little better than a vast sand and gravel pit, bounded by broken hills, bald and arid except on a few summits that support a scanty growth of scrub pines. The cattle had eaten off all the bunch-grass within three or four miles of the road, and a poor substitute for it chiefly in the shape of a bluish weed or shrub, called 'sage grass' or 'sage brush' has taken its place.'

Mile 85–90: The canyon narrows into what is known as **Jaws of Death Gorge**. Look down to the racing waters of **Suicide Rapids** at Mile 87.

Mile 90–95: Rainbow Canyon The walls of the cliffs are suddenly striped with pinks, greens and greys creating a beautiful rainbow effect.

ROUTE GUIDE & MAPS

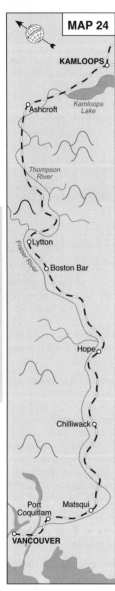

MAP 24

KAMLOOPS

Ashcroft

Kamloops Lake

Thompson River

Lytton

Boston Bar

Hope

Chilliwack

Port Coquitlam   Matsqui

VANCOUVER

Mile 97: Lytton This is where the Thompson River meets the Fraser River which the train follows nearly all the way to Vancouver, through the **Fraser Canyon**. It is said that you can sometimes see a clear line dividing the Thompson's clear waters from the Fraser's murky waters for some distance after they meet.

In *The Queen's Highway* Cumberland described the impressive scene in 1887: 'Six miles below Lytton a gulch, deeper and broader than any of the preceding ones, presents itself. To cross it by an ordinary bridge would be impossible, and a cantilever bridge, 96 feet above low-water mark, has been constructed at a great cost for the purpose.

'As one crosses the bridge a magnificent scene presents itself in thus being suspended over the surging, maddening river, increased in force by the waters of the North Thompson River, and with a full view of the gloomy canyon through which we have passed.'

Mile 103: The train crosses the Fraser River on one of the **Cisco Bridges**, a spectacular crossing high above the river's turbulent waters.

There are two bridges side by side – one built by the CPR in the 1880s, the other by the CNR about thirty years later. As you cross the CNR bridge, look behind for a view of the beautiful cantilever CPR bridge.

Mile 125: Boston Bar* This village was established by fortune-seekers of the Fraser River gold rush of 1858.

───────────────── **RAILWAY SUBDIVISION** ─────────────────

Mile 7: Don't miss the dramatic **Hell's Gate** where the river is forced to squeeze through the narrowest point of the gorge at high speed.

The narrowing was caused by a huge landslide triggered off by an explosion during the construction of the CN line. The landslide, blocking the sockeye salmon run that annually ascends the river, had a catastrophic effect on the fishing industry; fishways have since been constructed in an attempt to remedy the problem.

Totem Poles

Everyone knows what a totem pole is but not everyone knows that they are made almost exclusively in North-West British Columbia by Indian tribes. Contrary to popular belief these carved cedar logs are not used for religious worship. Their functions are as diverse as marking a grave, supporting a roof, celebrating a house-moving, or ridiculing a local individual, whose likeness is painted upside down.

The tallest, brightest and most elaborately carved totem poles tell of family histories or legends using a complicated series of symbols, often in the form of animals or spirits. Each family has its own symbols, so interpretation of the story on a totem pole usually requires a narrator from the family that constructed it. Unfortunately the poles have a relatively short life span since the moisture of the climate rots the wood.

Mile 27: Keep an eye out for Lady Franklin Rock lying in the Fraser River, named after English explorer Sir John Franklin's wife who came searching for him after he disappeared in 1845 (see p223).

Mile 40: Hope* A fur-trading post was established here in 1848 but it was from the 1858 gold rush that the town grew affluent. At Hope the rugged rocks of the Fraser Canyon recede into the fertile Fraser Valley, surrounded by verdant mountains.

Mile 71: Chilliwack* This is a busy agriculture-based city of around 42,000 people. Its name is thought to mean 'Going back up' (probably from the river) in a local native language.

Mile 87: Matsqui* This stop is close to the town of **Mission**, originally settled in 1862 by a Roman Catholic priest who aimed to convert the Indians. It was also the site of Canada's first train robbery.

Mile 111: Port Coquitlam The train passes an enormous CP railyard here (N); it covers 468 acres and can hold 3700 rail cars.

Mile 131: Vancouver The journey ends in Canada's third-largest and fastest growing city. For more information on Vancouver, see pp164-80.

YELLOWHEAD ROUTE: JASPER TO VANCOUVER

The Yellowhead route is not described here as it is covered elsewhere: you will find a description of the section from **Jasper to Kamloops** in the guide to *The Canadian* on pp210-3, while the section from **Kamloops to Vancouver** is described above in the guide to the Kicking Horse route (pp231-3).

FRASER DISCOVERY ROUTE: WHISTLER TO JASPER

[Map 25]

Mile 73.7: Whistler (MT) The old 'Cariboo Dayliner' route (operated by Pacific Great Eastern/BC Rail) actually began in North Vancouver, not Whistler – and that's why Whistler is Mile 73.7 and not mile 0. Today, the first portion of the 'Cariboo Dayliner' route is covered by *The Whistler Mountaineer*; see p237-8 for a description.

When the line was constructed in the early twentieth century, Whistler – in the heart of the Coast Mountains – was a little mountain hideaway visited by in-the-know locals; these days it's one of the largest and most famous ski resorts in North America and will host the Winter Olympics with Vancouver in 2010. The resort also offers plenty of summer activities too, such as whitewater rafting, mountain biking and golf.

Heading out of Whistler, the train follows the **Green River** down into the lush Pemberton Valley, home to Douglas fir, hemlock and cedar.

Mile 80: Look out for the glacier-fed **Green Lake** (W), with its vivid jade-green water.

Mile 87: The valley narrows to a slender canyon; Green River's waters hurtle down the dramatic **Nairn Falls** at Mile 91 (E).

Mile 95: Pemberton An agricultural town famous for its enormous potatoes and turnips.

Mile 99.4: Mt Currie The Mount Currie Reservation is BC's largest native reserve, home to the Lillooet people.

Mile 100: The train climbs up towards the town of **Birken**, alongside the salmon-rich Birkenhead River.

Mile 113: Shortly after passing **Birkengates Lake** (E), the train begins its descent into the dry side of the Coast Mountains, characterized by its desert-like landscape. The brown sagebrush and tumbleweed form a striking contrast with the lush temperate rainforests on the coastal side of the mountains.

Mile 123.8: Keep your camera at the ready for the beautiful **Anderson Lake** (E), which the track skirts for 15 miles.

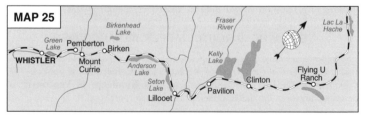

MAP 25

Birkenhead Lake · Green Lake · Pemberton · Birken · WHISTLER · Mount Currie · Anderson Lake · Seton Lake · Lillooet · Fraser River · Kelly Lake · Pavilion · Clinton · Lac La Hache · Flying U Ranch

Mile 141: The train follows the banks of another picturesque lake, the moss-green **Seton Lake** (W), flanked by vertical cliffs looming over the tracks.

Mile 157.5: Lillooet In the 1850s and 60s, Lillooet sprang up as a base for prospectors who headed first for the gold-rich sand bars of the Fraser River, and then for British Columbia's Cariboo region when gold strikes in 1862 precipitated the **Cariboo gold rush**. The town's boom-and-bust years led to a lot of fortunes being made and lost overnight. Just outside town, the macabre 'hanging tree' was the site of desperate suicides, as testified by several nearby graves.

──────────── **RAILWAY SUBDIVISION** ────────────

Mile 160–192: Leaving Lillooet behind, the train crosses the 242m/800ft-long Fraser River Bridge onto the east side of the Fraser River and climbs steeply up the Fraser Canyon – by Mile 180 you are vertiginously high above the river, on one of the most dramatic stretches of rail track in the Rockies.

Mile 192.2: Kelly Lake Overlooked by the beautiful Marble Mountains, this lake (W) makes a striking sight.

Mile 203: Clinton Once a major stagecoach stop on the Cariboo Trail from Lillooet (a wagon road built by prospectors during the gold-rush days), Clinton marks the beginning of the **Cariboo Plateau** – a flat, wide-open area between two mountain ranges, home to many ranches. The most common tree found on the plateau is the trembling aspen, whose leaves turn a dazzling golden colour in autumn.

Mile 206: A long trestle bridge takes you over the Fiftyone Creek canyon.

Mile 215.2: As you cross the Sixtyone Creek Bridge, look east for a brief glimpse of the ten-thousand-year-old **Painted Chasm**: a deep channel cut through the rock by the meltwater from receding glaciers. The walls of the Chasm are streaked by many vivid colours, thanks to the rich minerals of the rock.

Mile 236.3: The **Flying U Ranch** is Canada's oldest working guest ranch. Look east and you might spot a few ranch-hands riding their horses along the trail that runs parallel to the train track.

Mile 273.4: The train skirts the shore of **Lac La Hache** (E), whose exceptionally transparent waters are packed with trout. The wetlands around the lake also provide a home to many birds, including the loon, which appears on the $1 coin. Loons, incidentally, are said to be reliable predictors of storms – when one is on its way, a loon will often become very agitated, flap wildly above the lake and fly into the wind.

ROUTE GUIDE & MAPS

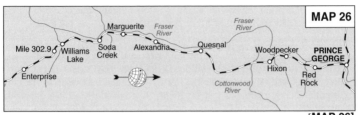

[MAP 26]

Mile 302.9: This tiny stop originally served the Cariboo Indian School, established by missionaries in the 19th century.

Mile 313.9: Williams Lake A busy livestock centre, Williams Lake is famous for its annual stampede, held here every July.

———————————— RAILWAY SUBDIVISION ————————————

Mile 330: Snaking its way up the Fraser Canyon, the train crosses the dramatic **Deep Creek Bridge**, the second-highest railway bridge in North America at 94.5m/312ft above the water.

Mile 384: Quesnal This is where you get off the train for your **overnight stop** in a nearby hotel. The largest town in the Cariboo region, Quesnal (pronounced 'Kwa-Nell') is a big sawmill and pulp-mill centre. It was the 'temporary' terminus of the rail line for 30 years, due to the difficulty of getting the track over the Cottonwood River.

Mile 398: Fourteen miles north of Quesnal, the **Cottonwood River** held up the completion of the rail line for three decades, owing to the difficulties of building a bridge on the unstable river banks. The bridge you cross was finally built in 1952 at a cost of $1 million.

Mile 462.4: Prince George When the track from Quesnal to Prince George was completed on 31 October 1952 (forty years behind schedule), celebrations were held throughout the city. For a brief description of the town today, see p216.

On to Jasper: From Prince George, *The Rocky Mountaineer* continues east to Jasper along the tracks used by VIA Rail's *The Skeena*: you will find a route guide for this portion of the journey on pp214-6.

The Whistler Mountaineer:
Vancouver to Whistler

The Whistler Mountaineer follows the first portion of the old Pacific Great Eastern (later BC Rail) 'Cariboo Dayliner' route from Vancouver to Prince George, started in 1912 and not completed until 1956. The three-hour journey to Whistler covers 73 miles of glorious scenery, including the stunning Howe Sound.

[MAP 27]

Mile 1: As you pull away from the North Vancouver terminus, look out for the totem poles in Stanley Park (see p178) to the south. You can also admire the fantastic waterfront houses of West Vancouver.

Mile 11: The train goes through the 1700-foot-long **Horseshoe Bay Tunnel**, deemed so long that a special rule was created for it: 'Train crews are limited to a maximum of 45 minutes in the tunnel. If this time is exceeded, self-containing breathing apparatus must be used. All windows are to be kept closed and crewmen walking in the tunnel should go in pairs (buddy system).'

Mile 14–39: For 25 miles, the train hugs the shore of **Howe Sound**, a stunning fjord studded with islands. It's a fabulous stretch of track: on one side (E) the Coast Mountains rise steeply above you; on the other, the views across the fjord to the mountains are breathtaking.

Mile 36.1: Look east for a good view of the **Shannon Falls**, the third-highest in BC at 335m/1100ft.

Mile 40.4: Squamish The train passes through the rail yards of the West Coast Railway Heritage Park, home to the famous ***Royal Hudson* steam train** which for many years travelled between Vancouver and Squamish during the summer season – until BC Rail (who operated it) was sold to CN Rail in 2005, with all passenger services discontinued.

Mile 40–75: The train begins its climb over the Coast Mountains, gaining almost 610m/2000ft. At Mile 47, look west as you cross the Cheekye River for stunning views onto the snow-capped **Tantalus mountain range**, which takes its name from the Greek myth of Tantalus, tortured by Hades and plunged into ice cold water with fruit dangled just out of his reach (giving rise to the word 'tantalize').

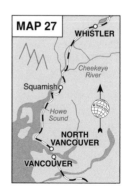

Far below, you can make out the whitewater rapids pounding through the canyon.

Mile 53: There are dizzying views for the next three miles as the track clings to a vertiginous ledge carved out of the side of the sheer **Cheekamus Canyon**.

Mile 65.3: Brandywine Falls (E) This is the only bit of rail track in Canada to cross over the top of a waterfall – look down for great views onto the thundering water.

Mile 73.7: Whistler The journey ends at the first-class ski resort (and year-round holiday resort) of Whistler. For comprehensive details on accommodation, things to do and other information, check Tourism Whistler's own website at ⌨ www.tourismwhistler.com.

ROUTE GUIDE & MAPS

APPENDIX A: TIMETABLES

The timetables given below are the latest available but are, of course, subject to change. Check with VIA and the Rocky Mountaineer. VIA's website (⌨ www.viarail.ca) has downloadable timetables in pdf format. Note also that although VIA give distances in kilometres, the CN subdivisions are still marked by mileposts at the side of the track.

OCEAN: HALIFAX–MONTREAL

Station name	Km from Halifax	Westbound Day 1 Ex Tue	Eastbound
Halifax	0	12.35	16.20
Truro	103	14.13	14.48
Springhill Jct*	200	15.33	13.24
Amherst	227	15.58	13.02
Sackville	243	16.15	12.46
Moncton	304	ar 17.00	dp 11.59
		dp 17.20	ar 11.44
Rogersville*	397	18.22	10.44
Miramichi	433	18.58	10.10
Bathurst	504	20.09	08.54
Petit Rocher*	521	20.25	08.29
Jacquet River*	549	20.45	08.07
Charlo*	574	21.03	07.48
Campbellton	605	21.50 (AT)	07.16 (AT)
Matapédia	624	21.40 (ET)	05.02 (ET)
Causapscal*	681	22.28	04.15
Amqui	703	22.50	03.55
Sayabec*	727	23.11	03.33
Mont-Joli	774	23.59	02.48
		Day 2	
Rimouski	803	00.31	02.11
Trois-Pistoles	864	01.41	00.52
Rivière-du-Loup	907	02.32	00.23
			Day 2
La Pocatière	975	03.15	23.37
Montmagny*	1035	03.48	23.03
Charny	1099	ar 04.40	dp 22.07
		dp 04.55	ar 21.52
Drummondville	1246	06.35	20.18
Saint-Hyacinthe	1292	07.10	19.27
Saint-Lambert	1339	07.48	18.52
Montreal	1346	08.15	18.30
			Day 1 Ex Tue

* Flag stop. The train will stop here only when someone wants to get on or off.
AT = Atlantic Time, ET = Eastern Time

CORRIDOR: MONTREAL–TORONTO (WESTBOUND)

Station name	Km	No 53 Ex Sun	No 57 Daily	No 61 Ex Sat	No 65 Ex Sun	No 67 Ex S/S*	No 69 Daily
Montreal	0	06.55	0940	11.40	15.40	17.00	18.15
Dorval	19	07.15	10.04	12.00	16.00	17.20	18.36
Cornwall	111	08.01	10.58	12.47	16.46		19.27
Brockville	204		11.48				20.14
Gananoque	249						
Kingston	285	Ar 09.19	12.33	14.07	18.04		20.58
		Dp 09.22	12.36	14.10	18.07		21.01
Belleville	357		13.20				21.42
Cobourg	426		13.59				22.18
Oshawa	488	10.57	14.39		19.42		22.56
Guildwood	518		14.57	15.58			23.14
Toronto	539	11.28	15.20	16.17	20.13	21.16	23.34

CORRIDOR: TORONTO–MONTREAL (EASTBOUND)

Station name	Km	No 52 Ex S/S*	No 56 Ex Sat	No 60 Daily	No 64 Daily	No 66 Ex Sat	No 68 Ex S/S*
Toronto	0	06.55	09.30	11.30	15.10	17.00	18.35
Guildwood	21	07.15	09.50	11.53			18.56
Oshawa	51	07.33	10.08	12.13	15.44		19.15
Cobourg	113	08.06	10.41	12.51			19.52
Belleville	182	08.43	11.14	13.29	16.46		
Kingston	254	Ar 09.18	11.49	14.08	17.21		21.03
		Dp 09.21	11.52	14.11	17.24		21.06
Gananoque	290						21.28
Brockville	335	10.06	12.38	14.58			21.54
Cornwall	428	10.53	13.23	15.48	18.44		22.42
Dorval	520	11.39	14.09	16.40	19.31	20.58	23.31
Montreal	539	11.56	14.26	17.07	19.48	21.15	23.49

* **Ex S/S** = excluding Saturday and Sunday

CANADIAN: TORONTO–VANCOUVER

Station name	Km	Westbound Day 1 Tu Th Sa	Eastbound
Toronto	0	09.00	20.00
Washago*	143	11.08	17.49
Parry Sound*	241	12.58	16.17
Sudbury Jct*	422	15.58	13.21
Capreol	444	Ar 16.35	Dp 12.55
		Dp 17.00	Ar 12.30
Laforest*	493	17.52	11.11
McKee's Camp*	494	18.00	10.57
Felix*	521	18.16	10.41
Ruel*	527	18.27	10.37
Westree*	547	18.40	10.14
Gogama*	583	19.20	09.44
Folyet*	683	20.40	08.19
Elsas*	739	21.28	07.32
Oba*	859	22.58	05.58
		Day 2 We Fr Su	
Hornepayne	921	Ar 00.25	Dp 05.05
		Dp 01.00	Ar 04.30
Hillsport*	989	01.51	03.19
Caramat*	1046	02.45	02.31
Longlac*	1084	03.15	01.59
Nakina*	1133	03.49	01.24
Auden*	1222	04.54	00.24
			Day 4 Fr Mo We
Ferland*	1265	05.32	23.50
Mud River*	1273	05.45	23.41
Armstrong*	1314	06.50 (ET)	23.05 (ET)
Collins*	1348	06.25 (CT)	21.29 (CT)
Allanwater Bridge*	1401	07.03	20.42
Flindt Landing*	1421	07.16	20.28
Savant Lake*	1440	07.30	20.17
Sioux Lookout	1537	Ar 09.05	Dp 18.55
		Dp 09.25	Ar 18.35
Richin*	1621	10.25	17.07
Red Lake Road*	1652	10.54	16.33
Canyon*	1682	11.19	16.07
Farlane*	1720	11.51	15.28
Redditt*	1735	12.13	15.11
Minaki*	1758	12.37	14.49
Ottermere*	1780	12.59	14.31
Malachi*	1784	13.02	14.26
Copeland's Ldng*	1788	13.03	14.23
Rice Lake*	1796	13.11	14.13
Winnitoba*	1801	13.16	140.7

CANADIAN: TORONTO–VANCOUVER (cont'd from p241)

Station name	Km	Westbound	Eastbound
Ophir*	1806	13.21	14.02
Brereton Lake*	1826	13.36	13.46
Elma*	1854	14.16	13.27
Winnipeg	1943	Ar 15.45	Dp 12.25
		Dp 16.55	Ar 11.20
Portage la Prairie*	2032	18.05	09.56
Brandon North*	2150	19.15	08.35
Rivers*	2173	19.40	08.23
Melville	2394	22.30	05.50
		Day 3	
		Th Sa Mo	
Watrous*	2602	00.40	03.23
Saskatoon	2702	Ar 02.05	Dp 02.10
		Dp 02.30	Ar 01.45
Biggar	2792	03.45	00.30
		Day 3	
		Th Su Tu	
Unity*	2885	04.46 (CT)	23.02 (CT)
Wainwright*	3017	05.17 (MT)	20.45 (MT)
Viking*	3089	06.06	20.00
Edmonton	3221	Ar 08.05	Dp18.20
		Dp 08.55	Ar 17.30
Evansburg*	3331	10.10	15.50
Edson*	3430	11.24	14.38
Hinton*	3518	12.34	13.35
Jasper	3600	Ar 14.05	Dp 12.20
		Dp 15.30 (MT)	Ar 11.00 (MT)
Valemount*	3721	16.34 (PT)	07.49 (PT)
Blue River*	3814	18.02	06.08
Clearwater*	3923	19.59	04.14
Kamloops	4038	Ar 22.10	Dp 02.25
		Dp 22.45	Ar 01.50
		Day 4	**Day 2**
		Fr Su Tu	**We Sa Mo**
Ashcroft*	4117	00.16	23.57
Boston Bar*	4240	02.43	
North Bend*	4265		21.30
Hope*	4305	04.02	
Katz*	4308		20.10
Chilliwack*	4355	04.42	
Agassiz*	4360		19.52
Matsqui*	4380	05.04	
Mission*	4405		19.15
Vancouver	4466	07.50	17.30
			Day 1
			Tu Fr Su

* Flag stop. Requires 48-hours advance notice
ET = Eastern Time, CT = Central Time MT = Mountain Time, PT = Pacific Time

SKEENA: JASPER–PRINCE RUPERT

Station name	Km	Westbound Day 1 We Fr Su	Eastbound
Jasper	0	12.45 (MT)	16.00 (MT)
Harvey*	106	13.38 (PT)	13.09
Dunster*	142	14.12	12.35
McBride	174	14.44	12.03
Goat River*	217	15.41	11.02
Loos*	232	15.58	10.45
Dome Creek*	262	16.32	10.10
Bend*	265	16.36	10.06
Penny*	285	16.56	09.45
Longworth*	301	17.11	09.29
Hutton*	314	17.24	09.15
Sinclair Mills*	319	17.30	09.09
McGregor*	331	17.43	08.56
Upper Fraser*	341	17.52	08.47
Aleza Lake*	349	18.01	08.38
Willow River*	378	18.31	08.08
Prince George	409	Ar 19.08	Dp 07.30
		Day 2 **Th Sa Mo** Dp 08.00	**Day 2** **Th Sa Mo** Ar 20.29
Vanderhoof	520	09.55	18.35
Fort Fraser*	560	10.32	17.57
Endako	594	10.50	17.25
Burns Lake	650	11.58	16.32
Houston	734	13.08	15.22
Telkwa*	780	13.52	14.37
Smithers	795	14.20	14.24
New Hazleton	869	15.37	12.58
Kitwanga*	912	16.27	12.08
Cedarvale*	933	16.51	11.44
Dorreen*	957	17.12	11.19
Pacific*	967	17.21	11.07
Usk*	988	17.40	10.48
Terrace (Kitimat)	1007	18.05	10.25
Kwinitsa*	1084	19.09	09.17
Prince Rupert	1160	20.25	08.00 (PT) **Day 1** **We Fr Su**

* Flag stop. The train will stop here only when someone wants to get on or off

HUDSON BAY: WINNIPEG–CHURCHILL

Station name	Km	Northbound Day 1 Su Tu Th	Southbound
Winnipeg	0	20.13	08.38
Portage la Prairie	88	21.16	07.36
Gladstone	148	22.03	06.45
Plumas	169	22.36	06.12
Glenella	191	23.05	05.43
McCreary	224	23.42	05.06
Laurier	238	23.56	04.52
		Day 2 **Mo We Fr**	
Ochre River	262	00.15	04.34
Dauphin	283	00.43	04.20
Gilbert Plains*	315	01.14	03.33
Grandview*	331	01.30	03.17
Roblin	385	02.23	02.25
Togo*	412	02.51	01.56
Kamsack	446	03.27	01.21
Veregin	459	03.40	01.07
Mikado	473	03.52	00.55
Canora	484	04.16	00.43
			Day 3 **Th Sa Mo**
Sturgis	520	04.57	23.53
Endeavour	549	05.27	23.23
Reserve*	586	06.03	22.36
Hudson Bay	636	06.55	21.55
The Pas	777	Ar 08.50 Dp 09.30	Dp 20.00 Ar 19.20
Cormorant	843	10.44	18.05
Wabowden	996	13.10	15.45
Thicket Portage	1073	14.45	14.25
Thompson	1149	Ar 16.25 Dp 17.55	Dp 12.35 Ar 11.05
Pikwitonei	1220	19.40	09.20
Ilford	1337	22.10	06.55
Gillam	1401	Ar 23.20 Dp 23.50	Dp 05.45 Ar 05.15
		Day 3 **Tu Th Sa**	
Weir River	1477	02.05	03.00
Herchmer	1540	03.55	01.05
			Day 2 **We Fr Su**
Belcher*	1603	05.44	23.21
Churchill	1697	08.30	20.30
			Day 1 **Tu Th Sa**

* Flag stop. The train will stop here on demand only.

APPENDIX B: FRENCH WORDS AND PHRASES

Many travellers are astonishingly ignorant about the importance of the French language in Canada. A group of backpackers I met in Toronto were flabbergasted when I introduced them to a Quebecker whose English was quite poor – they had assumed that all Canadians speak English as their main language. The fact is that, in theory at least, French has equal status with English; they are the country's two official languages. Over six million Canadians speak French as their first language. These are concentrated in, but not confined to, Quebec. There are also sizeable groups of Francophones in parts of Nova Scotia, New Brunswick, Ontario and Manitoba.

Apart from being a matter of common courtesy, speaking (or attempting to speak) French to a Francophone displays a cultural sensitivity that will be greatly appreciated by your listener, especially in Quebec. Even the clumsiest efforts will be rewarded with smiles and encouragement, and will definitely enhance your experience of French Canada.

MEETING PEOPLE

Hello	*Bonjour*
Good evening	*Bonsoir*
How are you?	*Ça va?* (informal); *Comment allez-vous?* (polite)
I'm fine, thanks	*Ça va bien, merci*
Yes	*Oui*
No	*Non*
Maybe	*Peut-être*
Please	*S'il vous plaît/s'il te plaît*
Thank you	*Merci*
You're welcome	*De rien/bienvenu*
Excuse me (in a crowd)	*Pardon*
Sorry	*Je m'excuse*
Okay	*D'accord*
No problem	*Pas de problème*
I'm called...	*Je m'appelle...*
What's your name?	*Comment vous-appelez vous* (polite)
	Comment t'appelles-tu? (informal)
I'm British/American	*Je suis Anglais(e)/Américain(e)*
I'm Australian/Japanese	*Je suis Australien(ne)/Japonais(e)*
I'm from New Zealand	*Je suis de la Nouvelle-Zélande*
I'm Swiss/Swedish	*Je suis Suisse/Suédois(e)*
I'm Italian/German	*Je suis Italien(ne)/Allemand(e)*
I'm Dutch/Danish	*Je suis Hollandais(e)/Danois(e)*

DIRECTIONS

I'm looking for the tourist office	*Je cherche le bureau de tourisme*
Where is the ...?	*Où est le/la ...?*
train station	*la gare*
town centre	*le centre-ville*
airport	*l'aéroport*
bus stop	*l'arrêt d'autobus*
metro	*le métro*
museum	*le musée*
washroom (toilets)	*les toilettes*

DIRECTIONS (cont'd)

Is it far to walk?	*C'est loin à pied?*
straight ahead	*tout droit*
near to	*près de*
in front of	*devant*
behind	*derrière*
to the right	*à droite*
to the left	*à gauche*
here	*ici*
street	*la rue*
bridge	*le pont*
square	*la place*
building	*l'immeuble*

ACCOMMODATION

hotel	*l'hôtel*
youth hostel	*l'auberge de jeunesse*

Do you have a room for	*Est-ce que vous avez une chambre pour*
one/two people	*une personne / deux personnes?*
for one night / two nights	*pour une nuit / deux nuits*
with a bathroom?	*avec salle de bain?*

Is breakfast included?	*Est-ce que le petit-déjeuner est compris?*
How much is it?	*C'est combien?*
Do you have anything cheaper?	*Est-ce que vous avez quelque chose moins cher?*
May I see the room?	*Pourrais-je voir la chambre?*
I'll take it.	*Je la prends.*

NUMERALS

1	*un(e)*	14	*quatorze*	60	*soixante*
2	*deux*	15	*quinze*	70	*soixante-dix*
3	*trois*	16	*seize*	71	*soixante-et-onze*
4	*quatre*	17	*dix-sept*	72	*soixante-douze*
5	*cinq*	18	*dix-huit*	80	*quatre-vingt*
6	*six*	19	*dix-neuf*	90	*quatre-vingt-dix*
7	*sept*	20	*vingt*	91	*quatre-vingt-onze*
8	*huit*	21	*vingt-et-un*	100	*cent*
9	*neuf*	22	*vingt-deux*	105	*cent-cinq*
10	*dix*	30	*trente*	200	*deux cents*
11	*onze*	31	*trente-et-un*	500	*cinq cents*
12	*douze*	40	*quarante*	1000	*mille*
13	*treize*	50	*cinquante*	1000,000	*un million*

MONEY

bank	*la banque*
money	*l'argent*
travellers' cheques	*chèques de voyages*
credit card	*une carte de crédit*
ATM	*distributeur automatique*

FOOD AND DRINK

water	*de l'eau*
orange/pineapple juice	*un jus d'orange/ananas*
wine	*du vin*
beer	*la bière*
(white) coffee	*café (au lait)*
tea	*le thé*
menu	*le menu*
salmon	*le saumon*
chicken/pork/ham	*le poulet/porc/jambon*
vegetables	*les légumes*
eggs	*des oeufs*
salt/pepper	*sel/poivre*
milk/sugar	*lait/sucre*

RAILWAY

timetable	*l'indicateur / horaire*
reservation	*une réservation*
connection	*une correspondance*
platform	*le quai*
ticket	*le billet*
ticket office	*la billetterie*
one way	*aller simple*
return	*aller retour*
sleeper class	*la classe voiture-lits*
Silver & Blue class	*la classe Bleu-Argent*
economy class	*la classe économique*
conductor	*le chef de train*
an upgrading	*un surclassement*
a refund	*un remboursement*
cancel	*annuler*
checked luggage	*bagages enregistrés*
hand luggage	*bagages à main*
luggage trolley	*un chariot à bagages*
bedding	*la literie*
late	*en retard*
on time	*à l'heure*

APPENDIX C: BIBLIOGRAPHY

Beattie, Owen and Geiger, John *The Fate of the Franklin Expedition 1845-48*
Berton, Pierre *The National Dream* and *The Last Spike* (1975)
Butler, W F *The Great Lone Land* (1872)
Cumberland, Stuart *The Queen's Highway* (1887)
Dorin, Patrick *Canadian Pacific Railway* (1974)
Dumond, Don *The Eskimos and Aleuts*
Gibbon, J M *Steel of Empire* (1935)
Grant, Rev George M *Ocean to Ocean* (1873)
Hurtig, Mel *The Betrayal of Canada* (1992)
Innes, H A *A History of the Canadian Pacific Railway* (1923)
Lavallée, Omer *Van Horne's Road* (1974)
Lotz, Jim and McKenzie, Keith *Railways of Canada*
MacEwan, G *The Battle for the Bay* (1975)
Macmillan, Alan *Native Peoples and Cultures of Canada*
McKee, Bill and Klassen, G *Trail of Iron*
McNaught, Kenneth *The Penguin History of Canada* (1988)
Mitchell, David *All Aboard* (1995)
Morton, Desmond *A Short History of Canada* (1994)
Pullen-Burry, B *From Halifax to Vancouver* (1912)
Radwanski, George and Luttrell, Julia *Awakening the Canadian Spirit* (1992)
Richler, Mordecai *Oh Canada! Oh Quebec!* (1992)
Roper, Edward *By Track and Trail Through Canada* (1891)
Stephens, D E *Iron Roads* (1972)
Stevens, G R *Canadian National Railways* (1960)
Woodcock, George *A Social History of Canada*

INDEX

TREKKING GUIDES
Europe
Trekking in Corsica
Corsica Trekking – GR20
Dolomites Trekking – AV1 & AV2
Trekking in the Pyrenees
Scottish Highlands – The Hillwalking Guide
(and British Walking Series: see p257)

Africa
Kilimanjaro

South America
Inca Trail, Cusco & Machu Picchu

Australasia
New Zealand – The Great Walks

Asia
Trekking in the Annapurna Region
Trekking in the Everest Region
Trekking in Ladakh
Nepal Mountaineering Guide

The Inca Trail, Cusco & Machu Picchu *Richard Danbury*
3rd edition 320pp, 65 maps, 35 colour photos
ISBN 978-1-873756-86-7, £11.99, US$19.95

The **Inca Trail** from Cusco to Machu Picchu is South America's most popular trek. Practical guide including detailed trail maps, plans of Inca sites, plus guides to Cusco and Machu Picchu. This expanded third edition includes new guides to the **Santa Teresa Trek** and the **Choquequirao Trek** as well as the **Vilcabamba Trail**. *'Danbury's research is thorough... you need this one'.* **The Sunday Times**

Scottish Highlands – The Hillwalking Guide
Jim Manthorpe 1st edn 312pp, 86 maps 40 photos
ISBN 978-1-873756-84-3, £11.99, Can$26.95, US$19.95

This new guide covers 60 day-hikes in the following areas: ● Loch Lomond, the Trossachs and Southern Highlands ● Glen Coe and Ben Nevis ● Central Highlands ● Cairngorms and Eastern Highlands ● Western Highlands ● North-West Highlands ● The Far North ● The Islands. Plus: 3- to 4-day hikes linking some regions.

Trekking in the Pyrenees *Douglas Streatfeild-James*
3rd edition, 320pp, 97 maps, 60 colour photos
ISBN 978-1-873756-82-9, £11.99, Can$29.95, US$19.95

All the main trails along the France–Spain border including the GR10 (France) coast to coast trek and the GR11 (Spain) from Roncesvalles to Andorra, plus many shorter routes. 90 route maps include walking times and places to stay. *'Readily accessible, well-written '* **John Cleare**

New Zealand – The Great Walks *Alexander Stewart*
1st edn, 272pp, 60 maps, 40 colour photos
ISBN 978-1-873756-78-2, £11.99, Can$28.95, US$19.95

New Zealand is a wilderness paradise of incredibly beautiful landscapes. There is no better way to experience it than on one of the nine designated Great Walks, the country's premier walking tracks which provide outstanding hiking opportunities for people at all levels of fitness. Also includes detailed guides to Auckland, Wellington, National Park Village, Taumaranui, Nelson, Queenstown, Te Anau and Oban.

Kilimanjaro: the trekking guide to Africa's highest mountain
Henry Stedman, 2nd edition, 320pp, 40 maps, 30 photos
ISBN 978-1-873756-97-1, £11.99, Can$24.95, US$19.95

At 19,340ft the world's tallest freestanding mountain, Kilimanjaro is one of the most popular destinations for hikers visiting Africa. It's possible to walk up to the summit: no technical skills are necessary. Includes town guides to Nairobi and Dar-Es-Salaam, excursions in the region and a detailed colour guide to flora and fauna. **Includes Mount Meru.'** *Stedman's wonderfully down-to-earth, practical guide to the mountain'.* **Longitude Books**

Trans-Siberian Handbook *Bryn Thomas*
7th edn, 448pp, 60 maps, 40 colour photos
ISBN 978 1 873756 94 2, £13.99, US$19.95
First edition short-listed for the **Thomas Cook Guidebook Awards**.
New seventh edition of the most popular guide to the world's longest
rail journey. How to arrange a trip, plus a km-by-km guide to the
routes. Updated and expanded to include extra information on travelling independently in Russia. New mapping. *'The best guidebook is
Bryn Thomas's "Trans-Siberian Handbook"'* **The Independent (UK)**

Siberian BAM Guide – rail, rivers & road
A Yates & N Zvegintzov, 2nd edn, 384pp, 22 colour photos
ISBN 978 1 873756 18 8, £13.99, US$23.95
Comprehensive guide to the BAM Zone in NE Siberia. Includes a km-
by-km guide to the 3400-km Baikal Amur Mainline (BAM) railway
which traverses east Siberia from the Pacific Ocean to Lake Baikal.
How to take the train and where to go in the BAM Zone, plus Lena
River and Kolyma Highway routes.
'...an encyclopaedic companion.' **The Independent**

Japan by Rail *Ramsey Zarifeh*   (Due June 2007)
2nd edn, 448pp, 60 maps, 30 colour photos
ISBN 978 1 873756 97 3, £13.99, US$19.95
New edition of this popular guide. The real secret to travelling around
Japan on a budget is the Japan Rail Pass, as explained in this guide.
Includes selected routes, strip maps, where to stay and where to eat,
practical information. Km-by-km route guides.
'Excellent guide' – **The Sunday Times**

Australia by Rail *Colin Taylor*
5th edn, 304pp, 70 route maps & town plans, 30 colour photos
ISBN 978 1 873756 81 2, £12.99, US$21.95
Fifth edition of this long-running guide. With 65 strip maps covering
all rail routes in Australia, city guides (Sydney, Melbourne, Brisbane,
Adelaide, Perth, Darwin and Canberra), and now includes the new
Ghan line from Alice Springs to Darwin. *'Benefiting from Taylor's 30
years of travel on Australia's trains.'* **The Sunday Times**

Indian Rail Handbook *Nick Hill & Royston Ellis*   (Oct 2007)
1st edn, 256pp, 30 colour, 10 B&W photos, 80 maps
ISBN 978 1 873756 87 4, £12.99, US$19.95
India has the most comprehensive railway network in the world, with
almost all tourist attractions accessible by rail. For most visitors travel by
train is the preferred means of transport, the ideal way to see the coun-
try. This new book is a wholly inclusive guide for rail travellers in India.
● Fully-indexed **rail atlas** of 80 maps with all 7326 railway stations
● **Rail travel for all budgets** – from the luxury of the *Palace on
Wheels* to 2nd-class berths for budget-conscious travellers
● **Timetables, suggested itineraries** and how to book tickets
● **Special trains** and **railway history**

Due 2008 (in same format as *Indian Rail Handbook*):
China Rail Handbook *Nick Hill*
1st edn, 256pp, 30 colour, 10 B&W photos, 80 maps
ISBN 978 1 905864 05 8, £12.99, US$19.95

TRAILBLAZER GUIDES – TITLE LIST

Adventure Cycle-Touring Handbook	1st edn out now
Adventure Motorcycling Handbook	5th edn out now
Australia by Rail	5th edn out now
Azerbaijan	3rd edn out now
The Blues Highway – New Orleans to Chicago	2nd edn out now
Coast to Coast (British Walking Guide)	2nd edn out now
Cornwall Coast Path (British Walking Guide)	2nd edn out now
China Rail Handbook	1st edn Jan 2008
Corsica Trekking – GR20	1st edn May 2007
Dolomites Trekking – AV1 & AV2	2nd edn out now
Hadrian's Wall Path (British Walking Guide)	1st edn out now
Himalaya by Bike – a route and planning guide	1st edn Nov 2007
Inca Trail, Cusco & Machu Picchu	3rd edn out now
Indian Rail Handbook	1st edn Oct 2007
Japan by Rail	2nd edn May 2007
Kilimanjaro – the trekking guide (with Mt Meru)	2nd edn out now
Mediterranean Handbook	1st edn out now
Nepal Mountaineering Guide	1st edn July 2007
New Zealand – The Great Walks	1st edn out now
North Downs Way (British Walking Guide)	1st edn out now
Norway's Arctic Highway	1st edn out now
Offa's Dyke Path (British Walking Guide)	1st edn out now
Pembrokeshire Coast Path (British Walking Guide)	1st edn out now
Pennine Way (British Walking Guide)	1st edn out now
The Ridgeway (British Walking Guide)	1st edn out now
Siberian BAM Guide – rail, rivers & road	2nd edn out now
The Silk Roads – a route and planning guide	2nd edn out now
Sahara Overland – a route and planning guide	2nd edn out now
Sahara Abenteuerhandbuch (German edition)	1st edn out now
Scottish Highlands – The Hillwalking Guide	1st edn out now
South Downs Way (British Walking Guide)	2nd edn out now
South-East Asia – The Graphic Guide	1st edn out now
Tibet Overland – mountain biking & jeep touring	1st edn out now
Trans-Canada Rail Guide	4th edn out now
Trans-Siberian Handbook	7th edn May 2007
Trekking in the Annapurna Region	4th edn out now
Trekking in the Everest Region	4th edn out now
Trekking in Corsica	1st edn out now
Trekking in Ladakh	3rd edn out now
Trekking in the Pyrenees	3rd edn out now
West Highland Way (British Walking Guide)	2nd edn out now

www.trailblazer-guides.com

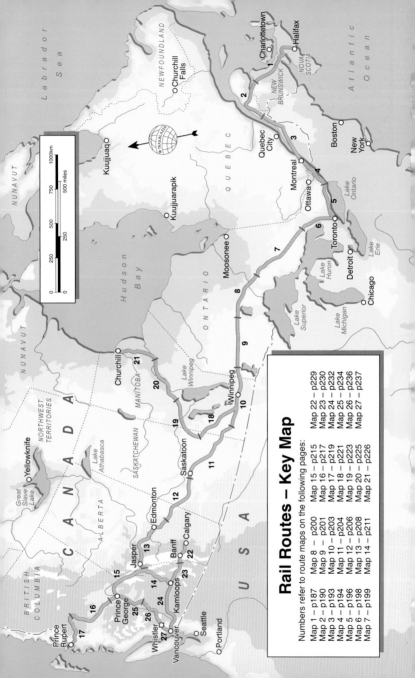

Rail Routes – Key Map

Numbers refer to route maps on the following pages: